PSYCHOANALYSIS AND SOCIAL WORK

Psychoanalysis and Social Work

Edited by

Marcel Heiman, M.D.

Preface by

M. Ralph Kaufman, M.D.

With contributions by:

David Beres, M.D.
Viola Bernard, M.D.
Peter Blos, Ph.D.
Henry A. Bunker, M.D.
Felix Deutsch, M.D.
Abraham A. Fabian, M.D.
Adelaide M. Johnson, M.D.

Lillian K. Kaplan, M.D.
Emanuel Klein, M.D.
Lawrence S. Kubie, M.D.
Joost A. M. Meerloo, M.D.
Peter B. Neubauer, M.D.
S. Mouchly Small, M.D.
Raymond Sobel, M.D.

INTERNATIONAL UNIVERSITIES PRESS, INC.
New York   New York

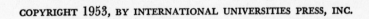

EDITOR

MARCEL HEIMAN, M.D.
Member, New York Psychoanalytic Institute

CONTRIBUTORS

DAVID BERES, M.D.
Attending Psychiatrist, Pleasantville Cottage School of the
Jewish Child Care Association of New York
Visiting Professor, College of the City of New York, Depart-
ment of Psychology
Member, New York Psychoanalytic Society

VIOLA BERNARD, M.D.
Associate in Psychiatry, Columbia University
Part-time faculty, New York School of Social Work
Psychiatric Consultant, Child Adoption Committee
Psychiatric Consultant, Ethical Culture Schools
Psychiatric Consultant, Bank St. College

PETER BLOS, Ph.D.
Teacher, Claremont Colleges, Harvard University
Teacher, Vassar College
Teacher, New School for Social Research
Consultant Psychotherapist, Child Guidance Institute
Jewish Board of Guardians, New York City

HENRY ALDEN BUNKER, M.D.
President, New York Psychoanalytic Society, 1948-1950
Faculty, New York Psychoanalytic Institute

FELIX DEUTSCH, M.D.
Former President, Boston Psychoanalytic Institute
Faculty, Boston Psychoanalytic Institute

ABRAHAM A. FABIAN, M.D.
Director, Brooklyn Juvenile Guidance Center, Brooklyn, New
York
Clinical Associate Professor, Psychoanalytic Medicine, State
University of New York, College of Medicine at New York
City
Associate Attending Psychiatrist, Kings County Psychiatric
Hospital

ADELAIDE M. JOHNSON, M.D.
Consultant, Department of Neurology and Psychiatry, University of Minnesota

v

Associate Professor of Psychiatry, University of Minnesota
In-Charge, Child Psychiatry, Section of Psychiatry, Mayo
Clinic
LILLIAN K. KAPLAN, M.D.
Staff Psychiatrist, Foster Home and Intake Department, Jewish Child Care Association
Consultant Psychiatrist, Girls' Club of B.H.O.A.
Assistant Attending Psychiatrist, Child Psychiatry, Roosevelt Hospital
M. RALPH KAUFMAN, M.D.
Psychiatrist to the Mt. Sinai Hospital, New York City
Director, Department of Psychiatry, Mt. Sinai Hospital
Clinical Professor of Psychiatry, College of Physicians and Surgeons, Columbia University
EMANUEL KLEIN, M.D.
Lecturer, New York Psychoanalytic Institute, School of Applied Psychoanalysis
Lecturer, New York Psychoanalytic Institute, Professional School
Attending Psychiatrist, Member of Medical Board, Hillside Hospital, New York
Consulting Psychiatrist, Board of Superintendents of the Board of Education of New York City
LAWRENCE S. KUBIE, M.D.
Faculty, New York Psychoanalytic Society
Clinical Professor of Psychiatry, School of Medicine, Yale University
JOOST A. M. MEERLOO, M.D.
Instructor in Psychiatry, Columbia University
Lecturer in Social Psychology, New School for Social Research
PETER B. NEUBAUER, M.D.
Director, Council Child Development Center
Psychiatric Consultant, Community Service Society
Instructor, New York School of Social Work, Columbia University
S. MOUCHLY SMALL, M.D.
Professor and Chairman, Department of Psychiatry, University of Buffalo, School of Medicine
Director of Psychiatry, E. J. Meyer Memorial Hospital, Buffalo
Consultant in Neuropsychiatry to the Surgeon General of the United States Army
RAYMOND SOBEL, M.D.
Instructor in Psychiatry, Columbia University, College of Physicians and Surgeons
Assistant Pediatrician, Presbyterian Hospital (Babies Hospital)

CONTENTS

PREFACE

There are two aspects of psychoanalysis. One, it is a system of human psychology, and the other, it is a therapeutic discipline. In both areas it has been responsible for revolutionary changes, and one can scarcely visualize any area in the social sciences of the present day that has not been profoundly influenced by both of these facets of psychoanalysis.

The field of social work which in itself is a relatively new area with an independent professional status has been particularly leavened by psychoanalytic concepts. This is true both as to its conceptual framework and in its practical application. The relationship between psychoanalytically trained psychiatrists and social workers has from the beginning been a very happy one. As two complementary professions, each has contributed abundantly to the other.

The main purpose of this book is to epitomize the contribution of the psychoanalyst to the field of social work. The professional stature of the editor and contributors is a warranty of the excellence of this volume.

—*M. Ralph Kaufman, M.D.*

The Mount Sinai Hospital
New York City
March 25, 1953

INTRODUCTION

Marcel Heiman, M.D.

Several years ago I was trying to set up a psychiatric teaching program for social workers in a family agency. I realized then the need to provide social workers with the fundamentals of those psychodynamic principles which are necessary in their daily work. Time and again I realized that social workers who were not too well steeped in the theory of psychoanalysis and its application to social work would almost precipitately enter deep layers of the psychic structure. Like persons exploring underground caves without adequate communication with the surface, they were lost when they found themselves confronted with material they could neither understand nor utilize constructively.

To some degree this state of affairs was facilitated by well-meaning psychoanalytic consultants who, in the attempt to instruct social workers, shared with them some of their rich knowledge which could not be utilized in the area of social work. If a social worker, stimulated by her contact with psychoanalytic ideas, turned to the literature to improve her understanding, she would find no specific text dealing with the application of psychoanalytic principles to her work. This book is an attempt to fill this gap by emphasizing those elements of psychoanalytic concepts which are applicable to the problems the social worker is called upon to handle. The chapters give evidence of the wide variety regarding both intensity and extensiveness of psychoanalytic knowledge used in different situations. In every case, to be sure, we find an application of Freud's prediction regarding alloying the pure gold of psychoanalysis. I believe it to be important that the original substance be pure because it makes the dilution so much more wholesome.

If we study the historical development of the mental hygiene movement in America we become aware to what extent psychiatry (out of which the mental hygiene movement sprang) was fathered and mothered by psychoanalysis and social work respectively. It is the very influence of psychoanalysis and social work upon psychiatry and upon each other which is largely responsible for America's leading position in the field of mental hygiene today. Before this took place psychiatry was shackled by a double chain, accounting for the relative sterility in which psychiatry found itself. The mental patient, isolated from the community and its social forces, was indeed considered alien. But similarly isolated was the person who took care of him, the alienist. At the same time psychiatry was static in its diagnostic and therapeutic approach to mental illness. With the help of the social worker this isolation was lifted and contact was made between the patient and the community as well as between the hospital and the outside world. This contact allowed for a study of social forces operative between the individual and his environment. Psychoanalysts then added a description of those dynamic forces which take place within the individual and his family.

If we wish to set a place and a date, when and where in this development we find a more concrete realization for such influence, the date is the year 1909 and the place New York City. It was in that year that the groping need for the establishment of a mental hygiene movement was finally materialized by the formation of the National Committee for Mental Hygiene. In the same year A. A. Brill formally introduced psychoanalysis to America by publishing his translation of Freud's "Studies on Hysteria."

Ever since that time psychoanalysis and social work have been traveling together. Mutually influencing each other and giving support to each other, the two traveling companions have only rarely become a burden or hindrance to each other, and as usual a voyage with an interesting companion proved to be an enriching experience. When social work was helpful in bringing an end to the isolation of mental patients in the asylums, the debt which psychiatry owed to social work was repaid by the contribution psychoanalysis made to the practice of social work. To quote Henry Alden Bunker (Chapter on "American Psychiatry as a Specialty" in *American Psychiatry 1844 to 1944*):

"Although, for example, the mental hygiene movement and the psychoanalytic movement might appear to have rather little in common, nevertheless the contribution of the latter to the former, no matter how indirect or unapparent, is unquestionable and fundamental. Indeed, in essentially every field of modern psychiatry, psychoanalytic principles—whether avowedly or not—have been implicit. They have been the little leaven which leavens the whole lump."

This book attempts to show just how much of a contribution psychoanalysis has made over the years to the field of social work. In the course of time social work has become a highly specialized field requiring many special skills. Wherever a professional person deals with individuals, understanding of psychodynamic concepts is of unquestionable value. Therefore social workers as well as other professional people will benefit from the chapters of this book dealing specifically with the psychoanalytic contribution to the development of personality and its functioning. In addition to that, however, social work has found itself confronted with areas so intricate and so complicated that the constant assistance of a psychoanalytically trained psychiatrist has been found to be not only useful but necessary as well. Certain areas of social work give good evidence as to the extent to which psychoanalysis has contributed to their growth. An example of this might be the development of child guidance clinics throughout the United States. On the other hand the psychoanalyst was provided with an opportunity to find a testing ground in practice for some of his theoretical concepts. There has been in the past and there still is at times some fear expressed lest the social worker and the psychoanalyst working so closely together might each lose their individuality and blend into something that represents a fusion of both. This fear is not warranted. I consider it essential beyond question that the social worker needs to have the knowledge of the principles of personality as supplied by psychoanalysis. It is true, however, that the temptation to use such knowledge in the contact with the client for purposes other than defined by social work are greater than in other fields. Similarly unjustified is the fear that the psychoanalyst would dilute the essence of the unconscious by adding some of the forces of the environment. The very reverse is the case. Those analysts who have studied children in their natural habitat have made important contributions to the theoretical concepts of psychoanalytic thinking.

Psychoanalysts who have been working as consultants with social work agencies show, not infrequently, a heightened awareness of the importance of the climate in the family. This climate is the stage on which the life of the individual is being played. Each person is an actor and reactor at the same time. The ability of the psychoanalyst to project from a patient's associations his actions and reactions upon the stage in which he lives is of importance in understanding his motivation and his unconscious drives. It is precisely because I feel that my horizon has been widened through my association with social work agencies that this book is presented as an attempt to repay a debt. I became more vividly aware of how social and family aspects are encroaching upon and invading the individual and his psychopathology.

The first part of the book deals with psychoanalytic theory. The first chapter by Dr. Kubie introduces the reader to evaluate behavior in terms of motivations rather than in terms of actions. His chapter brings clarity into an area where a great deal of confusion exists. Since the book has been designed to stress those aspects which are of practical importance, the second chapter by Dr. Bunker on the unconscious is short but precise. Chapters three and four by Drs. Beres and Klein, however, deal with aspects of the personality which the social worker has to understand as thoroughly as possible. They are complementary chapters which, together with the theoretical parts in some of the chapters on the practical application of social work, provide the professional worker in the field with a sorely needed foundation.

The second part of the book points up a selected number of areas of social work where significant contributions were made by psychoanalysts and social workers working together. In Chapter five Dr. Johnson describes her experiences in collaborative psychotherapy, while Dr. Neubauer's chapter demonstrates the family approach. Chapter seven by Dr. Fabian elucidates the structure as well as the function of the child guidance unit.

Chapters eight and nine by Drs. Bernard and Kaplan belong together functionally. Both the foster and the adoptive home provide us with an unusual opportunity to study the influence of environment upon the individual and vice versa.

Chapters ten and eleven by Drs. Blos and Sobel ought to be read together, since both deal with problems of the adolescent. Chapters twelve and thirteen by Drs. Deutsch and Small show the function of the medical social worker in dealing with psychosomatic conditions. It is suggested that they be read in this order because Chapter thirteen addresses the more experienced and more skillful social worker. Much remains to be learned regarding the mental economy and the dynamic resources of the aged. Therefore, Chapter fourteen by Dr. Meerloo, dealing with the aged, might assume greater importance as time goes on.

While planning the book and preparing it I received many valuable suggestions from the social workers I worked with and from the contributors to this book for which I wish to thank them. In thanking each of the contributors I wish to mention Dr. Henry Alden Bunker who died just before publication of this book. I am grateful to Dr. A. S. Kagan, the publisher, for his never-ceasing interest. I wish to acknowledge especially the many helpful suggestions and the assistance which I received throughout the preparation of this book from Miss Lottie M. Maury, editor of International Universities Press. My personal thanks go to Dr. M. Ralph Kaufman, my chief at Mt. Sinai Hospital.

Part I

THEORY

Chapter 1

THE CONCEPT OF
NORMALITY AND NEUROSIS[1]

LAWRENCE S. KUBIE, M.D.

Psychoanalysis is uncompromising in its concept of mental health. The analyst is not content with a statistical definition of normality as being that which "most people" do or feel or think. Common colds are illnesses, even though everyone catches colds; and dental caries is not "normal" merely because most of us have cavities in our teeth. The physiologist does not think that he has explained the subtle mechanism of the heartbeat by stating that everybody's heart beats. No more does the psychoanalyst feel that the mere fact that most people behave in a certain way makes it superfluous to seek the reason *why* they do so. The answer that "everybody does it" may be a statement of a fact, but is never its explanation.

Nor is the analyst content to use conformity to the cultural mores of any time and place as his criterion of normality. It will be shown below that neither conformity nor rebellion is necessarily or intrinsically normal. Neither do the usual medicolegal distinctions between the sane and the insane throw light on the essential contrast between normality and illness. These legal definitions deal only with the practical distinction between those people who for the good of the community should be held responsible for their conduct, and those who for any one of several

1 Adapted from Chapter III of Dr. Kubie's book *Practical and Theoretical Aspects of Psychoanalysis* (1950) and from "The Neurotic Potential, the Neurotic Process, and the Neurotic State" (1951).

reasons must be safeguarded, like children, from the consequences of their own impulses. Whether or not a man "knows the difference between right and wrong" in the archaic and unreal legalistic sense, or whether or not he believes that he knows both *what* he is doing and *why* he is doing it, is of limited significance. Many insane people know the difference between right and wrong quite as clearly as a clergyman; and many who think that they can fully explain their own conduct are merely deceived by pseudo-rational explanations. Nor does the difference between normal and neurotic conduct depend upon the degree to which an act contributes either to the welfare of society or to its destruction, or on whether the behavior is extravagant and fantastic or orderly and sedate. Certainly from the point of view of society all of these are important attributes of human behavior; but they are neither constant nor explanatory as a basis for the distinction between the normal and the neurotic process. Thus in the mere act of hand washing there is nothing eccentric or antisocial or deviant from any culture; yet it is not normal to wash one's hands thousands of times per day. This is not because the act itself becomes different when it is repeated, but because there is a fundamental difference in the purposes which the act serves. Similarly, to stand on your head in a tumbling act is normal, while to stand on your head in church is not, unless perhaps it is done to pay an election bet or as a hazing stunt. Evidently the critical difference lies not in the act, nor in its setting, but in the psychological mechanisms which determine the act. It will be shown that it is the nature of the inner forces which produce them which determines whether personality and behavior are normal or neurotic.

The Role of Conscious and Unconscious Forces

Through psychoanalysis we have learned that every moment of human life, and indeed everything that we do or think or feel, is determined not by one psychological force operating alone but by whole constellations of psychological processes. Some of them are conscious or readily accessible to our own unaided self-inspection. Others are usually on the fringes of consciousness, but can be drawn into conscious focus without special psychological instruments. (These are the so-called preconscious or descriptively subconscious processes.) Still others are actually inaccessible to conscious introspection. This is the "dynamic unconscious," to which Freud attributes the key role in psychopathology. Among the processes which are inaccessibly unconscious, those of which we have most information are those which have been subjected to active repression and which are blocked off from unaided self-inspection by active screening and disguising processes. At the same time there may be unconscious processes which have never been conscious, and which presumably have never been subjected to repression; but of these less is known. All behavior is a product of varied intermixtures of these three general categories of processes; i.e., the Conscious, Preconscious, and Unconscious systems.

Preconscious processes drop out of the central focus of consciousness through repetition. Thus all simple activities of life, such as breathing, sucking, excreting, moving, and crying, are originally random and often explosive acts. Early in life their purposeful execution is learned through repetition by which they become economically organized into synergistic goal-directed patterns. As any such act is fully learned, it can be initiated simply by the contemplation of the goal; and as this happens we gradually become unaware of the intermediate steps which make up the act. This great economy is achieved in the process of learning by repetition. It is in this way that we become able to walk without pondering each step, to talk without working out the movements by which we enunciate each word. It is in this way that the violinist and the juggler and the athlete learn complex chains of synergic movements. It is in this way that our thinking processes acquire seven league boots, i.e., the ability to leap over many intervening steps as we perform complex arithmetical processes. This is the source of intuitive thinking whether in science or the arts. In each case the intermediate steps drop into the background and disappear from consciousness. Yet they remain accessible to conscious self-examination. They are what William James called the "fringe of consciousness," or what Freud called the *preconscious,* as contrasted with the *dynamic unconscious.*

The dynamic unconscious, however, is no mere limbo of shadows; it is an area of hidden force or rather of whole constellations of forces in psychic life. Such unconscious processes are constantly at work in our lives; yet we cannot become aware of them by ordinary methods of self-observation, because they are hidden from us by vigorous opposing forces within ourselves. Throughout life these processes exercise a powerful influence on human behavior; and it is out of their influence that everything that is neurotic in human affairs has its origin. In this sense everything that we say and do and think and feel serves multiple functions and represents symbolically the conscious, preconscious and unconscious levels of psychologic organization. From this we may go further and conclude that if the psychologic conflicts of infancy and childhood could take place in the full light of consciousness, then the neurotic process could never be launched in human life.

Starting from these basic facts, psychoanalysis has made it clear that human behavior is normal precisely to the degree to which it is determined by conscious and preconscious forces, and neurotic in so far as it is determined by unconscious forces. This holds true equally for individual acts and for personality traits as a whole.

At this point the reader might ask why it makes so much difference whether conscious and preconscious, or unconscious processes drive the engine and steer the car. It is because the processes of which we are conscious can be influenced by appeals to reason, by argument and exhortation, by success and failure, by rewards and punishments. Consequently that part of the personality which is determined predominantly by conscious and preconscious processes has the capacity to adapt flexibly to external realities and to learn from experience. To the extent, therefore, to which conscious processes govern our lives we are free, free to learn and to grow in wisdom and understanding. Such freedom, indeed, is the only psychological freedom which psychoanalysis recognizes; and it is the essential core of normality. In contrast to this, those thoughts, feelings, behavior and personality traits which are determined predominantly by unconscious psychological processes are for that very reason rigid and inflexible.

Precisely because the determining forces are unconscious, they cannot be swayed by argument or reason, by exhortation or persuasion, by appeals to feelings or to loyalty, by rewards or punishments. Furthermore, since unconscious forces pursue the symbolic representations of unknown goals which they can never attain, those cravings which are determined by unconscious forces are insatiable; and the behavior which expresses such needs must repeat itself endlessly, repeating errors as frequently as successes, regardless of the happiness or unhappiness which it occasions. Consequently to the extent to which behavior is driven by unconscious forces it can learn nothing from experience, and can never develop or change or grow. In the truest sense of the word, it is enslaved (Kubie, 4, 5).

That is why the relative roles of conscious, preconscious and unconscious psychological processes in human affairs are perhaps the most important single fact that can be determined about human personality, human behavior, and human institutions.

Neither conscious, preconscious nor unconscious processes ever operate separately. A mixture is always at work; and the distinction between normality and neurosis is relative rather than absolute. The more preponderant is the influence of conscious forces, the more normal is the resulting behavior; and vice versa. It is a further corollary of this definition that there is no single human quality and no human act or thought or feeling which cannot be either normal or neurotic or both. Thus benevolence can certainly be both normal and valuable, but when it is compulsively overdriven by unconscious necessity, it can be destructive both to the giver and to those whom it attempts to serve, by defeating itself in the pursuit of unattainable unconscious goals. Similarly a high tolerance for pain, frustration, or uncertainty can be a most valuable human trait; but when it serves an unconscious need to suffer, the capacity to endure becomes a measure of illness and not of health. Similar reservations must be made about the human drive to work, to play, to eat, to fight—indeed, about anything that man can do. This brings us back again to our fundamental principle, namely, that it is not what we do but why we do it which counts. Or to put it more explicitly, it is not in the quality or value to others of an act or trait but in the inner forces which determine it that we find the essential distinction between psychological sickness and psychological health.

This is far from being a purely theoretical distinction. Quite on the contrary it has practical consequences from infancy to the end of life. Take as an example the disturbances of behavior which occur in the development of every child. Those which are determined by conscious and preconscious processes can be corrected quickly and easily by simple common-sense devices: e.g., by distracting the child, by punishing him or rewarding him suitably, by argument, by affection, by sternness, by flexible modifications of the situation, and the like. When, on the contrary, the identical behavior is determined predominantly by unconscious forces, it will resist all such efforts, and can be modified only if and as changes occur in the unconscious forces which produce the behavior.

Thus our unconscious needs and our conflicts over our unconscious needs become the source of all that is obsessive, rigid, and compulsive in human behavior. They enslave reason and subject it to their own purposes; and when reality frustrates them, or when they are deadlocked within us they give rise to all of the familiar manifestations of anxiety, depression, confusion, and anger which haunt men's lives. This implies that the neurotic in human nature causes all that is ridden with anxiety, driven by anger, paralyzed by depression, and lost in confusion. This occurs because our most important inner conflicts take place on levels to which our conscious self-perceptions cannot penetrate without outside aid.

Our consciously organized processes contrast sharply with this. Since they are conscious, the individual is able to consider them with clarity. He can gauge his chances of achieving his goals by one path or another. He can be experimental and adaptable in his efforts. He will appraise the difficulties realistically, and if they are too great, they will deter him from attempting the impossible or will spur him on in legitimate hope of success in the end. In short, the man who is normal in this sense can accept the guidance of reason, reality, and common sense. The outside world may be unyielding; but he remains flexible, modifiable, and educable, and therefore in a pragmatic sense, *free*. This indeed is the Fifth Freedom, which is the most important freedom of all, i.e., the freedom from the tyranny of the unconscious: It is the essence of the psychoanalytic concept of normality.

Why we "repress" certain psychologic processes in such a way as to render them unconscious is a question which will not be discussed here beyond pointing out that it happens whenever conscious or unconscious feelings of guilt and fear make it impossible for us to discharge internal tensions. When this situation arises we automatically render unconscious the tensions born of conflict, and then express them in disguised symbols, in the symptoms of the *neurosis*.

THE SYMBOLIC PROCESS AND THE NEUROTIC POTENTIAL

The symbolic process which I have in mind includes far more than the symbolism of dreams, which is only a special instance. The human being is capable of two related but different types of symbolic process. One gives him the ability to derive abstract concepts from his experiences, to represent these abstractions in symbols, and thus to express and communicate his purposes, needs, thoughts, and feelings through gestures, sounds, words, and their written symbols. The other symbolic process is the one by which man expresses in disguised forms those psychologic tensions which he is unable either to discharge or to face.[2] The first is the symbolic process of self-expression and of communication through language; the second is an unconscious effort to set misgivings at rest through the symbolic process of self-deception. In the developing infant and child these two symbolic processes have a common origin; and the ability to represent internal experiences through various forms of symbolic activity is the *sine qua non* equally of the neurotic process and of speech. It is not clear whether among lower animals either symbolic process is possible to a significant degree. This is why it is doubtful whether the so-called experimental neurosis in animals, which actually is an emotional disturbance that may occur in human neuroses as well, is identical with the neurotic process itself.

Between the two forms of symbolic representation there is a

2 *Editor's note*: See Chapter 2.

difference about which we can be quite specific. The difference between the representational process in communication and the representational process in the neurosis is primarily the difference between using a symbol for an internal experience of which we are or can be aware, and using a symbol to express an internal experience of which we are unable to become conscious. The capacity to create and use symbols is identical in both and is essential in both. The difference resides solely in the fact that the relationship of the symbol to the underlying psychologic process is conscious in language, and unconscious in the neurosis.

Therefore, if human beings were not able in the first place to abstract their psychologic processes and in the second place to represent these abstractions symbolically, and if in the third place they were not able to render certain unacceptable psychologic processes inaccessible to conscious introspection, there could be no such thing as a neurosis. Together then these three human capacities constitute the neurotic potential.

Thus this human vulnerability to the neurosis, i.e., *the neurotic potential,* arises out of our capacity for symbolic psychologic function, without which there could be neither a neurosis nor a thinking process, but merely dreamlike sensory imagery, passive echoes of previous perceptions. Like the neurosis, planful action and speech require symbolic processes by means of which sensory imagery can be taken apart and reassembled in new combinations.

THE NEUROTIC PROCESS

Out of this matrix the *neurotic process* emerges gradually and progressively. For each child, it starts the first time some psychologic experience becomes too painful to think about. It thereupon becomes repressed to such an extent that all that is accessible to conscious introspection and all that shows to the world is some combination of thought and behavior and feeling which stands as a symbol for what is buried. This representative or symbol will be simple at first, but with the passage of time and the gradual accretion of new buried problems which are more or less related to the first one, the initial symbol can come to represent many hidden psychologic states; and in turn there can be representatives of representatives, symbols of symbols of symbols, so that as the neurotic process evolves the ultimate linked chain of unconscious symbolic representatives can become very complex.

The neurotic process is always a symbolic process, and the split into parallel yet interacting streams of conscious, preconscious and unconscious processes starts approximately as the child begins to develop the rudiments of speech. This rudimentary speech is at first a language of action and not of words; but there is good reason to believe that the evolution of the capacity to use language is linked closely to the process by which we first repress and then represent our unconscious struggles. Consequently, throughout life everything we do and feel and think is always both symbolic and realistic; and the extent to which any piece of behavior serves as a symbol for something else measures the degree to which it has been shaped by unconscious forces. It may be accurate to say, therefore, that the neurotic process is the price that we pay for our most precious human heritage, namely, our ability to represent experience and communicate our thoughts by means of symbols, and through such symbols to discharge some at least of the psychic tensions which we bury in ourselves during our struggles with our instincts and our life experiences. Thus the highest potentialities of the human psyche and its susceptibility to neurotic distortion are closely related to each other; and all hope of any fundamental progress in human nature depends upon our learning how to preserve the creative potential which is inherent in the symbolic process, while limiting and controlling its potentialities for neurotic distortion.

The transient neurotic episodes which occur in every childhood are the first manifestations of this neurotic distortion of symbolic functions. Familiar examples are the nightmares, the commonplace facial twitchings and tics, the stereotyped behavior habits, the exaggerated loves and hates, the blind rebellion and equally blind submissiveness, the timidity, self-consciousness and shyness, the food phobias and eating compulsions, etc. These universal troubles of childhood are the larval manifestations of the process out of which adult neuroses evolve; and since at the present stage in the evolution of human nature these episodes are universal and are never wholly erased, some residue in adult years is also universal.

THE NEUROTIC STATE

The crystallization of the neurotic state out of the neurotic process may be illustrated with two cases. A courageous, artistic, and musical woman in her late fifties had been brought up in a cultured home. Through her attachment to her father, a man of learning, she had developed a spontaneous interest in literature and the arts. During her early years these preoccupied her almost to the exclusion of social life, but in later adolescence she married an older man of similar tastes and interests who had been one of her father's outstanding students. It was a good marriage and she gave herself to it wholeheartedly and happily. There were no portents of difficulty, except for a few "harmless eccentricities" of taste and dress. The years went by, however, and in the course of time her husband died, one son was killed in the war, and two of her children had to live on the other side of the world. All of this she weathered, but when her youngest daughter made a happy and suitable marriage, the woman broke down and had to seek help. Retrospectively it then became clear that her devotion to literature and the arts and even to her family had served two groups of inner purposes: one healthy and the other neurotic. From her early years, she had suffered from a secret fear of social challenges. In early childhood she would always vomit before going to a children's party. Without realizing it, her studies, her marriage, her home, her children, and her intellectual and artistic interests, and the eccentricities referred to above had served to mask her phobia almost completely. Consequently, during the long happy years of her marriage, she had been wholly unaware of her lurking neurosis, and it was not until the defenses provided by home and family were removed that she again found herself confronted by the unresolved neurotic terrors of her childhood. When this happened, the severity of her anxiety in all social situations forced her to retreat into an unwanted isolation. Her loneliness now depressed her so that she lost her ability to enjoy even the inanimate beauty of music, paintings, or a sunset. Gradually she developed various psychosomatic disturbances, an intractable insomnia, and finally a profound depression. Eighteen years of happy marriage had served her family and community well, but had served the patient badly by masking the highly charged neurotic process which was the hidden legacy of an untreated and unresolved childhood neurosis.

Another woman had grown up with an intense and hostile rivalry with her older brother, of which, however, she was totally unconscious. Because the original hostility was unconscious, she failed equally to realize that it had spread to include all men, so that every relationship with a man was poisoned by unconscious hatred and burdened with a confused inner conflict. In her early adult years this rivalry had masked itself tolerably in the life of a socially active, bachelor-girl, with talented writing and a vigorous participation in liberal politics and other community affairs. Ultimately, however, this same hostile rivalry with men led her to marry a gifted but weak man, who turned out to be impotent. Again because she had not realized the antecedent steps, she did not realize that she had been drawn to him by the weakness which was a part of his impotence, and which both frustrated her and intensified her secret feelings that to be a woman is to be unlovable. After two years of this, her seemingly stable adjustment broke down. Her previous activities could no longer serve their original unconscious purposes. She shut out her many friends, turned away from all community activities, became completely blocked in her writing, and lapsed into a severe neurotic depression.

These examples should make it clear that in spite of a virtual absence of any of the conventional signs and symptoms of a clinical neurosis, an unconscious process may be at work below the surface, the neurotic nature of which proves itself as soon as appropriate circumstances light up the patient's deep problems.

In summary we can say that the neurotic potential exists as an inevitable consequence of our essentially human capacity to represent symbolically all psychologic experiences, even those of which we are ourselves unconscious; that the neurotic process is an equally natural evolution out of this neurotic potential under the influence of unconscious guilt and fear; and that the symptomatic or clinically categorized neurotic state is nothing more than an episode which may be transitory or recurrent or persistent, in which the automatic symbolic language in which our unconscious struggles seek expression are accentuated and highlighted.

BIBLIOGRAPHY

1. GLOVER, E. Medico-psychological aspects of normality. *British J. Psychol.,* 23:152-165.
2. HARTMANN, H. Psychoanalysis and the concept of health. *Internat. J. Psychoanal.,* 20:308, 1939.
3. JONES, E. The concept of a normal mind. *Internat. J. Psychoanal.,* 23:1-8, 1942.
4. KUBIE, L. S. *Practical and Theoretical Aspects of Psychoanalysis,* Chap. III. New York: International Universities Press, 1950.
5. KUBIE, L. S. The neurotic potential, the neurotic process, and the neurotic state. *Armed Forces Med. J.,* 2, 1951.
6. KUBIE, L. S. The distortion of the symbolic process in neurosis and psychosis. *J. Amer. Psychoanalyt. Assn.,* 1:59-86, 1953.
7. REDLICH, F. C. The concept of normality. *Amer. J. Psychother.,* 6:551-576, 1952.

Chapter 2

THE UNCONSCIOUS

HENRY ALDEN BUNKER, M.D.

The concept of the Unconscious—or let us rather say, the realization that the human being harbors thoughts and wishes and feelings of which he himself may be entirely unaware—has a long history. As far back as the fifth century, B.C., we find more than a hint of such a conception in Plato's speaking in the *Republic* of "those appetites which bestir themselves in sleep—when, during the slumbers of that other part of the soul which is rational and tamed and master of the former, the wild animal part becomes rampant and endeavors to set out after the gratification of its own proper character. You know," Plato continues, "there is nothing that it dare not do, released and delivered as it is from any sense of shame and reflection." Similar adumbrations, although few so explicit, are to be found elsewhere in the literature of antiquity. More modernly, and more strictly proponents of a theory of the unconscious, we have such philosophers of the seventeenth to the nineteenth centuries as in particular Descartes (1596-1650), who could well be considered one of the great thinkers of all time; Leibniz (1646-1716); Schopenhauer (1788-1860); and Eduard von Hartmann (1842-1906), who in the vast spaces of his three-volume *Philosophy of the Unconscious* is said to have assigned a more important role to the unconscious than had any previous writer. With the nineteenth and twentieth centuries we pass from the philosophers to the psychopathologists—from the realm of largely *a priori* speculation to that of, as it were, laboratory demonstration: Charcot, Janet, Bernheim, Liebault, Mor-

15

ton Prince, Freud. Possibly it may not be inappropriate to conclude this briefest possible historical summary with a formulation of the unconscious from the pen of one of the last and greatest of the pre-Freudian psychologists, William James, who wrote in 1896 of his feeling "that we all have potentially a 'subliminal' self, which may make at any time irruption into our ordinary lives. At its lowest, it is only the depository of our forgotten memories; at its highest, we do not know what it is at all"; but who further wrote, a few years later, of the "subliminal" or B-region of the personality ("to distinguish it from the level of full sunlit consciousness"), that this B-region

> . . . . is obviously the larger part of each of us, for it is the abode of everything that is latent and the reservoir of everything that passes unrecorded or unobserved. It contains such things as all our momentarily inactive memories, and it harbors the springs of all our obscurely motivated passions, impulses, likes, dislikes, and prejudices. Our intuitions, hypotheses, fancies, superstitions, convictions, and in general all our non-rational operations, come from it. It is the source of our dreams. . . .

Admirable as this is as a piece of description, couched as it is in terms to which little exception could be taken as they stand, its phrases nevertheless illustrate how relatively empty, how largely sterile, is the concept of the unconscious as expressed thus purely descriptively rather than in the *dynamic* terms which Freud was the first to make fully possible.

Ernest Jones has remarked that to assume the existence of mental processes of which we are totally unaware—that is, of an unconscious mind—is "to take a serious step in thought which has far-reaching consequences." But since this assumption was made and this serious step taken centuries ago, actually, it would perhaps be better to say that it is only in the hands of Freud that they have had these far-reaching consequences; for it was Freud who first demonstrated, putting beyond any possible doubt, the effects exerted by unconscious upon conscious psychic processes, for example. Freud, as is well known, reached this unprecedented conclusion concerning the dynamic influence of unconscious upon conscious psychic processes through his pioneer observations upon (1) the "psychopathology of everyday life"— that is to say, the slips of the tongue (and of the pen), the forgettings, the unintentional acts, in a word, the "parapraxes" *(Fehlhandlungen)* of daily life; (2) the dream, that "royal road to the unconscious"—and Freud's illumination of the meaning of dreams will stand forever as his monument, even in the most unlikely event that all else were forgotten; and (3) the neurotic symptom—wherein we have, not the transitory loss of conscious control of thought or behavior of which (1) and (2) are in their various ways instances, but the more or less permanent disguised expression of unconscious, "ego-alien" impulses or wishes or thoughts. It is perhaps worth noting that it was Freud's discovery of the dynamic role played by the unconscious and its mechanisms in the creating of the neurotic symptom that led him to his formulation of the theory of dreams; and it was with the theory of dreams that psychoanalysis passed from being a psychotherapeutic method to being "a psychology of the depths of human nature" (Freud).

The three categories of psychic phenomena just cited represent each of them an escape into consciousness, in however disguised and distorted form, of an impulse or wish which is unconscious, an at least partial escape from repression of that which had been repressed. By repression, then, we mean the most important and most universal of those barriers, or *defenses,* against the incursion into consciousness, into the awareness of the ego, of unconscious, unwelcome, forbidden, "ego-alien" impulses and wishes. To effect a by-passing of these barriers, to make possible that "return of the repressed from repression" which is responsible for the parapraxis, the dream, and the neurotic symptom, various devices characteristic primarily of the unconscious mind are brought into play—various disguises are had recourse to, disguises put into effect by means of distortion, displacement, condensation, symbolization, for example. Such a disguise thus represents a kind of compromise arrived at in the conflict between the two opposing forces of repression and of escape from repression: as for example, the communicating force can indeed say what it wants to say, but *not* in the way it wants to say it—it can say what it wants to say *only* on condition that this be toned down, distorted, or in some way made unrecognizable. This unrecognizability may be achieved through *displacement,* whereby one affective object is substituted for another, the former a "neutral" one by comparison with the latter, or, similarly, affective emphasis is shifted from the significant to the insignificant (as in the "displacement upon the trivial" so characteristic of the obsessional neurosis). Another such device of the unconscious, encountered particularly in dreams, is that of condensation, whereby one conscious element may correspond to a number of unconscious elements, forming an undecipherable compression or synthesis of the latter— or also, even conversely. Still another and particularly effective means of achieving unrecognizability which is at the disposal of the unconscious mind is that of *symbolization,* whereby one idea can constantly and uniformly (and wholly unconsciously) represent or stand for another. No discussion of the unconscious could well omit particular reference to this striking capacity. For, by virtue of it, not only does the dreamer (for example) have at his command a symbolic mode of expression of which he knows nothing, and does not even recognize, in his waking life—so that "we have actually to believe in unconscious knowledge, thought reactions, and comparisons between different objects, in virtue of which one idea can constantly be substituted for another" (Freud), these comparisons being *ready to hand,* as we infer from their identity in different persons, sometimes even in spite of linguistic differences. Not only is this symbol-forming capacity the attribute of the individual unconscious, and the symbolic relations in question the characteristic of the dream work or of the neurotic symptom by which they are expressed; but on the contrary, the same symbolism[1] is employed as well in those creations of the unconscious, the myth and the fairy tale, in popular sayings and songs, in colloquial speech and slang, and in poetic fantasy. Space does not permit of an enumeration of even the commonest symbols encountered in psychoanalytic work; the whole extensive subject must be left with this passing allusion to the light which psychoanalysis has thrown upon certain aspects of

1 *Editor's note:* For a fresh approach to the problem of symbolization, cf. Chapter 1.

the unconscious with which psychoanalysis has, primarily, nothing to do.

The defenses set up with complete or incomplete success
against the irruption into consciousness of unwelcome, forbidden,
ego-alien impulses and wishes are effected by the ego. But they
are also automatic, "unconscious"; repression, for example, is a
wholly unconscious process. Thus it is clear that a *part* of the
ego is itself unconscious—its task, among others, that on the one
hand of either postponing or renouncing altogether the satisfaction of instinctual demands pressing as ever for gratification, or,
on the other, of turning its back on their existence by means of
the defenses referred to above. But, on the other hand, the ego
may also, under certain circumstances, permit the limited expression of certain ordinarily prohibited thoughts and wishes. Such
expression of these is provided in the dream—in which their
motor expression, however, is blocked off, and only the innocent
outlet of hallucinatory gratification remains open. But the dream,
transitory and "normal" though it is, is still the first member of
the series of psychological formations which includes as well
among its members the hysterical symptom, the obsession, and the
delusion. A second and extremely common, as well as usually
"harmless," outlet for forbidden or half-forbidden wishes toward
which the ego, now fully functioning, is permissive is exemplified
in the passing fantasies, the "daydreams," still to be kept within
certain bounds and clearly distinguished from reality, of ordinary
waking life—those fantasies which in the profitless character of
their imaginary wish fulfillment a colleague of mine once compared to the situation of the Austrian petty official, who "has
nothing, but at least he is *guaranteed* it."

If the id—that reservoir of instinctual drives which are with
such difficulty denied expression—is wholly unconscious, if an
important part of the ego is likewise unconscious, so too can this
be said of the third element in the structure of the personality as
psychoanalytically conceived, the superego—the unconscious part
of the conscience—formed from the internalizing (introjection)
of the child's upbringers *as the child sees them,* the latter furthermore colored by the child's own *projected* aggression. One evidence of the unconscious character of the superego is the fact that

it often behaves as though it were sealed off, like other elements which are unconscious, from the influences of maturing experience—its moral standards and rules of conduct usually quite strikingly impervious to the critical judgment which adult experience would ordinarily bring to bear; at its extreme, it is the instrument of a "nursery morality" (as it has been called) rather than of a more mature, a more contemporary, morality—of which the conscious conscience is in most of us a sufficient guardian, but the functioning of which has very little in common with that of the tyrannical (unconscious) superego: thus, for example, to disobey the injunction of the conscious conscience results typically in remorse, but to fall short of the demands of the superego gives rise to what is registered in consciousness as guilt feelings, depression, or a feeling of inferiority, however these feelings (since the whole process is *unconscious*) may be displaced, rationalized, attributed to wrong sources, and the like. It may well be true that conscience doth make cowards of us all; it is certainly true that even relatively "normal" persons are obliged to cope with a certain not inconsiderable amount of guilt feeling, which is connected only secondarily, almost needless to say, with the reality factors which the individual consciously believes to be its cause. Nevertheless it may be said that, on the whole, the stronger ego of the relatively "normal" person possesses more aggression with which to rebuff or fend off the reproaches of the superego; or, stated in the terms of the preceding paragraph, the id wish vetoed by the superego is repressed or maintained in repression by the unconscious ego, where it may remain further unheard from except as it may provoke dreams or possibly, under circumstances not well understood, form the raw material for sublimation. But in the less "normal," the more neurotic, person—bearing in mind that the difference between the two is in the last analysis one only of degree—the superego is "corruptible" (Alexander); that is to say, it can be "bribed" into permitting the expression (in disguised form) of the id wish by payment to it of a fee, usually considerable, in the form of depression, suffering, unhappiness; in a word, the enjoyment of the unconscious fantasy (in however symbolized or otherwise disguised form) is paid for by unhappiness (Bergler).

Let us conclude this necessarily far from comprehensive account of the unconscious with the reminder that nothing could better convey the crucial character of its role in the life of man than that which is intimated in Freud's familiar statement that the third of the grievous narcissistic injuries which mankind has suffered in the course of his evolution was the discovery that the ego is not master in his own house.

BIBLIOGRAPHY

1. FREUD, S. The interpretation of dreams. In *The Basic Writings of Sigmund Freud* (translated A. A. Brill). New York: Modern Library, 1938.
2. —— The psychopathology of everyday life. In *ibid.*
3. —— Papers on metapsychology. In *Collected Papers*, 4. London: Hogarth Press, 1925.
4. —— *An Outline of Psychoanalysis.* New York: W. W. Norton & Co., 1949.
5. GRODDECK, G. *The Book of the It.* London: C. W. Daniels Co., 1935.

Chapter 3

THE PSYCHOANALYTIC CONCEPT OF THE EGO AND ITS FUNCTIONS[1]

EMANUEL KLEIN, M.D.

HISTORICAL NOTES ON THE EGO CONCEPT

A great deal of psychoanalytic attention is currently being focused on the ego and its functions. The ego has become one of the "popular" topics for discussion. Some of this discussion represents part of the ever-present attempts to dilute psychoanalysis, to do away with the instinct theory, above all to minimize as far as possible the unconscious and the importance of infantile sexuality. But these attempts by no means cover all the work and attention that is being given to this subject. Analytic observations during analysis of neurotic disturbance, during the treatment of psychosis, in the analysis of children, is being supplemented by carefully controlled observations of young children and even of newborn infants, in an effort further to validate and supplement our older knowledge and to deepen it. This focusing on the ego became possible after Freud's theoretical formulations in the 1920's, in *The Ego and the Id* and *The Problem of Anxiety,* and after Anna Freud's *The Ego and the Mechanisms of Defense.* Until that time the major effort had to be directed toward working out the processes that take place in the unconscious, whose discovery was the basis of analysis. For a long time analysis was

---

1 *Editor's note:* This chapter should be read in conjunction with Chapter 4. Both complement and supplement each other, showing the relationship between the development of the ego and the corresponding phases of object relations.

thought of primarily as the psychology of the unconscious. The unconscious was a new territory that needed the most detailed investigation. This was accomplished through a study of the instinctual urges and their development. Only after this groundwork was laid could the major attention be fruitfully directed to the nature of the forces which accepted some impulses, repressed and rejected others, and greatly modified the expression of most of them.

It is a mistake to think that the concept of the ego was of recent origin in the history of analysis. In Freud's earliest papers, those that deal with hypnosis, there is already the concept of the conflict between the conscious mental processes (which he calls the ego) and an "unconscious memory," which the ego does not know about or is unable to interfere with, but which expresses its effects by bodily phenomena or morbid ideas. In 1893 Freud speaks of the ego as the repressive force and describes the neurotic symptom as the return of the repressed. He introduces the quantitative factor of the strength or weakness of the ego in dealing with or maintaining the repression. He speaks of the ego's struggle to cope with and ward off the derivatives of the originally repressed memories which have returned as the symptom. He observes how in conditions like paranoia, the ego accommodates itself to the repressed thoughts which have returned from the unconscious[2] and which now increasingly influence the thought processes of the ego and result in its change and deformation. From its very first beginnings analysis was based on the concept of the *conflict* between different aspects of the personality; on the temporary victory of the *ego* which succeeded in *repressing* the unwelcome idea or memory which became *unconscious;* on the *return of the repressed,* in distorted form, in the form of the symptom and the new struggle between the ego and the symptom. It is necessary to remind ourselves of these historic facts because many recent polemical works on analysis speak as though the concept of the ego was a late aspect of Freud's work, while others go still further and talk as though ego psychology had never been a subject of great interest to Freud.

[2] *Editor's note*: Cf. Chapter 2.

Nevertheless it is true that during the first twenty-five years most of the attention, though by no means all of it, was directed to an exploration of the unconscious impulses, their development, and their vicissitudes.

Three reasons for this shift in attention can be distinguished. In the first place, without an investigation of the unconscious impulses a scientific analytic view of the ego could not be formulated. In the second place, during the actual course of analytic therapy the role of the defenses as a barrier, which must be overcome before the unconscious wishes could be brought into consciousness, became increasingly clear. Persuasion, suggestion and encouragement that the patient voice all of his thoughts were helpful only up to a point. With the best conscious wish to cooperate, with the utmost encouragement by the analyst, the patient was still unable to obey the fundamental rule of free association when the emergence of new repressed contents mobilized his defenses. It gradually became clear that the defenses themselves must be analyzed in just as detailed a fashion as were the unconscious impulses. The third reason for the increased attention to the ego mechanisms lay in the fact that the psychological picture of the patient who came to analysis seemed steadily to change. Originally many of the patients seemed to have a relatively intact ego whose functioning was disrupted by the return of unconscious content with which it could not cope. When the repressive barriers were lifted and the unconscious material was made fully conscious, the ego was then able to assimilate the unconscious desires, deal with them in a new way, and regain its integrity. A change occurred when increasing numbers of patients with character disorders began to present themselves. In these conditions the ego itself had become permanently altered and a good deal of the neurotic illness consisted of just this alteration. In other words, the type of ego deformation that Freud had first observed in such grave disorders as paranoia, was found to be present in less grave illnesses, and even in the majority of patients who came to analysis. The old relatively "pure" cases of conversion hysteria and anxiety hysteria became increasingly rare and were replaced by every shade of character disorder. The reason for this change is still very obscure and a full explanation requires a great deal of further study. However, some tentative answers have been sought; e.g., that the change in the character of neurotic illness was the result of changes in the social and cultural conditions; the nature of these changes and how they brought about this result is still very problematic. It has been suggested that the changing attitude toward sex may have played a large role. Others have suggested that perhaps the change was not as great as it seemed to be, that perhaps in the earlier days, because of a lack of a proper theoretical framework, the observations of the ego and the character of the patients was less sharp.

In *The Ego and the Id* Freud suggested that our mental functioning can be divided into three related spheres of function which he called the *ich* (the German "I," which is usually translated into English by the Latin word *ego*), the *superego,* and the *es,* the German word for the "it" (which he borrowed from Groddeck) which is translated by the Latin word *id.* These words do not apply to different parts of the brain, although some aspects of the differences in the spheres of functioning roughly correspond to the distinction between some aspects of the functions of the cortical and subcortical regions of the brain. They do not correspond wholly to the distinction between the conscious and the unconscious, although many of the ego functions are conscious, and consciousness itself is one of the important aspects of a large portion of ego functioning. They do not refer only to the distinction between those parts of the personality that we call the self, although the self is often perceived as relating to the ego. They are not entirely separate from each other, although at times they may be in sharp opposition and then the cleavage between them may become clear and well demarked. They originally were one undifferentiated set of primitive functions, and the various functions only gradually organized themselves into certain modes of activity that sometimes complemented and sometimes conflicted with each other.

EARLY STAGES OF EGO DEVELOPMENT

During the first two months of his life the infant does not possess many of the capacities that we think of as the most elementary functions of the ego. He has very little control of his motility; he will reflexly grasp, kick, suck, cry, and smile. When distressed by strong, unpleasant stimuli which come from within himself, like hunger or bellyache, or by stimuli from without, like cold or noise, he will cry, scream, wave his arms and legs, and show clear signs of acute discomfort. When these stimuli are done away with, he does not become happy but rather he falls asleep. It is hard for anyone to believe that the smile of the newborn does not mean that he is happy, and surely no mother will believe it about her own child (which is just as well); yet during the first two months of his life the child may smile at the beginning of a bellyache, though as it continues to get worse he will cry. Toward the end of the first two months he will begin to smile in response to the sight of the full human face (but not to the profile); yet he will smile as readily when seeing his mother, a stranger, a masked face, or a nodding dummy.[3] Already at this early date he has made the first beginnings of the connection between the sight of the face and the pleasures of feeding or perhaps between the sight of the face and disappearance of the displeasure of hunger. He has begun to learn this through a process similar to that of the conditioned reflex; but as he gets a little older, this type of learning, which is the learning process of the animal, becomes increasingly displaced by a more complex process of human learning.

Though the connection between the smile and pleasure develops early, nevertheless there are mental states, in some cases of schizophrenia, where the regression goes so deeply that this connection is lost and the smile can at times be a signal of distress or at least a very unreliable guide to the state of the patient's emotions.

During the first two months the baby seems to oscillate between being at rest, usually sleeping, becoming disturbed and restless by hunger, sucking at the breast or bottle, and reverting to a state of rest. The striving at this point seems to be primarily a longing for the abolition of the state of inner tension and unrest rather than a longing for the pleasure of sucking. Barbara Low suggested the expression "Nirvana" principle for this state, an ex-

3 See Spitz and Wolf (26).

pression that was adopted by Freud. Out of this first stage there develops the pleasure principle which dominates the life of the child and which in modified form remains a basic principle throughout one's life.

The baby sucks his fingers from the first day; at first the sucking seems random, gradually the baby begins to suck when it feels hungry or distressed. There is a mounting inner tension, some kind of primitive memory trace of the absent breast, an attempt to gain satisfaction from sucking the fingers, failure of the attempt with mounting hunger and then crying. By the eighth month the baby has learned to differentiate the face of its mother from that of others to such a degree that it no longer smiles at the face of the stranger or the nodding dummy. It has learned a little patience, that is, it has learned to wait a little longer for its food without being immediately overwhelmed with distress. It has developed some measure of confidence that the appearance of the mother's face and the sight of her activities means that food will soon come. It has learned to get pleasure from the image of the mother and to anticipate the arrival of the breast or bottle.

Though these momentous steps in psychic organization take place very early there are many regressive states in which these capacities become gravely impaired. Some impulse-driven characters with oral fixation regress in some respects to that early state where it did not matter who furnished the milk as long as it was obtained. People of this kind may behave as though it did not matter from whom they can get what they wish as long as they can get it. They look on others as undifferentiated breasts and have no interest in the person connected with the breast, only in his readiness to furnish it. Frequently they are interested in the other one only while they are hungry; when the hunger is gone the interest is gone. We see some aspects of this behavior in severe alcoholics and drug addicts who look at the world primarily from the point of view that some people will furnish, or can be manipulated to furnish, or will tolerate seizure of, the money for the milk or alcohol or heroin. The "new milk" temporarily brings a series of pleasures with an increasing heightening of the feeling of self-esteem which finally approaches a state of perfect bliss, then becomes a state of nirvana.

Unhappily this becomes terminated by increasing tension, which only a fresh supply of "milk" can alleviate. In these people the ego is dominated by the oral desires for pleasure and for a restoration of the lost self-esteem which is brought about by the taking in of the "milk."

People who are dominated by these oral attitudes present many subdivisions. The oral optimist seems to feel sure that the milk will be provided for him. He usually behaves as though he entertained this expectation. When studied carefully it is frequently found that his optimism is not wholly based on confidence but on a denial of his perception of those aspects of reality which oppose his optimism. Optimism, genuine self-esteem and self-confidence, are found only in more mature types of people, where some aspects of oral attitudes are combined with, or where they color, a basically mature personality. The oral pessimist feels sure he will be denied[4] and is often quarrelsome, aggressive in his demands and frequently shows a self-centered, righteous indignation. These attitudes show a superficial resemblance to, but must be differentiated from, people with a strong sense of justice which is found in more mature individuals. Some orally fixated personalities seem to be intent on being denied because they constantly provoke denial. Such people seem to crave denial yet usually they really are demanding unconditional giving and they are driven to keep on testing the giver so that they may be able to identify him with a fantasy of the perfect ever-giving mother who would never refuse to give, regardless of the provocation. Only with such a mother could he really feel safe, despite the badness that he feels within himself. Naturally the usual result of this testing is that he again encounters the refusing bad mother, when the benefactor refuses to continue to tolerate the testing. It is true that in some persons some of the desire to receive is abandoned for the gratifications that come from being refused, the gratifications afforded by the opportunity to feel righteous indignation, to feel

---

4 *Editor's note*: "Denial" as used here must be distinguished from "denial" as used in psychoanalytic terminology where it specifically refers to a mechanism of defense. Cf. p. 44 of this chapter.

moral superiority, to demonstrate publicly that the mother is really bad but beneath all of these wishes the old desire to receive is still prominent and active.

NARCISSISM

The first state before the child is aware of the difference between himself and the outer world, is called primary narcissism. The first step in the development of a sense of reality is in learning the distinction between the child's own body and the outer world. This is a gradual piece-meal process. The body image is the first mental image of the "I" or the self and is the basis upon which later ideas of the self develop.[5]

In some psychoses this early distinction becomes blurred. The earth loses its solidity; the boundary between the person and his surroundings is weakened, the patient sees himself or aspects of himself all about him, feels external things and the thoughts of others inside of him. This occurs to all of us during sleep and dreams. It is also a common occurrence in states of ecstasy, religious and artistic, in which the person feels himself, in a mystical way, at one with the universe or with God. Something of the distinction between the self and the loved one is regularly lost during intense states of love. It occurs during pregnancy where in fact the distinction between the mother and the child growing in her develops only gradually. This loss of ego boundary is a prominent factor in pantheistic ideas and is often perceived as an "oceanic feeling."

The mental image that a person has of himself is often in sharp contradiction to his actual appearance. Many people who were regarded in childhood as thin and weak and who accepted these concepts as part of their image of themselves continue to have these thoughts about their appearance long after they have become strong and overweight. People who have grown quite tall after adolescence may continue to picture themselves as the "smallest one in the class." Many people retain a persistent picture of themselves of being as beautiful and charming to all the world, as they once were to their parents and other admiring

[5] *Editor's note:* Cf. Chapter 13, p. 298.

adults about them, and suffer a shock every time they look in a mirror or at a photograph and feel unable to connect what they see there with the mental image of themselves. This occurs not only with people who as children were greatly adored and admired by their parents and who have retained this image from childhood; it also occurs in children who have suffered derision for their appearance and have clung to an idealized wish-fulfilling picture of themselves.

The body image is carried over to various extensions of the body, in particular to clothing. A stain or a rip in a dress may be reacted to as though it were a bruise or a cut. Sometimes people even commit a kind of symbolic suicide by cutting up a dress. A patient who had a social experience in which she found other women more attractive and more popular felt strong envy with an unconscious desire to destroy the rival and to destroy her own inferior part. Both of these impulses were symbolically carried out when she came home from the party and tore her dress to shreds. People's choice of clothes depends in part on their body image of themselves, and when there is a great discrepancy between this psychic image and the real self the choice may be quite inappropriate. The pride that people take in their clothes and in their ability to choose them so well is part of the pride they take in the body. This attitude may reflect genuine self-esteem or may be compensatory in nature. Little girls regularly try to repair their damaged narcissistic feeling about their genital by shifting the narcissism onto their body as a whole and onto their clothes. In some people feelings of physical or genital inadequacy may result in the thought, "It does not matter what I wear, I cannot correct the deformity." Doubt and difficulty in choosing the clothes may result from oscillation in these attitudes. Some women lose their interest in clothes when they reach a certain weight; when they lose a few pounds, the interest returns.

The same extension of the feelings about the self occurs in relation to one's possessions; people extend their dread of bodily injury to the fear that their furniture may be scratched or damaged. Some individuals admire objects when they see them in the store but always find defects in them when they bring them home. The feeling that the body is damaged engulfs any possession that they make their own. A patient who as a child had been afraid that rough boys might harm him (as an extension of his oedipal fears) was very anxious as an adult when children visited him for fear they would scratch *his* part of the furniture—the radio, his bookcase and his books—but was much less worried in regard to "his wife's furniture"—the china, tables and chairs. Hypochondriacal patients often begin their symptoms with the thought that their clothes no longer fit them well. A patient with oral longings for the breast and penis, who later developed an obsessive idea of swallowing feces when he felt himself weak and small and was envious of others, complained a good deal that his collar was tight.

During artistic creation the writer or painter displaces much of his narcissistic feeling on to his creation; in fact it is probable that the capacity successfully to shift some of the narcissistic feeling from the self to the work is a prerequisite for success in creative effort.

In obsessional neuroses where the struggle against sexual impulses has become shifted by regression to a struggle against dirt, a major part of the attempts at cleaning the mind and the body are commonly directed by women to the process of house cleaning.

INTROJECTION AND PROJECTION

The first distinctions between the self and the outside world are carried out by the two ego functions of introjection and projection. Introjection is patterned after the process of feeding, which is the important childhood activity that requires the outside world in the form of the mother to come into close relation to the child. As the child drinks in the milk he drinks in the image of the mother, especially of her face. He drinks in her image through his gradually developing sense of vision, the taking into the mouth and the seeing are the basis of the child's first perceptions, and at the same time are the basis of the child's identification with the mother. The child's awareness that he has a face is based on his identification with the mother's face. Simultaneously the child becomes aware of his mother by imitating her movements. Through the imitative movements he both becomes aware of her and becomes like her. All of these processes take place simultaneously. He drinks the mother's milk, sees the mother, imitates her, takes after her, and becomes like her.

Before the distinction between the self and the outside world has developed, the child has a feeling of omnipotence. He and the universe are one. As the distinction develops the feeling of omnipotence is shifted onto the mother. By taking in the food that she gives, by looking at her, by imitating her, and by identifying with her, he shares in her omnipotence. He needs the mother both for the pleasure that she gives and the self-esteem that she fosters. The act of drinking in the food that she furnishes gratifies both these needs at the same time. As we grow older we become less dependent on the love, the praise and the approval of others for the maintenance of our self-esteem. Our self-esteem then does not depend exclusively on an external mother whose approval we seek but depends in part on the relation between the ego and the superego, which is an internalization of certain aspects of the parents. In some individuals the conviction that what they are doing is right and is in accord with their conscience will permit them to be self-confident in their course of action, despite the most intense opposition of those about them. Most people do not develop such a high ability to regulate their own self-esteem; the frowns of fortune in the form of the scorn of others, their indifference to our plight, the blows of fate bringing hardships and misfortunes, make most people lose some of their self-esteem and cause many to feel that they are weak and bad. Sometimes denial mechanisms may mask this feeling under a façade of belligerent self-assertion.

People who are fixated at these oral levels or those who have regressed to them remain very dependent on others for their self-esteem and often will go to any lengths to win the approval, praise and love of others, even drinking in eagerly rather obvious counterfeits of such love. One common type of such a person is the woman who feels small, weak, inadequate or unworthy unless she is in love with an idealized man who stands for her father (or at an earlier point, her mother), whose characteristics she tries to absorb so that she will again feel worthy or entire. In some women this leads to a series of infatuations during which the woman is completely absorbed in the interests of the man and loses her entire self-identity in him. Checkov in his short story "The Darling" very skillfully portrays such a woman. The person fixated at this level may try to gain these narcissistic gratifications by submission, by charm, by adoration, by an attitude of helplessness designed to appeal to the maternal feeling of the loved one, by force and violence, and most commonly by varying mixtures of these elements.

The child learns about the outer world by putting things into his mouth; those that are good he keeps there, sucks on them, chews them, and swallows them. All these processes are aspects of perception, of introjection, of incorporation, and of identification. Tasting, sucking, chewing, and swallowing remain not only as functions relating to food but as part of our relationship to experiences, to people and to knowledge. Most people retain a preference for learning by drinking in, through pictures, the radio, television, and light reading, that which can be sucked in with little effort, rather than to learn by hard chewing.

One of the child's first decisions is whether the thing that he has put into his mouth tastes good or bad, whether it should be taken in and kept there or should be spit out. This distinction between swallowing and spitting out corresponds to the psychological distinction between introjection and projection. Just as the bad-tasting stuff is spit out, so the unpleasant idea or feeling is projected onto another person and is then perceived as though it came not from within but from without. Since in the desires of this period oral wishes play a large role, in people with oral fixations, envy, which is based on a desire to take in the possessions of others, plays a large role. The envy is most acute when an older child sees the younger one at the breast. It leads children to watch the others' portions carefully at mealtime, to see that the others do not get a larger or better share. It gains direct expression when the child tries to seize the toys or food of the sibling or companion. Since these activities are prohibited or discouraged, the child learns to regard the feeling of envy as bad or threatening to him. He may then project the envy onto others and, experiencing it as coming from them, he will fear it, complain about it, and protect himself against it. The fear of the envy of others may lead one to abandon an activity in which one is in danger of excelling and therefore in danger of arousing other people's envy. It leads some children not to put forth their best effort or even to withdraw from areas in which they are gifted. One patient, a young violinist, did well until he began to surpass his father who was also a violinist, at which point he developed inhibitions and had to switch to a series of other musical instruments. People who project their envy often complain about the bad intentions of others and are in fear of being robbed of their possessions or of their ideas. One scientific worker was afraid to voice or even to write about any of his ideas that he considered valuable or original because of the fear of plagiarism and therefore often acted as though he were stupid. When asked his opinion he would parry the question by turning it back on the questioner or would hide in vagueness and uncertainty. Similar fear of other's envy leads some people to dress poorly and to spend far less on themselves than their income would justify. An elaboration of these fears may lead to paranoid suspiciousness and withdrawal.

In the Schreber case[6] Freud described how the patient who suffers from paranoia projects his love onto another man, a father figure. He says "I do not love him, he loves me." Since this thought still inspires anxiety, it is changed to "He hates me." This transformation can be understood if we realized that the love that the patient feels contains a large oral element. The patient loves the other man like the child loves the mother. He wants to take his penis (breast) into the mouth or anus. This love is ambivalent and includes the wish to get possession of the other's penis. The wish is therefore simultaneously perceived as a threat to the patient's own masculinity, because this love means that the person foregoes the use of his own penis and wishes to act as a woman to the other man; at the same time it is perceived and reacted to as a disguised and hostile wish to rob the other one of his penis. When the oral wish "I love him" is

<hr>

[6] (1911), Psycho-analytic notes upon an autobiographical account of a case of paranoia (dementia paranoides). In *Collected Papers*, 3:390-470. London: Hogarth Press, 1925.

projected and replaced by the thought "He loves me," this ambivalent love from the other one is perceived as partly threatening; the threatening aspect is stressed and then the thought "He
loves me" is easily changed to "He hates me."

The precautions taken against the evil eye consist of warding
off the ill effects of the oral envy of others. It leads the mother to
offer up a precautionary phrase when her child is praised, a
condensed prayer that God may protect the child and may prevent the envious one from hearing the praise.

The child projects not only painful thoughts and emotions
but painful inner sensations. He feels that the aching part of his
body is not part of himself but is something outside, or later
when his reality sense is greater, he feels that it is something
alien from outside that has gotten within him. We often retain
this attitude and refer to an aching back or foot as though they
were part of the outside or as though they were an evil one that
had gotten inside; germs and growths and illnesses arising from
them particularly lend themselves to this attitude.

By an extension of this mechanism the organ that has led one
to offend morally is sometimes regarded as an alien part. In
psychosis this may lead to self-destructive acts like attempts at
self-castration, the evisceration of the peeping eye, attempts to
scratch or cut the masturbating hand and finally to suicide. A. E.
Housman in his book, "A Shropshire Lad" voices these feelings
as follows:

> If it chance your eye offend it,
> Pluck it out, lad, and be sound;
> 'Twill hurt, but here are salves to friend you,
> And many a balsam grows on ground.
> And if your hand or foot offend you,
> Cut it off, lad, and be whole;
> But play the man, stand up and end you,
> When your sickness is your soul.

During the oral phase the ego of the child learns to develop
some of the relations between the self and its inner desires and
people in the outer world. These relations center around taking
and giving. Impulses around taking and giving are expressed
through ego activity, are organized so they can be gratified or are

postponed or are blocked. Oral desires continue directly as the quest for pleasure from kissing and other sexual activities involving the mouth, the pleasures of eating, drinking or smoking, of talking and singing. They continue as personality attitudes in the desire to get, in the form of optimistic expectations; they are sublimated into curiosity, the wish to learn and to absorb knowledge. They lend to the character a receptivity to new ideas and to the suggestions of others. If the oral desires have met with a good deal of deprivation, pessimistic attitudes are developed and the person expects to be refused. This often leads to mixtures of demanding and of denial of one's demands. If the person feels bitter toward the original refuser(s), a sadistic demand for redress for the wrong that one has suffered becomes directed to the world. Since these demands are based not only on the wish for love and pleasure but also on the need to gain reassurance and to maintain self-esteem, when the demands do not bring one the assurance he craves, the demands are insatiable and constantly grow larger. The child identifies with the mother's attitudes toward his needs. If he identifies with the giving side of his mother, he becomes generous and acts like a nursing mother to others. He will freely lend or give gifts to others, do things for them. Besides the identification with the giving mother, the giving is a magic gesture, a setting of an example to others, to encourage them to be generous and to give. If the identification is with the depriving aspect of the mother the child will be ungenerous and will automatically refuse to give and will regard all others as overdemanding. In some men this can lead to an inability to have an emission during sexual relations because of a reluctance to give the semen to the woman.

In general, oral characters are impatient, greedy, demanding, restless. They are talkative, active, impulsive, given to volatile changes of mood. The activity is directed toward the passive and dependent aims of being given. They are frequently charming, the charm being used to encourage others to give. Intermingled with these attitudes are opposing ones that represent indirect ways of achieving these ends, and of denying or mastering them. These ways of coping with the oral wishes lead to generosity and empathy. The struggle against passivity and dependence often leads to exaggerated activity and independence. The inability to accept even the necessary aspect of passivity is greater in men, because of the feminine coloring of passivity, and may lead to exaggerated masculine attitudes. Generosity and empathy contribute a great deal of warmth to the personality. Frequently there is also a receptivity to new ideas and a longing for change and variety.

IDENTIFICATION

Identification is originally a form of gratification, a way of taking in what one longs for, and keeping it there. It often takes place as a result of a disappointment with a loved one. Through identification with the lost loved one, one retains some aspects of him and in this way one makes up or tries to make up for the loss; thus it is a mechanism that is used by the ego to help safeguard itself against some of the anxiety and distress that arises from the loss of a loved one.

Later the child also identifies himself with the forbidden aspects of the parents. As a result of this he then develops a forbidding attitude toward those impulses that the parents had frowned upon. This type of identification thus becomes one of the ego's means of coping with forbidden wishes.

Anna Freud told how a girl defended herself against unpleasant affects through identification. When she felt the welling up of tenderness or longing or anxiety, each of which had for her a dangerous quality, she would react by making mocking remarks to her analyst and to herself. This came about by identification with her deceased father who had trained her in self-control by making mocking remarks to her.

A special form of the use of identification as a defense mechanism is involved in *identification with the aggressor.* Aichorn told of a boy who when frightened of his own impulses spontaneously imitated the angry face of the teacher who used to scold him. Anna Freud tells of a girl who was afraid of ghosts and who learned to overcome this fear by pretending that she was the ghost and in this way was again able to walk in the dark hall. This mechanism is a combination of identification, plus the turning of a passive experience into an active one. This occurs constantly in children's play and supplies a large part of the motive force for the play. The little girl metes out on her doll some of the punishments and prohibitions which her mother meted out on her. The boy who has been frightened by a visit to the dentist plays at being the dentist and cuts up objects or drills holes into things. Sometimes the mechanism is combined with projection as in the case of Anna Freud's patient who rang the doorbell loudly, was frightened at his audacity and, expecting a scolding, he then scolded the maid for taking so long to answer the bell. Anna Freud gives two further examples of this fusion of identification with projection in the account of the boy who projected his curiosity onto his mother, adopted what he took to be her forbidding attitude to it, and then scolded the mother for her excessive curiosity. In a similar example a girl accused her analyst of being secretive and scolded her for it.

When oral wishes are repressed eating difficulties are common. By extension one may develop inhibitions in speaking, in reading, in curiosity, and in the desire for knowledge. The corresponding personality attitudes may manifest themselves in an inability to ask for things, in a great reluctance to impose one's will, or in an impulse to refuse all offerings. Yet even when repressed the old desires often recur as a wish to get things for others. This leads to a quest for vicarious gratification through helping others attain their wishes. Identifying with the wishes of others and having renounced their own desires, such individuals no longer hesitate to be demanding or aggressive on behalf of others. All parents have something of this trait which gains expression as a wish that their children get the satisfactions and opportunities that were denied to them and on behalf of their children are able to make demands that they could not make for themselves. Something of this mechanism is involved in the capacity for empathy and pity.

REPRESSION

The child is born with some means of protecting himself against being flooded or overwhelmed with stimuli. It is likely that the undeveloped state of his sense organs and his nervous system acts as a partial barrier against his being overwhelmed in this way. Despite these barriers it seems fair to assume that during the process of birth the child is flooded by a high intensity of unpleasant sensations and that this condition is the prototype of later acute anxiety attacks in which a person feels himself utterly overwhelmed by feelings and sensations against which he cannot protect himself. Probably the same experience of sudden flooding by fear occurs during accidents that are followed by the development of a traumatic neurosis.

At first the child has no active way of increasing his defense against excessive stimuli. Since perception is at first closely related to motor reaction and since the child first perceives partly by imitation, by changing his body, the child gains a way of inhibiting the active aspects of perception. During attention a child heightens his perceptions. He then learns to shut off stimuli by shutting off his perceptions, just as he shuts off sight by closing his eyes. This shutting off occurs in a massive way during fainting and during sleep. Less extensive ways of doing this occur in repression, denial, and isolation.

Repression was the first defense mechanism observed by Freud and to some extent it is the prototype of most of the others. It is an active but unconsciously motivated form of forgetting, and of actively but unconsciously keeping something forgotten. It is directed against a forbidden wish, against memories involving the wish, and against the anxiety or pain that was connected with the wish or that was imagined as the probable consequences of the wish. The wishes that are most regularly repressed and that were the first unconscious wishes to be discovered, are the infantile sexual wishes for the parents. Why sexual wishes are commonly handled by repression whereas aggressive wishes are often handled by other modes of defense is not entirely clear. Fenichel has suggested that one factor is the circumstance that the subject of sex is often treated by the pretense that it does not exist whereas the existence of aggressive impulses is acknowledged, talked about, and denounced as wicked. These distinctions are relative: aggressive wishes are often fused with sexual wishes. In most pregenital strivings and in sadistic impulses, aggressive wishes arise against the love object as well as those

against the rival because of the sexual wish for exclusive possession of the beloved, and aggressive wishes from these sources are
also repressed.

In repression the ego renounces part of its important function
of remembering, and instead devotes its energy to keeping something forgotten. Repression is an unending process, requiring a
constant expenditure of psychic energy and if it is done on a
large scale, it causes a depletion of the ego and a serious impoverishment of its forces. During adolescence when a large part of
the ego's energies may be directed toward this task, other tasks
that confront the ego may be carried out with difficulty. The
chronic fatigue of which some individuals complain although
they have not done anything often arises from these continued
efforts at massive repression. When external events stimulate
the repressed wishes, more energy must be used to maintain the
repression and the patient feels still more tired. When the repressed impulse and the experiences and memories connected
with it are stimulated by a current experience or when there is a
weakening of the repressive forces of the ego, there is a tendency
on the part of the repressed impulse to gain partial expression in
relation to the new experience. Derivatives of the repressed impulses then make their way into consciousness and are, in turn,
subject to fresh attempts at repression, so that gradually larger
parts of one's memory and experience are removed from conscious recollection. When a boy represses his sexual love for his
mother, his ego usually permits a tender, partly desexualized
feeling to rise to consciousness. In some cases it may be necessary
for him to repress these also, with the result that he cannot recall any affection for the mother. When the sexual or tender
feelings then try to attach themselves to other women or girls,
it may be necessary to repress these also and the patient may be
unable to recall any experiences connected with sexual or tender
wishes to women or to girls. Usually repression alone does not
suffice and other mechanisms must be added to cope with the
feared desire.

In anxiety hysteria where repression plays so large a role, it is
generally supplemented by inhibition, displacement, and avoidance. The commonest form of inhibition concerns the actual sex-

ual function and includes the whole range of sexual difficulties from shyness with the opposite sex to the various degrees of impotence and frigidity. The simplest mechanism underlying these conditions is the unconscious attachment to the parent of the opposite sex. As a result the sexual partner is in some way unsatisfactory because she is not the mother, and is a sexually forbidden object because she is like the mother.

By extension, other functions may acquire a sexual meaning and therefore become forbidden, leading to varying degrees of inhibition. It is not always easy to recognize an inhibition, because it may be disguised as a preference, and substitutive activities may cover the inhibited ones. To bring out the varying degrees of inhibition I will refer to a composite case of a musician (actually based on several cases). The patient made a recording of his playing on the piano of a Bach fugue. It was beautifully played, and certainly on hearing it, one would never think that there was any question of inhibition involved. Yet this recording was the result of a long series of musical inhibitions and was followed by another series of them which resulted in a total abandoning of music at the time he came to treatment.

The choice of the music was itself partly a result of inhibition. The patient had become unable to play music that he felt was too sensual, or romantic or diffuse and had given up Chopin, Schumann and Debussy. The stricter musical form of the Bach fugue seemed to him more controlled, less chaotic and less sexual. The recording was made in his own home, with only the recording machine as audience. At one time he could play before an audience of strangers, then only before friends, for his family, for a recording machine, for himself alone, and finally not at all.

The choice of instrument was a result of a series of inhibitions. He began to play the violin as a solo instrument, then as first violinist in a quartet, as second violinist in a quartet, then switched to the (psychologically) less important viola, and finally to the psychologically more "feminine" piano. The choice of the "feminine" instrument was a result of an inhibition of the more "masculine" one, but the underlying conflict invaded this area also.

The simplest form of repression is illustrated by the temporary inability to recall a name which one knows very well, which is just at the tip of the tongue. The name has become connected with a forbidden sexual or aggressive urge, with a painful or humiliating experience, or with the possible consequences of a forbidden urge. The following are examples of words or names that could not be recalled by patients: "Dr. Fuchs," because of its connection with an obscene sexual word; "Shattuck," because of an anal association; "streptococcus," for similar reason; "Browning," because of a connection with a forbidden anal activity; similarly with "Suckling," "Piscator"; the word "fairly," because of its connection with fairy; the names, "Dr. Sharpe, Ripley," were connected with aggressive desires and fears. Sometimes because of repressed envy and hostility hardly any names can be remembered.

In successful repression, one may be able to gauge the extent of it only by noting the absence of ideas, desires or feelings that would ordinarily be present in a person and that re-emerge only when the repression has been lifted. Most cases of repression are not entirely successful, and some aspect of the repressed content tends to manifest itself in disguised form. These disguises result from the mechanisms of defense that are used to supplement repression.

OTHER DEFENSES

In anxiety hysteria the desires that arouse the anxiety are repressed, but the anxiety appears in consciousness; at first as a diffuse free-floating anxiety and later as a feeling bound to a special place, act or situation which stimulates the desire, or the fear of its consequences. The anxiety was intended as a warning signal to the ego that a longed-for act is dangerous. Due to the pent-up state, the warning signal quickly mounts to such a degree of anxiety that it overwhelms the ego and makes it helpless to cope with the situation.

Some aspect of the experience in which the initial panic occurred becomes tied to the attack and thus becomes a signal for a fresh attack. Before a process of displacement and selection has taken place, the anxiety is felt in a situation that directly would involve sexual or aggressive impulses, or in a situation of actual danger. Thus a patient has an anxiety attack at the prospect of having sexual relations, or in a situation in which he would become angry at someone, or in a situation of actual danger. By displacement the connection between the forbidden wish and its opportunity for gratification is disguised and bound to a specific situation which is then feared.

When the desire for sexual adventures with strangers is bound up with the desire to walk the streets, walking without a companion is frightening. The desire to be knocked down and raped yields to a fear of falling. The fear and hate of the father is displaced onto a horse, as in the case of "Little Hans,"[7] or the fear of the aggressive mother is displaced onto cats.

In general a desire or a punishment for a desire is displaced onto an external situation which is then avoided.

In anxiety hysteria projection also plays an important role. Little Hans projected his jealous hatred of his father onto his father and feared his father's attack on him. This was displaced onto a horse, whose bite he then feared.

Reaction formation, prominent in obsessional neuroses, is another way of supplementing repression. An impulse is not only repressed, but to reinforce it, the energy behind the impulse is used by the ego to engage in the opposite activity. The desire to smear feces is repressed, and in addition the person becomes compulsively clean. Envy is repressed, and the person becomes compulsively generous. Hostility is repressed and replaced by compulsive kindness. A preliminary stage of reaction formation is seen in anxiety hysteria where the mother represses her hostility to her child and replaces it by an exaggerated anxiety about the child's welfare. In the preliminary stage of reaction formation this exaggerated concern does not apply to all children. In reaction formation the process goes further, the ego's activities are modified to a greater degree, and the anxious concern applies to everybody. Of course in actual cases the process is very complex, and the original suppressed impulse gains covert expression even in the reaction formation. The compulsive

[7] See Freud, S. Analysis of a phobia of a five-year-old boy. *Collected Papers*, III. London: Hogarth Press, 1925.

kindness is used in an aggressive way: the overanxious mother torments the child, the compulsively clean one is constantly pre-occupied with dirt.

The ego function of attention becomes used as a defense measure in isolation. Attention involves a certain amount of isolating a perception or a thought in order to bring it into better focus. This process is used as a defensive action to enable one to remain unaware of the connections between an idea and its associations, or between an idea and its accompanying emotions. It is used most prominently in obsessional neuroses, when the patient is often aware of some of his forbidden thoughts, but the emotion that would accompany them is warded off by repression and displacement, or where the connection between the one set of ideas and another is broken.

All forms of defense can be regarded as a kind of denial. In repression one denies that one has or has had certain bad or painful ideas, desires or feelings. In reaction formation one points to one's abhorrence of such wishes and one's preoccupation with the very opposite. In displacement one denies that one is fearful of one thing by pointing to something else one is afraid of. In projection one denies a desire in oneself by finding it in another. In isolation one admits to an idea but stresses that it is not really felt. In addition to all these denials there are certain defensive measures that are specifically called denial. The simplest of these involves a denial of one's perceptions. "No! I did not see what was there; I saw the reverse." A little girl on seeing a baby's penis said, "He is nice and smooth in front." A little boy on seeing his baby sister's genital says, "What a lovely penis she has." In fetishism the patient's personality is split in its attitude. The patient says, "My mother has a penis," and he seeks confirmation of this thought when focusing on a woman's black-stockinged leg. Another part of his personality is well aware that she has no penis. When a sense organ is impaired by local damage, or by damage of the part of the brain where the perception is registered, denial is facilitated.

In some forms of conversion hysteria where a sense organ is involved, the entire perception of sight or hearing may be denied, or the inhibition of the function may only be partial.

In childhood, denial by fantasy and play is universally used to help the child endure the painful aspects of reality he cannot avoid. He copes with the envy of the father's power and strength by pretending he is big, strong and powerful. He kills off his enemies by toy weapons. He overcomes his limited powers of locomotion with toy vehicles. His ego tries to avoid anxiety and painful comparisons by make-believe in all of his games. He carries this still further by pretending that he is only pretending to be a little boy.

Children must give up this play at the demand of the parents, who ask them to take a bath, or come to dinner or go to bed. When there is too much anxiety to be mastered by the fantasies or the games, they develop a persistence that becomes a source of difficulty to the child. The child tries to cling to the hat or stick or toy which supports his make-believe at all times. He cannot abandon it even temporarily. This may be tolerated up to a certain age, but becomes increasingly difficult for the child as he gets older and associates more with other children. It leads to a stereotyped form of play without the necessary flexibility. It merges play with mannerism. In a child who copes with objects of anxiety by belittling them, it can lead to a constant clowning which denies his fear. Anna Freud (5, pp. 92-93) tells of a little girl who could not acknowledge the difference between the sexes. Instead of displacing her wish to exhibit to her body as a whole, or to her pretty clothes, she denied that she didn't have a penis and lifted her dress as though to say, "Look what a fine thing I've got." She reinforced this by constantly calling on others to come and admire something that was not there.

In childhood the ego mechanism of denial through fantasy is a basic necessity for the child's adjustment to life. The child cannot tolerate some aspects of his life, those that are brought about by the great gap between his insatiable, fantastic primitive, and contradictory wishes and the reality that confronts him. He cannot change his environment, or seek a new one, or endure the one he is in. He must cope with it by denial and wish-fulfilling fantasy, while he is gradually developing increasing tolerance for reality and the power to cope with it in other ways. If the reality he is confronted with at the beginning of his life is close to maximum indulgence and very gradually makes increasing demands on him at the pace at which he can best tolerate it, that is, at his own rate of maturation, he is more apt to develop a strong ego which can get along with increasingly less use of denial through fantasy, and the fantasies themselves become less primitive, and more aspects of reality are incorporated in them.

As the child grows older it becomes progressively more difficult for his maturing ego to deceive itself completely for long periods of time, because of the ego's increasing capacity for reality testing, synthesis, and integration. Denial through fantasy loses much of its force, and other ways are employed for coping with the gap between the inner urges, the self-observing and self-criticizing functions and outer reality.

Denial of reality and the substitution of wish-fulfilling fantasy as a major way of coping with life's problems returns only during deep ego regressions as in narcosis, intoxications, states of ecstasy, and in psychoses where it returns as delusion. Delusions are mixtures of wishes, fears, self-reproaches and projections of them. In the graver psychoses there is a tendency for the wish-fulfilling aspects to gain the ascendancy. The Schreber case is a familiar example. When Judge Schreber[8] was appointed to a very superior position as the head of a group of distinguished judges, some part of his personality recoiled from the lofty prospect before him. Probably inner feelings of unworthiness, self-doubts with regard to his capacity, and fear of the consequences of daring to fill so elevated a post must have assailed him. He was "wrecked by success." He began to envy women who did not have such demands put on them, and thought that it must be pleasant to be a woman in the sex act. In short, he renounced his masculinity because of castration fear and guilt feeling and his feminine, passive wishes came to the fore. But part of his ego was outraged at this regressive process that was taking place in the rest of his ego, and he projected his now strengthened passive, feminine homosexual wishes and complained that the attendants and doctors were trying to use him for homosexual

8 *Op. cit.* See note 6.

purposes. His own reproaches at his homosexual desires were projected and perceived as derisive name-calling by others who he thought were mocking him by calling him "prostitute" and "Miss Schreber." Then through the use of religious ideas in which complete submission to God was not a weakness but the supreme virtue, he decided that he was being used sexually not by the doctors but by God, for a divine purpose of creating a new race of men. In other words he reached back to his old identification with his mother and with the Virgin Mary who was linked in his mind with her. Under these new circumstances, with the ego gratification of serving a divine purpose, he accepted his feminine status, and locking himself in his room he dressed in woman's finery and admired himself as a woman. A delusional feminine wish fulfillment now put him beyond the possibility of castration for daring to serve in a position so lofty that it was reserved only for father.

Denial by fantasy is a complex process, and even in its simpler forms usually involves regression, projection, introjection, and often repression and isolation as well. Yet despite all this, it is by no means always a pathological process, even after childhood is left behind. On the contrary, it remains an essential ego function and its total loss or abandonment represents a marked ego impoverishment. Fantasy can be a substitute for activity or a spur to activity. In sexual fantasies especially, it is possible to carry them on by thought and deed to the point of substitute gratification, or they can lead one to try to realize them to some degree in reality. As one strives for distant goals fantasy merges with hope, optimism and anticipation, and thus is one of the sources of the energy for continuing to strive.

Fantasy is an essential ingredient in all forms of play and games. Even the most restricted personality engages in it every night during sleep. Some obsessional characters who are afraid of the fantasy element in play and whose superego is inimical to pleasure must justify games by practical considerations and stress the exercise aspect of outdoor games and must even justify sexual relations by the idea that they are healthful. Frequently they can tolerate only those group fantasies that have religious sanction.

Fantasy is closely related to imagination, and the child's defense mechanism of denial by fantasy matures into the imagination of the adult. In the child whose fantasy life becomes too threatening to him, the fantasies may be repressed, and defended against by a "flight into reality" or into "common sense," with restriction and impairment of the imagination. In school such children have great difficulty in writing compositions. If they are asked to write about "A Winter Day," they write that it is cold in winter and then they stop. They can answer a series of questions about a winter day but cannot elaborate the material by themselves.

In analysis such people have the greatest difficulty in free association. If they are asked to associate to "A Winter Day," they will give their first association, then go back to the original stimulus for more associations. They will say, "In winter it is cold. In winter it snows. In winter—that is all I can think of." They find it difficult to proceed in a series—winter—snow—sleigh riding—a sleigh-riding incident at six—another child involved in the incident—feelings about this child, etc. They find it hard to react to each new thought as a stimulus to another one, and must return to the first thought, which remains a topic from which they cannot spontaneously depart. An exaggerated self-critical faculty examines each nascent thought before it is voiced, or before it is barely formed, and automatically rejects it. Such people hate to write letters because "they have nothing to say." The intermittent recurrence of this mechanism in writers is one of the symptoms of "writer's block." One aspect of this attitude is to equate imagination with "lies."

Creative imagination, in the good artist or the good audience, involves what Kris (20) has called "controlled regression," and "regression in the service of the ego," and is similar to what Freud characterized as "the flexibility of the repressions." The good artist and the good audience must be able temporarily to gain access to the repressed, draw energy and content from it, without too much interference from a vigorous sense of reality, and then subject the material to critical analysis, secondary elaboration, and synthesis. Art is simultaneously an exploration and elaboration of reality and a denial of it. The denial is temporary in character. After one has finished the book, one discontinues one's identification with its characters.

Religion usually represents, in one of its aspects, a more or less permanent group denial of some aspect of reality. Many religions deny the fact of death, and try to give reassurance to their followers that what seems like death is but a rebirth to a new, more wonderful, spiritual existence. Undoubtedly this faith helps to sustain people when confronted with the fear of their own death, and of those close to them, or when faced with grief over the death of a loved one. Attendance at any funeral, however, permits one to observe that this mode of group denial is only partially effective; the grief-stricken faces of the family show that some parts of the ego do not accept the denial. Few are so firm in their religious beliefs that they truly sing with gladness at the approach of their own death or that of their family.

As is well known, Freud was implacably opposed to religion, partly because of what he felt were its harmful, reality-denying aspects. He believed that the group maintenance of such denial led to serious ego deformation, and militated strongly against the goal of "supremacy of the intellect." He felt that the sustaining effects of the denial of the painful aspects of reality through religion could be better attained by what he regarded as the more mature approach of facing reality in all its aspects.

A basic ego mechanism which has many aspects is flight. Fainting, sleep, intoxication and fantasy are all forms of flight, but none of them are an actual physical flight from the painful environment. Running away from home, moving from one place to another, changing one's job, marriage, profession, to varying degree involve flight. They contain elements of exchange of environment, exchange of relationship from one person to another and exchange of activity. Used in this broad sense we can find some aspect of flight in many of the healthy and pathological ways of coping with difficulties. Anna Freud (5) tells of the case of the pretty young girl who was rebuffed at her first dance by the boy she admired. She abandoned her interest in dancing and pretty clothes for books and study. This abandonment is brought about by the desire to avoid a situation that brings humiliation or a blow to the pride. Other activities may be avoided because they bring neurotic anxiety, guilt feelings, and varying mixtures of these three forms of distress. For the abandoned activity another is substituted. In childhood one can keep on finding new activities that to some extent make up for those abandoned. As one grows older this becomes increasingly difficult, and successful adaptation through the finding of new fields of endeavor becomes more unlikely of attainment. In the same way children respond to disappointments with their friends by seeking new ones to replace the old but as one matures it is more difficult successfully to replace older relationships, particularly the more complex ones involved in the relationship to one's first family of parents and siblings and one's later family of husband, wife and children. Flight in the narrower sense is the exchange of one environment for another. It varies from a literal running away from home, city or country to a more organized search for a new and better environment. Just as the exchange of one set of activities for another can range from neurotic restriction of the ego to a realistic awareness of one's limitations, so exchange of environment can range from panic-determined flight to a mature grasping of better alternatives. Usually flight contains varying degrees of admixture of these elements.

Basically ego functions are aspects of the process of adaptation —adaptation to the demands of the instincts, the ideals, and self-critical attitudes of the superego and the demands of outer reality. The function of the ego is to synthesize and integrate these varying demands, by taking each of them into account. The basic ego defense mechanisms are originally patterned after basic, instinctual or id mechanisms in the way that introjection and identification are patterned after the physiological act of swallowing and the related id mechanism of incorporation. These basic mechanisms are designed to cope with painful, instinctual states of tension and unpleasant aspects of the environment, or rather to cope with the discrepancy between the infantile, instinctual urges and the opportunity offered by the environment for gratifying them. These primitive defense mechanisms then are used by the ego in its more involved, more mature attempts at synthesis and adaptation. Any of the defense mechanisms can result in a pathological deformation of the ego, but even what began as pathology can in a secondary way be drawn into the ego's adapted functions (15). In the same way, however, the ego's adaptive functions can become increasingly maladaptive when as a result of a rise in instinctual tension, or a weakening of the ego's capacity in coping with them or an increase in environmental frustration, or a heightening of the sense of guilt, leads to an increased use of a primitive ego defense mechanism because of the breakdown of a sublimation. Neurotic illness can be defined as a change from the ego's capacity to sublimate to the ego's new need to re-emphasize old primitive defense mechanisms. Contrariwise the return to psychic health from neurotic illness can be characterized as a regaining of the powers of sublimation.

BIBLIOGRAPHY

For the most basic works on the ego and its functions, see (5-10). Many recent aspects and applications of current studies in ego psychology will be found in the various volumes of The Psychoanalytic Study of the Child, *especially Volumes 6 and 7.*

1. FRENCH, T. M. Interrelations between psychoanalysis and the experimental work of Pavlov. *Am. J. Psychiat.*, 12, 1933.
2. —— A clinical study of learning in the course of a psychoanalytic treatment. *Psychoanal. Quart.*, 5:148-194, 1936.
3. —— Reality and the unconscious. *Ibid.*, 6:23-61, 1937.
4. —— Defense and synthesis in the function of the ego. *Ibid.*, 7, 1938.
5. FREUD, A. *The Ego and the Mechanisms of Defense.* New York: International Universities Press, 1946.
6. FREUD, S. (1914) On narcissism: an introduction. In *Collected Papers*, 4. London: Hogarth Press, 1925.
7. —— (1921) *Group Psychology and the Analysis of the Ego.* London: Hogarth Press, 1938.
8. —— (1923) *The Ego and the Id.* London: Hogarth Press, 1927.
9. —— (1926) *The Problem of Anxiety.* New York: W. W. Norton & Co., 1936.
10. —— (1937) Analysis terminable and interminable. In *Collected Papers*, 5. London: Hogarth Press, 1950.
11. HARTMANN, H. Psychoanalysis and the concept of health. *Int. J. Psychoanal.*, 20:308-321, 1939.
12. —— Ego psychology and the problem of adaptation. In *Organization and Pathology of Thought* (translated and edited by David Rapaport). New York: Columbia University Press, 1951.

13. —— On rational and irrational action. In *Psychoanalysis and the Social Sciences*, 1:359-392 (edited by Géza Róheim). New York: International Universities Press, 1947.

14. —— and KRIS, E. The genetic approach in psychoanalysis. In *The Psychoanalytic Study of the Child*, 1:11-29, 1945. New York: International Universities Press.

15. —— —— and LOEWENSTEIN, R. M. Comments on the formation of psychic structure. *Ibid.*, 2:11-38, 1946.

16. —— —— —— Notes on the theory of aggression. *Ibid.*, 3/4:9-36, 1949.

17. HENDRICK, I. Ego development and certain character problems. *Psychoanal. Quart.*, 3:320-346, 1936.

18. —— Instinct and the ego during infancy. *Ibid.*, 11:33-58, 1942.

19. —— Work and the pleasure principle. *Ibid.*, 12:311-329, 1943.

20. KRIS, E. Art and regression. *Trans. N. Y. Acad. Sci.*, 6:236-250, 1944.

21. —— On preconscious mental processes. In *Psychoanalytic Explorations in Art*. New York: International Universities Press, 1952.

22. —— Opening remarks on psychoanalytic child psychology. In *The Psychoanalytic Study of the Child*, 6:9-17, 1951. New York: International Universities Press.

23. —— Some comments and observations on early autoerotic activities. *Ibid.*, 6:95-116, 1951.

24. SPITZ, R. A. Hospitalism: an inquiry into the genesis of psychiatric conditions in early infancy. *Ibid.*, 1:53-76, 1945.

25. —— Relevancy of direct infant observation. *Ibid.*, 5:66-73, 1950.

26. —— and WOLF, K. M. The smiling response. *Genet. Psychol. Monographs*, 34, 1946.

Chapter 4

THE PERSON AND THE GROUP: OBJECT RELATIONSHIPS

DAVID BERES, M.D.

Psychoanalysis has from its earliest days been deeply concerned with the question of the interaction between the person and the group, a question which it has considered under the concept of object relationships. The purpose of this chapter is to present a summary of psychoanalytic thought on this subject. The term "person" is used here in its broadest sense to mean a human being, but in a specific context it may mean the individual, the self, the body, or the ego, a meaning that must in each instance be made clear. The term "group" is used to indicate a number of persons, and may then involve the person and one other person, as the mother, the father, the lover; or the person in a larger group such as the family, the school, the church, the culture in which the person has developed or even mankind as a whole. The group is not merely the sum of two or more persons. When two or more persons are joined together in a group a new psychological phenomenon is established. Psychoanalysis, as well as other psychological disciplines that have studied group activity, has emphasized this broader dynamic relationship and has recognized that one must deal with the interactions of the person on the group as well as of the group on the person.

The psychoanalytic study of group dynamics does not supplant other psychological or sociological studies but rather adds to them. The specific contribution of psychoanalysis is the consideration of the unconscious factors as well as the conscious factors which influence the manifestations of the relationships between persons. The study of cultural, social, and economic factors has occupied the interest of workers in many disciplines and has built up a vast store of knowledge in anthropology, sociology, economics, and history, among others. Psychoanalysis, which has concentrated its research on the problems of psychic structure, the vicissitudes of the instinctual drives, dynamic unconscious mental processes, and the role of conflict in human behavior and mental development, approaches the subject of object relationships with these problems in the foreground. It correlates the manifestations of object relationships with all these factors and especially with that of the development of the ego and superego,[1] demonstrating the constant dynamic interaction between the various factors. As the individual grows from the amorphous unstructured self which is the newborn infant, under the complete domination of his instinctual impulses and basic needs, to the complicated social person living in a complex cultural group, the developmental process is constantly influenced by the nature of the cultural group. The parental and familial relationships, social and economic factors provide the substratum of a learning process which is added to the biological maturational process. The person, with his individual characteristics and his pattern of object relationships, is the product of this interaction of biological and cultural factors, a process with varying manifestations in the course of the individual's development. The infant is at first in relationship only with himself. The first outside relationship which begins immediately after birth is with the mother, and only gradually do his interests develop to include the father, siblings, other children, and in later life, friends, lovers, and social groups. In this chapter object relationships will be traced according to this developmental pattern from the autoerotism and narcissism of infancy, to the mother-child relationship, and further to the family, the child group, the love relationship and the community. Object relationships as they occur in the casework situation will also be considered.

[1] See the chapter in this book on ego development by Emanuel Klein.

AUTOEROTISM AND NARCISSISM

The child's earliest relationship toward himself may take one of two forms: (1) the act of gratification of a basic need, or instinctual drive, on his own body, which is called *autoerotism,* and (2) the love of the self, which is called *narcissism.* Autoerotism may persist into later life in the form of masturbation or its equivalents. In the small child autoerotism may be seen as thumb sucking, rocking, genital play, or play with feces. It is directed with notable emphasis on specific parts of the body, such as the mouth, the anal region and the genitals which have therefore received the special designation of "erogenous zones." Narcissism is a much more complicated concept which may manifest itself in a variety of ways.[2]

In the course of development the child's love energy (libido) is transferred in part from the self to outside objects; narcissism is replaced by object libido. Under certain circumstances the libidinal energy may again be directed from the object back to the self, once more therefore taking on the form of narcissism. One may view the relationship of the person to others about him in terms of this constant flow of love energy from the self to the object and back to the self, a process which goes on throughout life. The factors which determine the return of the love energy from the outside world back to the individual may be either normal or pathological. An example of normal regression to narcissism is sleep; an example of abnormal regression is the increase of narcissism in the course of organic illness. The distinction between narcissism and object libido does not mean that narcissism is abnormal. It is rather a matter of an optimal balance, both excessive or inadequate narcissism presenting potential dangers to the individual's adaptation.

Why does the infant need to go out of himself to satisfy his

[2] The self, the body, and the ego are each distinctive concepts. Since the love energy (libido) may be directed toward any of these different aspects of the person, the term narcissism will vary accordingly and it becomes necessary to define in what sense the term is being used in any specific instance. The reader who seeks more detailed elaboration of the theoretical implications of narcissism should consult Heinz Hartmann's paper "Comments on the Psychoanalytic Theory of the Ego" (5).

instinctual impulses? Why does the libidinal energy originally invested in the self pass out from the self to outside objects, from narcissism to object relationships? There are at least two factors that explain this phenomenon. One is an assumption based on the concept that the damming up of libidinal energy within the self (and the same applies to the damming up of aggressive energy within the self) leads to unpleasure, so that the love (or aggression) must be directed outward to relieve the tension. As Freud has said, "We must fall ill, if we cannot love." Another factor subject to more direct observation and study is that by the nature of his biological development the infant is thrown into a close relationship to another person, the mother, and the satisfactions of this primary mother-child relationship set a pattern for continued relationships with other persons. We turn now to this mother-child relationship.

The Mother and the Child

The infant at birth has a body, a self, but the concatenation of psychic functions which is called the ego is still to develop. The individual's object relationships are intimately tied up with this ego development, which in turn is critically influenced by the basic mother-child relationship. Before the ego appears the infant is dominated by his instinctual impulses of love and aggression, which demand immediate gratification. There is no capacity to accept frustration, no capacity to test reality, no capacity to effect gratification without the help of an outside person. These are all ego functions and until the ego develops sufficiently the mother is usually the outside person who assumes these functions. Her role becomes crucial in the child's development and survival. Certain ego functions and capacities such as perception, memory and thinking develop as part of the biological process of growth, the autonomous ego functions. Other functions develop out of the experience of the relationship with the mother. Daily experiences bring out frustrations which are unavoidable. Delays in feeding, demands for cleanliness, restraint of aggression force the child to recognize the difference between himself and the outside world, the nonself. That which is gratifying, good and without pain, is accepted as the self; that which is not gratifying, bad and with pain, is felt as the nonself. These are unavoidable deprivations and essential for the development of the ego. Without deprivation and conflict (actually an impossible situation) the distinction between self and nonself would not develop; if the deprivation is too severe there are serious disturbances in the development of the ego. What one seeks, and this is of course the central question in child upbringing, is the determination of the *optimal* degree of deprivation.

As the child develops a spiral form of interaction becomes evident—the continued satisfactory relationship to the mother promotes further ego development so that frustration is better tolerated and reality testing becomes more accurate; the increased growth of the ego in turn permits the individual to sublimate his libidinal and aggressive drives and so to form better object relationships.

IDENTIFICATION

The mother-child relationship is the first emotional tie of the infant and in the beginning it does not recognize the difference between persons. Its basis is the process of *identification*, which is of central importance in the psychoanalytic discussion of object relationships. Primitive thought in the child, the savage or the neurotic seeks out similarities; it tends to fuse persons and objects, to identify them according to their similarities, and to act on the basis of this identification. The child's imitative play, the savage's animistic magical practices, the neurotic's displaced emotional responses, contain each in its own way elements of the process of identification.

In these early relationships there is evident an urge to belong, a tendency for the psychological merging of the person with another person or with an abstract force. It is an obliteration of separateness, a denial of weakness and aloneness; it is a seeking for strength that comes from unity with another, a stronger being. The question arises whether the need to identify, the urge to belong, to be part of a group, is a biological or learned process. Some authors prefer to speak of gregariousness as a basic instinct, others prefer to emphasize "cultural" factors. The question cannot be answered fully with our available knowledge. What we do see is that the tendency to identification may already be noted in the infant's relationship to the mother and it remains as a characteristic of human relationship throughout the life of a person, though varying in its manifestations and its strength.

The organic prototype of identification is the process of feeding. The child learns about the world by taking it into himself. He makes the unknown known to him by bringing it into relation with that with which he is already familiar. He incorporates a bit of the outside world and he is then able to deal with the incorporated bit as a part of his known self.

There are important variations of the process of identification. In the small child and under certain pathological aspects of ego functioning, identifications are transient and superficial, though they may be very intense. Such superficial identifications can be easily replaced by others. It is only when the identification goes deeper, when there is a process of *internalization,* that identification produces permanent changes within the individual which can be recognized as his characteristic ego and superego. The relationship to persons in later life will vary considerably depending upon whether the individual characteristically identifies on a transient superficial level or on a deep, permanent level.

The importance of the mother-child relationship in the child's development and the role of identification have been studied by observing the effects of early separation from the mother (without the substitution of an adequate mother surrogate) and the effects on the child of a psychotic or rejecting mother. It is of course necessary to consider that the mother's attitude to the child must be evaluated not only in terms of her overt behavior and conscious attitudes, but also in terms of her unconscious attitudes. These studies[3] have shown that a disturbed mother-child relationship may eventuate in pathological character manifestations which may take the form of psychic infantilism, asocial character structure or other ego deviations. As a result of this pathological development, object relationships are also disturbed.

[3] See John Bowlby (1) for an exhaustive survey of the literature on this subject.

The psychic infantilism with its tendency to superficial and transient identification, disregard of reality, and demand for immediate gratification interferes with the relationships to other persons. An infant who has been separated from the mother but who is supplied with a satisfactory mother surrogate by the age of six months will probably avoid the developmental disturbance described.[4] Separation after this age is crucial and the effect will vary according to the age at separation, the period without a mother substitute and the quality of the mother substitute. The deleterious effects are, however, not entirely irreversible, though follow-up studies of such children show some degree of ego deviation as a universal finding.

Identification is one stage in the love relationships of an individual. Loving has been defined by Freud as the relation of the ego to its sources of pleasure, and it may assume many forms. Identification may be regarded as a step toward the love relationship which recognizes the loved person as a separate object, a type of love which can tolerate separation. This the child learns to do only gradually; at first he must be part of his love object and he must possess it. Even in later love when real object love is established, there is a constant tendency to regress to identification, to forget that the loved one is a separate person.

THE CHILD AND THE FAMILY: INFANTILE LOVE

As the child proceeds in his development he forms relationships to other members of his family which are transitional stages leading to later outside relationships and which set the patterns for these later relationships. From the exclusive attachment to the mother the child goes on to a relationship with the father and with the other children in the family. There develops a particular relationship between the child and his two parents, a constellation of sufficient ubiquity to warrant its designation as an entity, namely the *oedipus complex*. The child's relationship to the mother before the oedipal period (the *preoedipal* period), his relationships within the oedipal period and how

4 *Editor's note:* Cf. Chapter 9, pp. 177 ff., where Viola Bernard deals in detail with this problem, including pertinent research and bibliography.

he deals with both are all extremely important in determining his later relationships to persons outside the family.

We shall consider first the child's early relationships which precede his oedipal period. In this phase the manifestations of love do not express themselves in genital functioning, which in fact still will require a period of further maturation. This is the *pregenital* phase, but even during this phase, from early infancy, there is evidence of genital reactivity. This early love demands exclusive possession of the object, but at the same time the object is readily changeable for another. It is intense in its demands and expression, and at the same time is marked by contradictions —love and hate appear in rapid succession *(ambivalence)*. It demands immediate gratification and at the same time its aims are diffuse, ill-defined and incapable of complete satisfaction.[5] It is by its nature doomed to end in disappointment and the inevitable frustrations feed the ensuing ambivalent responses. Pregenital love, infantile love is best understood as a stage in development toward genital, mature love.

Early love is essentially love by identification. Its relationship to the object is in terms of the significance of the object to the needs of the individual himself. So for example, the object may serve to support the individual, to gratify the demand to be loved, in essence to continue in the idealized atmosphere of love, the feeding and nourishing relationship to the mother. To such a love the term *anaclitic,* ("leaning-up-against" type) has been applied. Infantile love also seeks to gratify in the object the need to love the self. An object is chosen in the image of the self or an idealized object is chosen with whom the child may identify himself and so share in the accomplishment and greatness of the object. This is narcissistic love and the process is described as *narcissistic object choice.*[6] In later life such a tendency may show itself in a man who loves a woman for the opportunity that she affords to gratify his need to show off, or in a woman who loves a man for the vicarious satisfaction she achieves by sharing in his power and strength.

[5] *Editor's note*: Cf. Chapter 1 for an additional reason why these demands must remain unfulfilled.

[6] Annie Reich discusses this subject in great detail in a recent paper (10).

A basic concept of psychoanalysis is that the love (libidinal) energies pass through specific phases of development from earliest infancy to adult life. This concept is based on clinical psychoanalytic experience and it has received strong confirmation by direct observations of children. The phases of libidinal development are described in terms of the areas of the body most prominent in their expression, the erogenous zones: oral, anal, phallic and genital. There is no sharp demarcation between these phases as development proceeds and each successive phase carries residua of the earlier ones. This tendency for earlier phases to persist in the love expressions of the individual is the phenomenon of *fixation;* and depending upon the degree and type of fixation the manifestations of love will be specifically colored. Aggressive impulses too enter into these pregenital relationships to an important extent and promote the manifestations of *ambivalence.*

So, for example, when oral elements are prominent in a love relationship, the lover's demands are all-absorbing; they insist on a merging with the love object, a denial of any individuality to the two lovers. The love is clinging and dependent. The anal component in love appears in the possessiveness, the domination, the attempts at mastery of the lover. The phallic components appear especially in exhibitionism and competitiveness. These various pregenital components enter into any love relationship to different extents and are not in themselves abnormal. What is important, is to understand their genetic basis, their roots in infantile love, their vicissitudes in the course of development and their place in the total picture. The effect of such components on later object relationships may be profound.

The child is in his early stages of development dominated by the need to gratify his basic instinctual drives, both sexual and aggressive. The maturing ego assumes the functions of testing reality, of postponing gratification, of adaptation, and as the ego learns to tolerate frustration the manifestations of aggression decrease. Also as the ego develops its capacity to neutralize basic instinctual drives and to sublimate them, their energies become available for adaptive purposes. A part of this process is the "fusion" of the energies of love and aggression, a concept that emphasizes the diminution of aggression by the influence of erotic impulses. In the child (or in the adult whose love relationship is essentially pregenital) aggressive impulses may erupt and the love relationship will be punctuated by outbursts of hostility. This is the basis of the ambivalence which in the child may be a passing phase of development, but in the adult may be an indication of psychopathology.[7]

From these more general aspects of early object relations, I turn again to the child in the family, this time to the role of the father in the family constellation. The early exclusive attachment to the mother is modified by the relationship to the father, and varies in the boy and the girl. The basic human family group of mother, father and child provides the first scene of action that permits the child to experience the interactions of love and conflict. The energy for both has its source in the instinctual impulses, libidinal and aggressive. There are drives that foster love and unity, there are primal aggressive impulses and there are unavoidable deprivations that foster responses of hostility. It does not seem necessary here to discuss the problem of the universality of the oedipus complex in different cultural milieux, but it is a fair assumption that wherever a child is brought up in a relationship to two parents (or to persons who represent these parents) there will be manifestations of love and conflict requiring resolution, and to these manifestations the term, oedipus complex, may be applied. The manifestations of this relationship will vary considerably in different cultures and even within a specific culture. Especially in our own complicated culture, the variations will depend upon such circumstances as whether a child has known a parent, the death of a parent, the influence of other relatives, and the attitudes of the parents to their children. But regardless of the cultural variations, of the variations within a specific family, there are always to be recognized basic expressions of the underlying triangular relationship, the oedipus complex. This consists essentially of love of the parent of the opposite sex and hostility toward the parent of the

[7] See the papers by Hartmann, H., Kris, E., and Loewenstein, R. in the different volumes of *The Psychoanalytic Study of the Child* (6, 7, 8) for a detailed exposition of the complicated factors that enter into psychic structure, development, instinctual drives, and object relationships.

same sex. This is called the *positive oedipus complex*. A common variation, and potentially a pathological one, is the *negative oedipus complex* in which the love is directed to the parent of the same sex and the hostility to the parent of the opposite sex.

In the boy under usual circumstances, there is a process which involves both identification with the father and hostility toward him, the mother remaining as the love object. In the girl there is a change of love object from the mother to the father which carries with it, again, a complicated response to the mother to whom the girl may remain attached in terms of her preoedipal relationship and toward whom she may manifest disappointment and hostility.

In dealing with the oedipus complex, which is usually present in its greatest intensity in the ages from about four to six, the child goes through a process of identification particularly with the parent of the same sex. In this process the boy gives up the love of the mother, substitutes for it a feeling of tenderness and is free to go on to develop other object relationships with persons of the opposite sex. This phenomenon which is spoken of as the "passing of the oedipus complex" becomes of paramount importance in the determination of the child's later relationships outside the family. If the boy does not free himself from his infantile attachment and love to the mother and his hostility and hate of the father, these disturbed feelings will influence his character structure and his later relationships to men and women, not only with regard to love relationships, but also to social and work relationships. However, the passing of the oedipus complex is a quantitative phenomenon. It is a process through which every individual must pass with more or less success, and it is a moot question whether one can ever speak of a total resolution of this problem.

Another important aspect of object relationship within the family is that among siblings. This may take on a number of forms depending upon such factors as the relative ages of the siblings, circumstances surrounding the birth of the siblings and the sex of the siblings. A sibling who is born at a time when a child is enjoying the full love and attention of the mother and who interferes with this idyllic relationship cannot but engender profound feelings of rivalry and hostility. The attitudes of the parents to this hostility will effect the expressions of the rivalry which may take the form of overt manifestations of hostility and conflict, or its opposite, passivity and reaction formations of solicitousness and consideration, beneath which however there may be the roots of conflict and neurotic disturbance. The relationship to a sibling who is much older and who may occupy the role of a substitute parent may complicate the manifestations of the oedipus complex. The relationship to siblings, particularly if unresolved, may have profound effect upon the individual's relationship to other persons in his later life. For example a co-worker may be related to in terms of a hated brother and a wife treated as a beloved sister, the former with irrational hostilities, the latter with the inhibitions of incestuous love.

THE CHILD AND HIS COMMUNITY

From his relationships within the family the child steps out toward his relationships within the community. These concern relationships with other children, relationships with adults, and relationships to society. In his earliest relationships to the group the child expresses only his own needs. He recognizes the presence of other children but uses them for his own purpose. However, some recent observations by Anna Freud and Sophie Dann (3) are of special interest because they indicate how much is still to be learned in this field. They describe an experience with six children who were German-Jewish orphans, the victims of German Nazism, all of whom lost their parents during the first year of life, and who were brought to the concentration camp at Tereszin between the ages of six and twelve months. There they were inmates of a ward for Motherless Children, where they received such care as was made available by other inmates of the concentration camp. The authors say:

They had no toys and their only facility for outdoor life was a bare yard. The Ward was staffed by nurses and helpers, themselves inmates of the concentration camp and, as such, undernourished and overworked. Since Tereszin was a transit camp, deportations were frequent. Approximately two to three years after arrival, in the spring of 1945, when liberated by the Russians, the six children with others were taken to a Czech castle where they were given special care and were lavishly fed.

Subsequently these children were brought to England where they came under the care of Anna Freud at Bulldogs Bank. At that time they ranged in age between three years and three years and ten months. The interesting point about their behavior as a group is described by Freud and Dann in terms of a clinging together of the group, a disregard of adults and outsiders, positive relations within the group with absence of envy, jealousy, rivalry and competition, though with some discrimination among group members and antipathies and friendships among the group. Only gradually did these children develop a positive relationship toward adults, with manifestations of sharing, consideration, and equality with adults, helpfulness to adults, sensitiveness to them, and finally more definite personal relationships.

It appears from this study that in these children at the age when they were observed, the need to belong and the identification with the group were stronger than the self-centered isolating tendencies, the "egocentrism" of Piaget. The severely disturbed relationships of these children in the first year of their lives and later were deciding factors in this development. The authors consider this question:

> The children were without parents in the fullest sense of the word, i.e., not merely orphaned at the time of observation, but most of them without an early mother or father image in their unconscious minds to which their earliest libidinal strivings might have been attached. Consequently, their companions of the same age were their real love objects and their libidinal relations with them of a direct nature, not merely the product of laborious reaction formation and defenses against hostility. This explains why the feelings of the six children toward each other show a warmth and spontaneity which is unheard of in ordinary relations between young contemporaries.

What appears basic is the need to identify whether with a parental figure as is the usual case or with a group of contemporaries as in this extraordinary instance.

The earliest relationship to the mother is built up on a pattern of identification and, with the later identification to the father, becomes the basis of the development of the child's character and personality. These earliest relationships determine the pattern of later relationships, but are also subject to modification by later identifications with figures in the environment such as teachers, leaders, or even abstract persons or ideals supplied by national, religious or educational forces. This constant interaction between the basic core of personality which develops out of the early childhood experience within the family and the later modifications from contact outside of the family goes on for the rest of the person's life.

Confusions in a person's relationships may result from confusions in his early identifications both within the family and outside. The absence of a parent, inconsistencies of a parent's attitudes, inconsistent attitudes between parents, will all have profound effects in producing confusions within the child regarding his personal identity and will express themselves in his disturbed personality and character development. To this basic disturbance there may be added further confusions that result from inconsistencies in the social environment beyond the confines of the family group. There are many examples of such social factors which may influence later development and object relationships: the second generation child in this country who finds conflicting attitudes between the school and the home; the victim of the enforced migrations imposed by Nazism who must readjust to new pressures and new economic standards; the African native or the American Indian who leaves his own people to live in a metropolis; all suffer confusions of identity which influence their behavior and their relations to others.[8]

The basic "need to belong" shows itself in the tendency of the adolescent to join a group. The adolescent group may be formed for different purposes—intellectual, athletic, social or even antisocial. The emphasis on the antisocial group, "the gang," may lead to the neglect of the fact that even in the antisocial group

[8] See Erikson's, *Childhood and Society* (2), where this question is given special emphasis.

there is the basic need to belong of the adolescent,[9] a need which if it is recognized and utilized, can be directed toward satisfactory social adjustment. The adolescent joins with others of his age to form groups for at least two reasons: one is to break away from the parental ties, to deny his dependency upon his parents; the other is to deal with the tensions and anxieties which result from the sudden increase at this time, in the strength and prominence of the instinctual impulses, sexual and aggressive. Being part of a group permits the adolescent to share his guilt, to lessen his anxiety, and within the activities of the group to achieve some gratifications, both sexual and aggressive, that he could not achieve by himself. It becomes the task of the worker to recognize these needs and to permit the adolescent the proper balance between gratification and deprivation that will permit development and sublimation. Conflict cannot be avoided, but it can be kept within optimal bounds.

In this adolescent group we find the characteristics of any group formation. The specific contribution of psychoanalysis to the study of group dynamics and group activity is the recognition that in group dynamics there are two sets of factors, conscious and unconscious. A group may be formed for conscious reasons, to organize a dance, to form a football team or to read poetry together—all conscious ego activities. But at the same time there enters into the formation of the group, no matter what its conscious purpose may be, the unconscious motivations which permit the expression of id and superego functions. In any group there exist between the members of the group unconscious emotional ties and identifications which keep the group together. These ties are the basis of social feelings. Freud (4) has emphasized that the nature of this emotional tie is particularly influenced by whether or not the group has a leader. The relationship to the leader is on both conscious and unconscious levels, but it is particularly the unconscious components which give a group its specific significance. The relationship to the leader is an expression of the individual's relationship to his superego and in-

---

[9] *Editor's note*: Cf. Chapter 11, where Raymond Sobel shows how this need for identification is utilized in the program of residential therapy with adolescents.

fluences his relations with other members of the group. He surrenders to the leader a part of his superego, and to that extent, as a participant of the group the individual surrenders a part of himself. By this surrender he wins the approval of the leader; he shares in his strength and omnipotence (often fantasied); he gains release from anxiety and guilt; he achieves social acceptance. But for these gains he pays the price of regression. His emotions become intensified, his ability to think becomes impaired; the individual in the group will act and think in a way that is different from his acting and thinking when away from the group. He faces the dangers of the breakdown of the group, the panic and confusion that follows the breakdown of the mutual ties between its members or the loss of the leader. This is not necessarily abnormal or maladaptive; regression has a definitive adaptive value under appropriate circumstances. The group may be formed primarily and consciously to accomplish socially desirable aims and the leader may function to achieve the same goal. In such a case the regressive surrender of the individual in the group is subject to re-evaluation and reversal, even as a person who permits himself the regressive pleasures of art and play can, when necessary, bring back into action his more developed ego functions. Kris and Leites (9) compare democratic and totalitarian groups and show that in both there are identifications with leaders, but the different unconscious responses are crucial in determining the resultant manifestations. They say:

> In a totalitarian state these identifications concern, to a large extent, id and superego functions. These identifications facilitate the gratifying completion of impulses, as superego functions have been projected upon the propagandist, and as he is idealized in an archaic sense: Omnipotence, omniscience and infallibility are attributed to him.
> In democratic states, the corresponding identifications concern, to a large extent, ego functions which are delegated to the propagandist. Amongst these functions, the scrutiny of the existing situation and the anticipation of the future are of predominant importance. While the propagandee relies upon the propagandist for the fulfillment of these functions, he retains a critical attitude in relation to him.

Group formation is a basic phenomenon of human behavior—
the complexities of its manifestations and the social consequences
are in great part in causative relation to the unconscious mental
activities of the individuals in the group.

BEING IN LOVE

An important expression of group activity is the individual's
behavior in the love relationship. Psychoanalysis considers love as
much broader in scope than sexuality and certainly broader than
genitality. Love thus includes the relationship of the individual
to his love object in terms of other factors than sexual union,
including idealization, tenderness, considerateness, provision for
care and common interests. The emotional responses of love also
require consideration, but as a modern philosopher has said of
poets, novelists and even other philosophers who attempt such
consideration:

> The conscious quality of this passion differs so much in
> various races and individuals, and at various points in the
> same life, that no account of it will ever satisfy everybody.[10]

In the same book the author adds:

> Two things need to be admitted by anyone who would not
> go wholly astray in such speculation [about love]; one, that
> love has an animal basis; the other, that it has an ideal ob-
> ject. Since these two propositions have usually been thought
> contradictory, no writer has ventured to present more than
> half the truth, and that half out of its true relations.

Since these words were written, psychoanalysis and particularly
Freud's own contributions have presented both propositions as
parts of an integral concept.

The development of love from its earliest manifestations as
love of the self (narcissism) to love of another person (object love)
goes through a series of phases, into which many factors, both
biological and cultural may enter. Psychoanalysis emphasizes particularly this developmental aspect of love. The sexual behavior

10 Santayana, G. The life of reason. *Reason in Society*. New York, 1905.

of an individual is in direct correlation with his social behavior
and an individual parallels in his social behavior his basic sexual
strivings. The individual who, for instance, is fixated at the infantile sexual level of orality will express oral tendencies in his
personal relations with all persons. He will demand that all
persons love him; he will become inordinately jealous of a fellow
worker who is praised by the boss; he will become dispropor-
tionately depressed by a minor criticism, because his self-esteem
requires insatiable replenishment. So too other pregenital manifestations will appear both in the love relationships and other
social contacts. Of particular interest are those individuals whose
basic love relationships are disturbed by the unsatisfactory resolution of their aggressive impulses. Here sadistic and masochistic
components appear as tendencies to hurt others or to be hurt.
Every social worker has the experience of dealing with an individual who suffers one misfortune after another, seeking at the
same time to place upon the outside world the full blame for the
tragic series of misfortunes. It soon becomes clear that at least
a part of the difficulty lies within himself and that there is a
pattern of bringing upon himself these unfortunate occurrences.
This pattern, which is familiar to the psychoanalyst in the concept of moral masochism, cannot be dealt with adequately if the
emphasis is placed only upon the external factors.

Love relationships of special importance are those in which
the individual seeks his gratifications only in fantasied relationships. His pattern is one of acting out with a series of persons
the fantasy which he seeks to gratify. His choice of an object to
love is determined by neurotic needs and only rarely can such a
choice meet with satisfactory resolution in real life. An example
is the person who seeks to gratify his need for dependence on the
mother in every woman he loves. In the less common instance in
which such a person chooses as his love object an individual who
has a need to give love to an infantile object, a semblance of
adjustment may be achieved, but more usually this is not accomplished.

The "narcissistic" type of love relationship is one in which the
individual seeks perpetually to love himself by loving another
person who represents himself. Homosexuality is particularly

characterized by this type of love. The woman who seeks in her husband the gratification of her own masculine strivings is another example. The parent who seeks in his child the achievement of his own frustrated ambitions is expressing in his parental love a form of narcissistic love.

When one turns from the aberrations of love to the consideration of "mature" love, one does well to remember Santayana's wise and charming warnings of the difficulties to be encountered. The developmental approach to love assumes goals toward which the development tends: immature love becomes mature; pregenital love becomes genital; ambivalent love becomes postambivalent; narcissistic love becomes object love. These goals are ideals and it may be questioned if they are ever fully achieved. Even as with the concepts of "normality" and "health," psychoanalysis prefers to be cautious about offering a precise definition of mature love until many still obscure questions are clarified. Allowance must also be made for the widely varied expressions of so profound a relationship. A further difficulty comes from the fact that regressive factors are evident in the ordinary manifestations of love which are clearly not pathological. Pregenital foreplay, narcissistic identifications, in fact many characteristics of immature love have their place in normal love activities. It is not the presence or absence of these characteristics alone that determines the level of maturity but additional factors such as the balance between the component activities, the accompanying guilt or anxiety, the nature of the gratification, the extrasexual behavior and the place of the relationship in the social adaptation of the two persons.

TRANSFERENCE

The individual who brings to his object relationships his fantasied needs and who gives to the object fantasied qualities, is manifesting the phenomenon of transference. This means that he is transferring to a real person feelings, attitudes, and fantasies which come from his unconscious mind and which are residuals of his infantile experiences and conflicts. What are "transferred" are unconscious instinctual impulses, sexual and aggressive, unconscious attitudes, and unconscious fantasies. It is important to emphasize that this phenomenon of transference occurs to a greater or lesser degree in all persons at all times, and that in each response to an object there enter both the expressions of transference and the realistic awareness of the object. When an individual in his behavior to other persons predominantly transfers infantile wishes and attitudes, then his object relationships will be at a level of clinical disturbance. The psychiatrist or social worker does not produce or create a transference; the patient or client is only too ready to do this himself. It is true, however, that the therapeutic situation or the casework setup fosters the overt expression of transference phenomena. It is the function of the psychiatrist or caseworker to recognize the transference manifestations and to deal with them. A specific example would be that of an individual whose object relationships are characterized by a tendency to transfer to any person with whom he comes in contact his aggressive feelings toward his parents. In his ordinary life situations he will meet with an immediate response to this aggression, namely, counteraggression. One might speak of this counteraggression as countertransference, except that an individual who is subjected to an aggressive act is entitled to respond aggressively even though the instigator of the act is behaving under the motivation of an unconscious need to be aggressive. The psychiatrist, the social worker, and other persons who are professionally engaged in dealing with human beings, such as teachers, and jurists, should however be required to deal differently with these transference manifestations—they must be expected not to give expression to their counteraggression. When a professional person does respond with counteraggression, he is at that moment not recognizing his professional role and is acting from his own unconscious, that is with countertransference. To avoid this undesirable response the professional worker must pay close attention to the phenomenon of transference. Similar considerations apply to fantasied feelings of love that are transferred to the object and which may activate countertransferences. When the transferred feelings are ambivalent, as is so often the case, special problems of countertransference arise.

There are three stages in dealing with transference which require progressively increasing levels of training and experience. These are: (1) understanding the transference, (2) utilizing the transference, and (3) interpreting the transference.

Understanding of the transference will permit the worker to understand the behavior of the individual and to recognize its significance in terms of his developmental experience and his present unconscious needs. It gives to the worker added data that permit the fuller integration of other factors—the present behavior and problem, the environmental forces, the past experiences and earlier object relationships.

The utilization of the transference is a technique available to the caseworker, the value of which will depend on his understanding of the phenomenon. Utilization of transference is an everyday phenomenon. It explains many "cures" of emotional disturbances by life situations, by fortunate relationships with other persons, by faddists and cultists. A good friend who intuitively reassures an unhappy man may help to lift a depression without any awareness on his part of what he is doing. The professionally trained person who utilizes the transference should, however, do so with an awareness of the dynamics involved. The recognition of a transference-need permits the establishment of a relationship between a caseworker and a client which allows for the utilization of such techniques as suggestion, advice, counseling, and education. Transference is the basis of, but not identical with, rapport. The development of a negative transference, that is, the expression of hostile, infantile, unconscious impulses introduces great difficulties in dealing with a client, and it is therefore preferable to avoid the provocation of such a reaction except in intensive therapy. Where it does appear it requires skillful handling.

The interpretation of the transference, that is, confronting the individual with the awareness that his behavior is the repetition of a specific unconscious infantile constellation is definitely part of psychoanalytical therapy and requires the preparation of the individual by the careful analysis of his unconscious defenses. Otherwise one would be dealing here with the too frequent experience of "wild analysis." In some instances the transference manifestations are so obvious that their "interpretation" requires no

preparation, but this is not usually the case. The premature interpretation of a transference phenomenon will in fortunate circumstances produce no effect whatever because of the individual's
defenses; in less fortunate instances it may produce severe manifestations of anxiety or guilt. Where it appears that interpretation of transference is essential for progress in a case, then direct
psychiatric therapy is indicated.

A significant aspect of object relationships that will concern
the social worker is that of the psychotic or prepsychotic client
who in his relationships utilizes the mechanisms of his psychotic
illness and transfers unconscious demands to other persons. For
example he seeks in his relationships unrealistic magical gratifications or he introduces paranoid projections and blames others
for his own difficulties.

THE PERSON AND SOCIETY

A frequent misconception regarding psychoanalytic formulations about object relationships is that because psychoanalysis
emphasizes the developmental basis of object relationships, their
origin from instinctual impulses, sexual and aggressive, it therefore pictures man in society as a base and despicable creature.
This is actually far from the truth. Psychoanalysis in its emphasis
on ego and superego development, on sublimation, on the development of object relationships from narcissism to object love, has
recognized and emphasized the importance of the manifestations
of positive social relationships. Psychoanalysis shares with a
French poet of the last century the thought: "Man has henceforth this cause of pride: that he has bethought himself of justice
in a universe without justice, and has put justice there."[11] Psychoanalysis has recognized the role of co-operation, altruism, kindness and mutual dependence. Its task is to study all the phenomena of human behavior including the relationships between persons, to trace their origins, their unconscious roots, and their
development. It does not assume the task of setting up standards
of values. To understand object relationships, to gather their full

[11] This quotation from Jean Lahor is borrowed from George Santayana's
Poetry and Religion in which a chapter is devoted to the ideas of the poet.

importance and to exploit their usefulness require a total approach—the study of biological, genetic factors and the study of cultural factors, within the family and outside it. Psychoanalysis, it may be said, has made a definitive contribution to these studies by its delineation of the problems of the unconscious and of psychic development.

BIBLIOGRAPHY

1. BOWLBY, J. *Maternal Care and Mental Health.* World Organization Monograph Series No. 2, 1951.
2. ERIKSON, E. H. *Childhood and Society.* New York: W. W. Norton & Co., 1950.
3. FREUD, A. and DANN, S. An experiment in group upbringing. In *The Psychoanalytic Study of the Child,* 6:127-168, 1951. New York: International Universities Press.
4. FREUD, S. *Group Psychology and the Analysis of the Ego.* London: Hogarth Press, 1922.
5. HARTMANN, H. Comments on the psychoanalytic theory of the ego. In *The Psychoanalytic Study of the Child,* 5:74-96, 1950. New York: International Universities Press.
6. —— and KRIS, E. The genetic approach in psychoanalysis. *Ibid.,* 1:11-30, 1945.
7. —— —— and LOEWENSTEIN, R. M. Comments on the formation of psychic structure. *Ibid.,* 2:11-38, 1946.
8. —— —— —— Notes on the theory of aggression. *Ibid.,* 3/4:9-36, 1949.
9. KRIS, E. and LEITES, N. Trends in twentieth century propaganda. In *Psychoanalysis and the Social Sciences,* 1:393-410, 1947 (edited by Géza Róheim). New York: International Universities Press.
10. REICH, A. Narcissistic object choice in women. *J. Am. Psychoanal. Assn.,* 1:22-44, 1953.

Part II
PRACTICE

Chapter 5

COLLABORATIVE PSYCHOTHERAPY: TEAM SETTING

ADELAIDE M. JOHNSON, M.D., Ph.D.

In this chapter I intend to describe a highly refined procedure of therapy so far not widely used or understood. I shall be concerned, for the most part, with collaboration between two therapists. Two psychiatrists, or one psychiatrist and a social worker, may participate, as a minimum. At times three therapists may be intimately concerned. In this kind of therapy, the procedure no longer is limited to the psychiatrist interpreting the structure and needs of a patient and advising the social worker to do thus and so, with occasional conferences to understand the movement of the case.

The Functions of the Members of a Team

The concept that the psychiatrist always has the greater knowledge and experience is purely academic. Actually, the extent of one's knowledge depends only upon training and experience. It is no academic matter, however, that legally the psychiatrist must bear the final responsibility for the therapeutic task undertaken.

In this team procedure as I have experienced it for many years, every therapeutic hour by each therapist is reviewed fully with the other and the dynamic interplay of patient with patient, and each with her or his therapist, is fully discussed. Although this procedure first evolved where a child was concerned, it has been extended just as carefully in certain cases where the two patients are adults. By such collaboration in psychotherapy, the psychiatric social worker at times may contribute any of the multiple functions she fulfills in case work. Such activity would be in addition to the highly refined psychotherapy in which she participates in the office. Collaboration of the kind described can be a part of case work, then, and I can see no reason for sharp lines of demarcation between the prerogatives of workers in certain cases.

In observing clinically the mutual therapeutic responsibility, several features become evident. The question immediately arises as to the rationale for, or benefits accrued from, such a collaborative procedure. Such benefits cannot be observed in all cases—in fact in many cases only damage might evolve from the introduction of two therapists into the life of one patient or into the lives of two members of a family.[1] This is a problem that warrants careful diagnostic scrutiny in every case.

Furthermore, the earlier procedure whereby the psychiatrist always treated the child, and the social worker treated the mother or father, has been greatly modified in a more rational direction. The needs of the patients—in a family those who need help might be only the two parents or some other two adults—and the training and experience of the members of the team should decide the question of procedure. I hope that the earlier dubious concept that the child needs a more dynamically experienced and trained therapist will go by the board as a generalization. The new direction has evolved along with increasing knowledge of how intricately the parent-child pathologic condition intermeshes in an etiologic symbiosis. The age of the patient cannot decide the issue of the introduction of a dynamic therapy.

Likewise, the sharp demarcation between definitive uncovering therapy and supportive therapy,[2] limited respectively to the psychiatrist and the social worker, seems obviously untenable. At present it is believed that good supportive therapy demands as thorough a knowledge of dynamics as does uncovering therapy. Even in interviewing a mother or father or spouse on a so-called "simple reporting" level, real skill is required to maintain the tempo. Similarly, if the curative process requires fairly definite

---

1 *Editor's note:* Cf. Chapters 6, pp. 114 ff., and 7.
2 *Editor's note:* Cf. Chapter 7, pp. 131 ff.

uncovering therapy by the psychiatrist, together with extra-office calls by a woman social worker who will explore the patient's social or recreational life, the role of this latter person, to be effective, demands the keenest understanding. This is true in an institution or outside of one. It may be that the roles of the participant therapists are reversed in a particular case, especially if the psychiatric social worker participating in such close teamwork is experienced. I encourage social workers to work with the transference and resistance as the case demands, and as the capacity of the workers makes possible, just as I encourage any senior resident in psychiatry. Needless to say, many residents and many social workers never will be able to work with transference and resistance, and never can become successful members of highly sensitive collaborative psychotherapy teams. It is a fact, however, that the social worker has to do much of the taxing leg work in dealing with the environment, such as court work, interagency contacts, making housing and housekeeping arrangements, conducting home studies, and so forth, largely because she has had the training and experience in many of these areas which usually the psychiatrist has not had. When she does psychotherapy, whatever the approach to definitiveness of it, this is only part of her function in case work.

I have covered sketchily only a few of the problems which arise concerning a collaborative team. Now, however, it is possible to consider fundamentals and I think it has been made evident that what I am about to discuss applies equally to both situations regardless of whether the team consists of two psychiatrists or a psychiatrist and a social worker.

THE NEED OF RESPECT AND FRIENDLINESS WITHIN THE TEAM

It is impossible to achieve much for the patients if, within the team, respect and mutual friendliness are lacking. The patient or patients soon sense competitiveness, narcissism and defensiveness or overprotectiveness in the therapist and further progress is prevented. For instance, two parents may be put at loggerheads or they may be led into apologizing for one another; under such circumstances it is impossible to get very far with their child. If there were no unresolved blind spots in either therapist, to speak hypothetically, then there would be no clinical need for the two members to get together to discuss their cases or case; only for research would this be necessary. However, there *are no* therapists without blind spots. The benefit achieved, therefore, from frequent discussion of cases is, in addition to research, the assistance one gives another to see what he might not see because of countertransference difficulties. In the course of discussion, resistance frequently springs from overidentification with one's patient. Therefore, collaborative conferences, to be of clinical value, must transpire, as has been said, in an atmosphere of friendliness and respect. In many instances benefit may accrue to the patient from my colleague's suggesting a point of view of which I have been unaware. At times I may be rendered very uneasy or irritated by his or her suggestion. The latter is characteristic of every collaborative enterprise, but the persons concened must be so friendly and conscientious that they will be willing to explore the sources of such irritation. Such exploration obviously involves no confession to one's collaborator—such insight is one's own personal affair—and the collaborator should be concerned only with the renewed progress of treatment. Every good therapist grows somewhat in the course of each case even if working alone; he grows even more with each successful collaborative experience.

The psychiatrist, because of his own problems or inexperience in an enterprise in which he is collaborating with a social worker, may be anxious and hesitant about the social worker's therapeutic efforts. This feeling quickly is conveyed to the social worker and, whether she becomes irritated or not, the fullest use of her skills will be jeopardized unless she is a highly stable and experienced person. The reverse likewise is true. Tensions of the sort described should be aired mutually as soon as they are sensed by either partner. The psychiatrist, who for so-called philosophical or empirical reasons feels uneasy about collaborating with a certain other psychiatrist or with a certain social worker, should avoid entering upon such an enterprise. In other words, each member of the team *must* become aware of his own and of the other's assets, skills and limitations and the two must be able, as has been said, to deal with these openly, in a friendly atmosphere, or the procedure is doomed to failure. Often each must search for some time to find the collaborator with whom he can do the best work. The limitations otherwise can be too destructive on either side.

In my first attempts to advance the useful technique of collaborative therapy, I was most fortunate that an old and valued friend from medical school days happened to be in the same child guidance clinic. Thus, S. A. Szurek and I were able early to deal frankly with each other and to work in a friendly atmosphere. Having achieved real gratification and confidence thus, it has been relatively easy since to establish similar relationships with a number of social workers and with other psychiatrists.

I do not wish to be overly optimistic but, by and large, I have encountered circumstances wherein social workers and I have functioned with mutual pleasure. I have had the good fortune to teach in a number of the leading schools of social work and thus have had the opportunity, on the spot, to observe with the greatest respect their excellent and difficult educational and training programs. Therefore, because I was not ignorant of the philosophical concepts and clinical training imparted in such schools, I did not become anxious about the aptitude of their graduates. Furthermore, I had no fear of their attempting to maneuver me into a position of sanctioning their assumption of clinical responsibility for which they could not take the final legal responsibility. This I have never experienced. Social workers have taught me much about law and agency functioning; I have taught them something of the dynamics of the personality. In research there is no qualitative line of demarcation in mutual psychotherapy even though, in research, both partners cannot always be highly experienced.

THE SETTING FOR COLLABORATIVE THERAPY

As for the situations for possible employment of such a team, I can be brief. Such collaborators could work in children's agencies; family agencies; public health agencies; guidance clinics; medical, surgical and psychiatric hospital settings, and under the purview of the psychiatrist in a private setting. I have worked on teams with social workers and psychiatrists in every one of these settings and with real comfort.

At the risk of appearing to repeat myself, I must make clear a conviction which applies especially in the private setting. I am completely opposed to nonmedically trained persons doing psychiatric therapy, even though it involves only so-called environmental manipulative therapy, without the supervision of a psychiatrist. The shortage of psychiatrists is a spurious argument for this practice. The more that is known generally by the public of emotional disorders, the more complicated become the defenses (as the conflicts are pushed deeper). Thus, psychosomatic symptomatology of a deeper and more complex nature is increasingly seen. Grand hysteria has largely disappeared in the more sophisticated urban areas and more complicated psychologic and somatic solutions are apparent. Many new organic diseases are likewise recognized from year to year and the interrelationships with psychogenic factors are so complicated that even the medically trained psychiatrist is in for trouble if he does not recurrently turn to the internist or surgeon for help in the proper evaluation of the symptomatology presented by his patients. Just the routine of sending the patient who is receiving psychiatric treatment to an internist once a year is no guarantee of safety, although it is better than nothing. Thus, as I said, no matter how highly gifted or experienced in psychotherapy a person without medical training may be, I am opposed to his undertaking care of a patient without the closest collaboration with a psychiatrist. On the other hand, if a gifted and experienced psychiatric social worker is functioning under my supervision, I set no more limits to the extent to which she treats her patient than I would set for a senior resident or a colleague of my level of experience.

I wish to reiterate that collaborative therapy does not imply occasional review with the psychiatrist of the status of the social worker's patient but regular conferences covering their mutual therapeutic hours in detail. This should be emphasized, since the procedure I have in mind has little in common with a tendency which I question although I do not condemn it; namely, referral of a patient by a psychiatrist to a psychiatric social worker who conducts treatment and who only occasionally consults with the psychiatrist.

SELECTION OF PATIENTS

Selection of patients best adapted to collaborative psychotherapy demands careful diagnostic study. Generalizations do not apply. Much of what I shall discuss below is still open to question. Some declarations, however, can be made with considerable confidence. In three large groups of cases intensive research has been done and for these collaborative therapy is to date easily the most effective procedure. This is not by any means to maintain that it works in all such cases, but nothing else seems so nearly adequate.

1. All little children or adolescents who are acting out seriously, in an antisocial manner, and who are living at home, are hazards to others and usually it is futile to try to treat them unless the significant parent[3] also is being treated. If placement of the child or treatment of the parent is out of the question, then it is less damaging to the family situation if a therapist does not undertake treatment of the child. Etiologically many of us who are in this work believe that the child acts out because the parent has a need to achieve vicarious gratification through the child for his own poorly integrated, forbidden impulses. This is more often unconscious than conscious on the parent's part. At the same time, the destruction of the child's stability in his society is also an unwitting expression of the parent's hostility to that child. Often just one child in the family is selected to be the scapegoat, and the reasons for his selection must be understood in each case. If the parent is consciously or unconsciously con-

---

[3] In any case, one or both parents may be concerned in the pathologic state. For convenience, however, I generally shall use the singular. Moreover, because the parent who needs treatment more often is the mother, usually I shall use a feminine pronoun to refer to "the parent." Likewise, I generally shall use a feminine pronoun to refer to the psychiatric social worker because this worker almost always is a woman. On the other hand, usually I shall employ a masculine pronoun to refer to the psychiatrist because, thus, the task of distinguishing between psychiatrist and social worker will be simplified.

doning the child's behavior and brings the child for help only to avoid his expulsion from school or to propitiate or beguile the law, through the therapists, treatment of any nature is practically hopeless unless the child can be removed from the home. If a therapist succumbs to the situation of unconscious sanctioning by treating only the child, then the acting out often becomes far worse. Increasing acting out on the part of the child may occur because the therapist has been unwise in his technical handling of the case but often another potent factor is that the parent, for multiple reasons, unloads the responsibility for any deviation into the therapist's lap, thus giving increased rein to his own pathologic sanctions of the child's acts. This is not the place to go into this matter in detail, but such unloading never fails to happen if only the child is treated. Case material later in this chapter will illustrate this concept. Further relevant discussion also is to be found in *Searchlights on Delinquency,* wherein Szurek and I have written chapters (7, 1), and in a more recent paper of ours (5). Collaborative therapy seems a necessity in cases such as have just been described.

2. Another large category of patients whose condition some have found difficult to alleviate except by collaborative effort is composed of those troubled by prolonged fixations. In these cases, diagnostically, a child seems fixated at some instinctual level for a long time—either having regressed to such a point or never having moved beyond it.

In a normal family, if a child regresses after the death of a member of the group, or in the course of the child's own organic illness, or with the advent of a new sibling, support and kindliness at home, with or without therapy, usually restore the child relatively rapidly to his previous more mature level of adaptation. When, in the face of such reality, or beset by fantasy, a child remains obstinately fixated, my experience indicates that search should be made for what, in one or both parents, may be fostering the fixation. When a child remains arrested in his growth, or, when older, becomes unable to reach adjustment with his parents and regresses, it is important to search for something in the parents which frightened him at the higher level, but also to determine whether, at the fixation level, something may be giving the parent unconscious gratification. To illustrate this point the following might be described:

Johnny, aged six, gets a new baby sister. Soon Johnny begins to soil his clothes and this soiling continues. Finally he is brought for treatment by the less involved parent. Intensive analysis of the child alone may fairly well clear up the rivalry with the sister—the double oedipal conflict—so that Johnny is co-operating fairly well with parents, school and friends. The soiling, however, obstinately remains. It looks as if he has considerably by-passed this pathologic characteristic of his growth for the time being.

How is this explained and what can be done about it? Close scrutiny almost always reveals that at least one parent, for multiple reasons, has continued through the child an instinctual gratification and it takes the form of condoning arrested or regressive development as exemplified in soiling. The child feels a powerful obligation to the parent to continue to supply this gratification and case analyses reveal clearly what he sees in the face, hears in the voice, and observes in the behavior of this parent that conveys to him what he must do. A child so involved in a parent's guilty demand and sanction of the child's antisocial acts feels as guilty and frightened about modifying his behavior as would a normal child who was being seduced by an outsider to steal. Often such a pathologic situation can be observed and successfully treated only if treatment of both child and parent is undertaken. Again, case material will help to clarify these claims, which I originally incorporated in a paper read before the American Psychiatric Association in May, 1952.[4]

The most difficult cases the therapist encounters, except those which exemplify actual psychosis, fall into the foregoing two numbered categories. Until, in both groups, the details of the pathologic symbiosis were perceived and resort was had to mutual concomitant therapy, often the attempt at cure failed miserably.

[4] The paper was entitled "Collaborative Psychotherapy as a Research Tool in the Study of Fixation; it has been expanded and will be published soon under the title "The Etiology of Fixations."

3. Something of the third category, namely, psychoses, will be discussed later under more theoretical implications.

These, then, are the three types of situation in which treatment is most difficult. Cases in group 1 require immediately tactful identification of which parent is unwittingly fostering the acting out. Cases of group 2 necessitate detailed scrutiny into what enrages the parent about the child's achievement at a normal level, plus what instinctual needs the parent is gratifying, through the child, at the fixation level or levels. And, as has been said, comment on cases of group 3 is deferred.

Many cases do not require the intensive uncovering and special therapy that have been described. On the other hand, in many cases, benefit results from collaborative efforts directed toward a different goal and geared to a different form of operation from those described. For instance, a neurotic woman or man may live inextricably in a miserable reality situation. After all, therapists cannot change the world and must often attempt to help patients so immured. Such a situation is familiar to any family agency. The best that the psychiatrist can do with it is to employ some degree of uncovering and supportive therapy and the best that the psychiatric social worker can do is to give more or less environmental manipulative help. Even in the selection of a housekeeper, the social worker should act on the basis of a great deal of dynamic understanding. Sometimes an adolescent girl whose mother is dead or ineffective may profit 'from definitive psychotherapy, but only if it is accompanied, at a certain phase, or throughout, by the peripatetic resources of an experienced and trained real mother figure. A worker who can function as such a figure will be called on many times to handle, verbally or not, many dynamically pertinent factors that are bound to form a part of even the most distinctly extra-office relationship.

Another group of patients of whom there are all too many are either adolescents or adults who suffered great physical brutality as children but whose mistreatment was of such a nature that, instead of acting out, they submitted masochistically. Analysis of such intensity and depth as would free these patients can be made only if there are available the economic and geographic resources to hospitalize them at various phases of their analysis when they become suicidal or act out. If such resources are not available, chaos may result. Therefore, in many such cases my goal is a limited one as far as cure is concerned. A collaborative setup, highly flexible and uncontaminated by narcissistic ambitions of either therapist, often can operate fairly successfully for years, making life less destructive for these patients. Only the team and the particular assets of its members can control the decision as to who might be seen by the psychiatrist or the social worker. If a very masochistic parent, physically misused early, has a disturbed child, the child might be accessible for highly definitive therapy, whereas only support for the parent, dynamically comprehended, may be—and I think should be in many cases—the instrument of choice. In a situation such as has been described, if two therapists are working concomitantly, the most careful collaboration is necessary to cope with the hostile envy of the parent while, at the same time, care is being taken not to endanger the defenses that are successfully damming back the parent's homicidal and suicidal impulses. Social workers and psychiatrists know from experience that environmental help, some degree of abreaction and so on, can carry such a parent, *if* the therapist knows how to limit every possible cause for regression. Many highly masochistic egos can be kept working if the therapist gives his treatment in careful doses, not too frequently, and if he has no need within himself to foster the patient's undue dependence and regression. Many therapists working intuitively get into such a tangle. Also analytic therapists—especially the very young or the very old—lose for a time or forever their confidence in bringing to bear on the issues what resources intuitively they used to employ with real sensitivity and success. The net result is that their patients frequently regress more easily than do many who are handled by the sensitive, intuitive, nonanalytically trained man.

Actually, the cases that lend themselves especially to collaborative therapy are some of the most difficult ones. When I analyze either an adult or a child, and no one else in the family needs serious help, the case usually is not so taxing as some others are. Take an example similar to one I used earlier in this chapter:

A child or an adult has lived in a normal family but has had long organic illness, or early in the life of the family a crucial member of it has died, such as a mother. The analysis may be long and stormy and may cause the patient the greatest misery; still it presents a problem that is far easier dynamically than if the pathologic state of a family is genetically significant.

When the question of collaborative therapy arises after careful diagnostic study, an immediate practical problem is: How can the significant parent be brought into treatment? This entails a brief discussion of the degree of insight of the parent.

1. Some parents have insight and ask for help for themselves as well as for the child.

2. Some parents pay only lip service to the idea that they may need help, having heard lectures and read many articles.

3. Some parents can accept the fact of psychologic aberrations in the child but are extremely resistant to seeing their own role in the neurotic symbiosis.

Those of the first category come relatively readily into treatment. Those of the second group often will accept the proposition that the therapist see them as well as the child, to evaluate better their feelings in the whole situation and the extent to which such feelings may be clarified. It may not be necessary to say to such a parent: "You are a patient also." This type of parent will be likely soon to recognize this himself.

It is with the third category of parents that, in the beginning of their clinical experience, many therapists seem uneasy as to just how to proceed. Many questions arise which to them seem difficult; they believe that they are involved as therapists in a question of ethics and procedure.

Let it be remembered that in many cases, when the parents complain about the child, the motive for their coming is involved with their own pathologic state. Such parents, in their symbiosis with the child, have come to the point at which the ledger of gratification no longer balances equally or in the parents' favor. This is really the complaint and the motive for coming. Thus, the therapeutic responsibility is disrupted by any overidentification with child or with parents. Yet the following confusions arise in the minds of therapists.

Suppose the parent comes complaining of the child. The therapist knows that in time work must be done with one or both parents. Should he be silent about the role of the parent then, and start with the child? Later, when he tries to include the parent in treatment for one or more reasons (jealousy of the parent, resistance of the parent to losing the gratification she obtains through the child, blocking by the parent of the child's new attempts at growth), what will be the result? Many parents then feel that to draw them into therapy for which they never asked is to betray them. Their sense of being cornered may or may not be successfully analyzed. If the attempt at analysis in this direction fails, whether the parents remove the child from therapy or permit him to remain, the therapist, feeling that it would be a blow to the child to dismiss him, is saddled with a situation which never will be successfully resolved. This sequence of events has been part of every therapist's experience. The following has been observed, and can be correctly maintained: After the preliminary diagnostic evaluation has been made, and the mutual, or common, pathologic state has been briefly but frankly discussed with the significant parent, and it has been suggested that treatment for child or parent or both would be helpful, but the parent is not ready for such an approach, she will withdraw the child from possible treatment. The child, then, possibly will be deprived of treatment for years—because the parent was frightened by the proposal made to her.

I have raised many of the difficulties that may arise from the opening discussion with a particularly resistant parent. How can resolution be achieved, to the benefit of all? When a therapist encounters a difficult situation in which neither of two technically possible approaches seems feasible, it is frequently helpful for the therapist to concentrate on a question: May there be some problem of countertransference which makes the difficulty seem insoluble? In my own experience, much improvement in my technique in dealing with a highly resistant parent has come about through resolution of some countertransference resistance in myself. In a case involving a highly resistant parent, the therapist could, of course, take the attitude that if the parent is going to feel tricked or betrayed, the child may have to suffer and be deprived of treatment until the parent comes to her senses. Or, if the therapist overidentifies with the child, he may feel it is justifiable to allow the parent to feel cornered and betrayed so that at all costs the child may be rendered safe from a destructive symbiosis. But neither of these attitudes really solves the difficulty.

It will be profitable in this connection to think further of what transpires in the course of an adult's analysis. This will entail some review of what has been said. The patient, in his anxiety, may ask for a blueprint of what is going to happen. After a few interviews with him it can be perceived that he will have many terrifying and miserable periods. He will rage at the therapist for not having warned him of the severity of the ordeal. He will charge that he was trapped and so on. Yet this is not explained to him ahead of time because he might not believe what he was told anyway, or he might be frightened away from treatment. In time, transference to the therapist will carry him through his ordeals whereas, at the beginning of treatment, he could not possibly know of this transference and its strength to help him. It is part of the therapist's job as a physician to accept the patient's feelings. In time the patient knows that the therapist's conscience is clear, for later the patient realizes the strength of the transference and how it makes his ordeal bearable. *If,* however, an inexperienced therapist has not the fullest emotional appreciation of what he was obliged to do to save his patient, he will be so guilty and frightened by the accusation of trickster or traitor, that only chaos can result. Tricks are tricks when the perpetrator uses a technique for a selfish or narcissistic reason or out of ignorance.

Thus, in dealing with parents who obviously are without any insight, I feel perfectly guiltless about not telling them at the outset that they must be patients. The mother, for instance, at first may talk only about the child. Soon she may be talking more about herself. When, however, resistance develops, then she protests that she never asked for treatment; it is then that she charges betrayal and so forth. Here again the skilled therapist counts on the development of transference as a support when resistance has to be analyzed. The plan may not always work, but the technique is increasingly fruitful as experience increases. Parent and child both are likely to continue with treatment.

As time has gone on, then, it has become increasingly clear to me that much of what, in my early work, I called frankness with patients or frankness with resistant parents, stemmed from my fear that some day I would be called to account and that, should the day come, feelings of guilt might spring from many sources which had no rational bearing on the issue at hand. The therapist can feel very guilty about his ignorance or lack of experience, or about his purely selfish wish to set up a treatment situation as he wants it, so that it will be easy on him and things will work out "his way." If he is conscious of these sources of his guilt and admits as much to the patient, order takes over where chaos reigned.

Thus, today, rather than frightening parents into withdrawing from all help for their child and themselves, I can without guilt tell a highly resistant parent that I will try to help the child if the parent will join in the therapeutic enterprise and will see a colleague who will add, in the case, whatever knowledge she can acquire of how things move at home. An experienced colleague soon will have the parent talking more and more about herself or himself. I do not emphasize that the parent is to be a patient too. When, later, the parent becomes anxious and angry her therapist helps her to understand what is frightening her and why she doubts my good intentions. This recalls my earlier statement that the parent's real motive in bringing the child for help is that the mutual neurosis (when it *is* that) is shifting the balance of gratification so that more pain than gratification is being felt by the parent member.

There are varied points of view of this single set of problems which I have briefly covered with regard to the diagnostic and planning responsibilities of the team. Undoubtedly my thinking, as well as that of others, will change with greater experience and study.

In the cases now to be discussed I am concerned primarily in elaborating how a team can actually function in the therapeutic task at hand. In this presentation, in limited space, it will be impossible to attempt to describe the variations in technique that are necessary in cases of all the large categories wherein collaborative therapy is advantageously applicable.

ILLUSTRATIVE CASES

Let it be said that a child apparently has been fixated for a long time at a certain instinctual level. This level, say, is more malignant than that at which a child might be fixated who by death or illness had been deprived of a member of his normal family but who had received intensive therapy alone or else splendid support at home.

Case 1.—Four-and-a-half-year-old Eddie was brought for treatment because he wanted to be a girl and because, with the exception of a few months when a housekeeper was in the home, he continued to soil. For the previous year and a half his soiling had been according to a ritual; he had to defecate into a diaper when lying on the bathroom floor. Eddie abhorred odors and had to be cleaned immediately. He was the terror of the neighborhood and had no friends. He had a sister, two years old, who was much more the mother's favorite, as she spontaneously admitted. Realizing that the mother was a very neurotically ill woman who would need long analysis, we decided to start intensive analytic treatment for the boy, leaving the mother untreated for the time being.

The boy was permitted to regress to the infant level, to a pre-ambivalent state. The therapist was permissive of the boy's dependency needs, and Eddie soon realized that he did not wish to be a girl but a baby. Without pressure to grow up, and with indulgence, he became rapidly satisfied; he no longer wished to be a baby or a girl, and began to grow up to the level of a child five years of age with a five-year-old's problem of ambivalence toward both parents. Within a year and a half, Eddie was a happy child, possessed of friends, progressing well in kindergarten, competing normally for his age with his father, no longer victimizing his sister and so on.

One island of trouble, however, remained absolutely fixed— the soiling ritual in the bathroom. On a simple reporting level the mother told how Eddie had said, "What would you do if I used the toilet?"

She told him, "I don't know."

When Eddie said, "When I'm six, I'll probably use the toilet," she said she could think of nothing to say.

This woman was paralyzed, so to speak, concerning an appropriate response. Nevertheless, the fact that Eddie now was asking such questions, and in play was insisting that Hopalong Cassidy and all his heroes go to the bathroom after breakfast, showed that he was beginning to try to solve his problem. About this time his sister, then three-and-a-half-years-old, was reported to be developing the same soiling difficulties.

For research reasons and to avoid another long course of treatment, it was decided to try to engage the mother in treatment, but of as limited extent as possible. At first she was excessively sweet and ingratiating. After a time she talked regularly to her therapist about the children's bathroom habits, recurrently asking advice but discarding it before ever it was given. One day her therapist commented that the mother seemed troubled about being at all definite or firm about these functions in the bathroom. The mother then told that when her little daughter had seemed hesitant to urinate in the bushes with the neighborhood children, the mother had gone out and showed her how to do as the other little ones did. When the therapist asked the mother if she knew why she did this, the patient became defensive and very angry.

The mother than talked at length of many Pacific tribes "who can soil all their lives." She gave a considerable anthropologic summary. When the therapist then suggested that possibly the mother had some feeling, not fully known to herself, about the soiling impulses of people, the mother vehemently denied this. Immediately, however, she recounted, with many angry tears, that from her early childhood through late adolescence her own mother had permitted the family home to be unclean. The patient's father, a passive, inadequate man, and the mother, had allowed the latter's alcoholic father and three alcoholic brothers to live with the family and the house was "constantly smeared with, and smelling of, vomitus and urine." The patient had been humiliated so often by this that finally she had ceased to bring friends home. To condense the material drastically, she had not been conscious of her rage at her mother for permitting all this "mess" and, making an identification with her mother so that she would be relieved of her feeling of hostility toward her mother, was finally achieving ambivalent gratification through the soiling habits of her son and now of her daughter. Of course, she was crippling them as well.

In other words, the mother, having repressed her rage toward her own mother, was trying to solve the problem in this way: "I don't have to hate my mother for permitting that outrageous mess made by my uncles and grandfather, if I can be messy too—through my children." Fostering this in the children also gave vent to much of her hostility; it was transferred to the children and was destroying their adjustment with everyone concerned.

Finally, when Eddie *did* begin to sit on the toilet to defecate, it was soon clear to his therapist that the heckling by his mother persisted—that he still was far from pleasing her. The mother awarded him a large candy bar for a big "B.M." and a small piece of candy for a small "B.M." Arguments, of course, ensued over size of "B.M." and the merited award. His therapist found Eddie confused and angry. She first of all had to clarify the realities for the child; namely, that nobody can decide to have a large or a small "B.M.," which was counter to the mother's assumption. The anger against his mother, the anger against the therapist as a transference figure and also as a person having a different view from his mother, had to be analyzed. The mother's therapist, apprised of this new form of unconscious attack and disapproval at home, could quickly identify it in the mother's vague and extremely distorted material. Undoubtedly the mother's therapist, having been warned by the child's therapist, could see through the mother's disguises more rapidly than she could have done if she had been working alone, and could accelerate the mother's progress. The mother volunteered the story of the awards and bickering about the size of the stools and of course the therapist encountered intense maternal resistance following inquiry as to why the awards had been given.

There were many indications of great confusion in Eddie's mind about realities, promises and deceptions. It became increasingly clear to the mother's therapist that her patient might tell three different stories about one incident. The therapist never could be sure when the mother was falsifying outright, so she took this up directly with the mother. The patient went on to tell how her own mother frequently would lie to spare her daughter from having to face definite and inevitable painful realities. Gradually the patient became able to deal with realities and to avoid deceiving herself, her therapist and her children. The immediate effect on Eddie was evident. It was gratifying, from that time on, to see this mother work sincerely at her treatment and to observe a real personality emerging from the previous mist and fog of vagueness, isolation and anxiety. Her treatment continued long. Eddie became well long before the mother's therapy terminated.

It might be interesting to discuss the work of a collaborative team in an acute emergency situation.

Case 2.—The service was asked to send someone to see a boy, twelve years old, who was in a hospital and who had regressed to the level of a two- or a three-year-old. He was soiling, was eating only a little fluid and was whining like a baby. The history included the information that the boy had been brought to the hospital partially blind. One evening an orderly had begun to shave his head. The boy had protested and the orderly had told the boy that his brain was to be operated on. Next day, in fact, a brain tumor had been removed. The boy had recovered all his neurologic faculties. There was no possibility that injury to the brain or edema of the brain was a factor in his state by the time the psychiatrist saw him and heard from him about his terror concerning the operation. While the boy was still in the hospital, his therapist bent all efforts toward comfort and mobilizing the anger which was associated with his terror and with his sense of having been betrayed. In the course of the second hour of treatment the boy said spontaneously, "Maybe the doctor will come back and cut off my diddle (penis)."

The anger came out in rages against doctors and nurses. The terrifying experience through which the boy had passed was particularly destructive in his case because he had been reared by a passive father and a tyrannical mother who had good reason to despise her own father; moreover, from the time of the boy's birth, she had consciously not wanted him and had hated him. He was considered a sweet boy who "never once talked back." In other words, this child had tremendous castration anxiety and doubts about any consistent love from the mother before what he considered his betrayal in the hospital. The boy's therapist hoped to gain his confidence and to help him back gradually to his previous adjustment while he was in the hospital away from his mother. This was not possible, however, since the parents were abjectly poor financially although the mother's father was wealthy. The parents left the hospital telling all the physicians they were returning home where help for the boy was unavailable.

Six weeks later, however, the parents called, saying that they were living in one rented room in the town where the operation had been performed because they had been too anxious to go home. The boy was then in worse condition than when he first had been seen in the hospital. He threatened to kill his mother, displayed a complete sleep reversal and refused most food since his mother insisted that he eat specific things and amounts. The father was exhausted. He had been afraid to sleep for fear that the boy would become violent against the mother. At this point the collaborative team began to plan and operate.

What were the possibilities of breaking into the vicious circle of anxiety and rage that was paralyzing this family? The mother was far too ill and inaccessible to enter even the most superficial therapeutic relationship. The father, extremely dependent and feeling very guilty for not having brought the boy to the hospital before the blindness was far advanced, seemed the only hope.

It seemed imperative to get the boy out of his regression and to preserve his ego. This was impossible with the mother heckling him constantly. It was decided that one therapist would be most sympathetic in an interview with the father and would give him a mild sedative to enable him to relax a little. In the interview, a strong immediate dependent transference and the father's sense of guilt about the boy were utilized. The father then was strongly advised that he must take a stand with the mother and send her home to rest while one therapist worked with him. Another therapist was to work with the boy, seeing him in his room at first, utilizing only a few simple interpretations and, for a time, responding to his needs mainly with great indulgence on a preverbal level. The father was advised to cater to the boy's whims about eating. If the boy wished only popcorn for two days, popcorn he should have. And he should be allowed to eat when, what, and only as much as, he wished. If the boy did not care to walk outside, if he wished to scold and swear, he was to have his way. Real destructiveness or physical battles were to be prevented if at all possible.

The father quickly put into effect all of the foregoing. Typically, he went out at midnight to get a radish sandwich which the boy requested. He carried the child to the bathroom as demanded; he urged nothing. The boy once swore and shouted for thirty-six hours straight. The next day he did this for an hour but it never happened again. The father, with his sense of guilt and his strong belief in his therapist, was extraordinarily flexible. No attempts were made to analyze the father's conflicts toward the boy and wife. After about five weeks the boy had grown up considerably. He was eating well and spontaneously. He was walking to the bathroom and outside. Nevertheless, he remained angry and said very little. His therapist, therefore, went to his room and repeated firmly and definitely the interpretations given in the hospital pertaining to his shock and terror, his rage against the doctors, his fears of real castration, his rage at the parents for abandoning him to the doctors without discussion and his rightful feeling that no one in the world at that time had protected him or seemed to love him. The boy was furious during all this discussion, but the next day the patient walked into his therapist's office smiling and behaving more like any boy twelve years old. Certainly he was more jaunty and more free of hostility, although he was adequately aggressive, than he had been, according to reports, before the operation.

When the mother returned to town, the father and the boy were far better able than they had been to stand firmly against her. Fortunately, moreover, her father had capitulated and gave all necessary financial help. Follow-up letters from the parents have indicated that the boy was like any twelve-year-old and talked up to his parents regardless of his mother's resentment.

Undoubtedly an experienced single therapist could have treated both father and boy. However, fairly young therapists were working on the case and it seemed better all around if each patient had his own therapist. Needless to say the father was completely won over to the idea that the boy was not losing his mind because he behaved as he did. Additionally, the landlady was most understanding to permit the shouting and cursing for the necessary six weeks of rehabilitation.

Presumably, the boy eventually will die of the malignant tumor. The frightful predicament of the mother as she sees him finally growing helpless can easily be imagined. Her bitterness, sense of guilt and depression will be tremendous and, at that time, possibly a therapist can enter the situation sufficiently to help her to ward off some psychotic break directed toward herself and possibly against the child.

Such an acute emergency situation as developed in case 2 lends itself well to management by a collaborative team. The father received, largely, dynamically understood support. The child received, for the longest period, largely nonverbal contact, rationally used by his therapist and tremendous indulgence on the part of his father. Only later, when a base line of confidence in the world again had been established in the boy, were the interpretations of his predicament offered and constructively accepted.

I should like to describe another challenge to a collaborative therapy that many therapists will encounter and which I believe cannot be handled otherwise. Both patients come for therapy because of an acute, hazardous state. To be sure, one very experienced therapist might be able to do the task alone but two therapists certainly can salvage many more patients than are being saved now by only one partner of the symbiosis being treated.

The following case typifies a hazardous undertaking unless careful collaborative planning is given, especially if both patients are to remain in the home. The case falls within the category of acting out but could move in the direction also of psychosis if given the right balance of forces.

Case 3.—The parents brought their son, fifteen years of age, for help. The boy came willingly for he was very anxious. He had had episodes of extreme panic contingent on the fear that he would kill his mother. Such episodes had been especially terrifying at night, when his destructive impulses also had been directed, to some extent, against his thirteen-year-old brother. The boy was a fine student but had no companions. His mother was "his girl," he said.

The mother was very apprehensive about her son's impulses and was easily observed to feel guilty. To condense the material drastically, she fostered his getting into bed with her and her husband and often alone with her, even though she observed her son to be uneasy about his erections. She unwittingly encouraged his isolation from colleagues and, in one interview, the experienced therapist could observe the sadistic sexual gratification which the mother achieved from her relationship with her older son. In a few interviews, the background of her behavior became obvious.

It was believed that this boy, in one of his recurrent episodes of panic, could act out or break down, depending on the direction in which the mother might swing the balance of her power. The father, a most ambivalent man, could not be trusted to help. It seemed wise to have the boy live in the medical section of a hospital for a few days, where his therapist could see him. The boy would sleep in the hospital but would go out to school. At the same time the mother would begin treatment with her therapist. It seemed dangerous to have the two living together until some strengthening transference had been aroused in both. During the days that the boy resided in the hospital, his therapist found that he talked readily about his mother's being "his girl" and that he needed no other. The therapist was direct in telling the patient that as long as he remained so close to his mother he would be angry toward both parents, since his father was in the closest relation to the mother. It was explained to the boy that he had tried to solve this problem by being less grown up than he really was. It was added that this kind of solution also angered him. The therapist stated that there was another solution; namely, to stay out of the mother's bed and to work with the therapist about matters that worried him. In fact, the therapist was emphatic that getting into bed with his mother must stop at once. Soon much anger emerged toward the therapist, but gradually the boy became more relaxed and, the mother having been similarly prohibited by her firm therapist, the boy was sent home after five days of residence in the hospital.

The boy made rapid strides with his therapist, many defenses were analyzed, while necessary educational measures were introduced. The mother, a typical hysterical personality with all her sadomasochism toward males very close to the surface, developed a strong ambivalent transference to her therapist, a man. Her son, feeling freed of obligation to her neurotic emotional needs, soon worked sincerely at his therapy, and quickly acquired many male and female friends. When, finally, the boy wanted to interrupt his treatment since he was enjoying life, this was permitted—for years there had been too much demand on him that he be regressed and obligated to an adult. We knew he would need further therapy later, but with many adolescents interruptions for experimenting in growth are helpful and lead to ego change. At the same time, both collaborators agreed that great vigilance must be exercised by the mother's therapist to ensure her not using the boy again to escape her problems with her male therapist. In spite of such vigilance, for a time one could see her attempting to use the younger brother for her purposes, and he, formerly an outgoing popular boy, was quickly pulled into an anxious, regressed state. Increased therapeutic hours for the mother, and greater activity in analysis of her motivations, gradually freed this second boy. She then began to turn her destructiveness toward her husband, a more equal match, as her problems were further analyzed. Needless to say, this type of woman would need long treatment with variable amounts of help for her husband.

The foregoing case (case 3) is typical of the background in many of those relationships that lead to tragic acting out and homicide. The brutal murder of a mother by an adolescent son was spread all over the newspapers in the country about two weeks after our patients began therapy. Their anxiety as they identified with this tragic outcome was prominent. With the boy, his therapist emphatically professed no concern that his patient would ever act on his impulses. The mother felt so guilty about her destructiveness toward her son that, of course, she considered that she deserved to be destroyed by him and unwittingly fostered destruction. To understand where the

mother received the unconscious sanctions for her behavior with
her son, took only a short time to discover in her relationship
with her parents.

Case 4.—A boy, two and one-half years of age, was brought to
the clinic because he was constantly clutching his genitals. Even
the most cursory observation of the child showed that this was
not any masturbatory consideration but obviously protective.
Analysis of adult males often reveals that, fearing their own hostile sexual impulses, they experience distressing contraction of
the cremasteric muscles and upward retraction of the testicles.
One interview with each of the parents demonstrated clearly the
mother's tremendous unconscious hostility toward males. At the
time they came to the diagnostic clinic, the marriage, at least
consciously, was working moderately well. It was clear, from the
fantasies inadvertently expressed, that the husband was being
spared the wife's hostility, since it was being directed toward the
child, subtly but potently, all overlaid with sweet reasonableness
on the part of the mother. The little boy's own fantasies demonstrated clearly that his unconscious knew what was going on and
he was greatly confused and frightened.

This mother showed sufficient flexibility and insight during
the diagnostic interviews to warrant our advising the parents
that we might be able to help by seeing Jimmie, and also the
mother with regard to some of her feelings. Collaborative therapy was begun. Jimmie immediately loved his play hours and the
therapy, although it was obvious that he was fearful and inhibited about any aggressiveness. Every hour with each patient
was reported in each seminar so that the significance of each
patient's problems, as they impinged on the problems of the
other, could be understood clearly. Jimmie's clutching was associated with any fearful situation in which he found himself
with the therapist and it subsided completely, or worsened, as
the mother's ambivalences manifested themselves in her own
treatment. Of course, as in any such case, when she analyzed her
conflicts with men, the husband began to experience her hostility; this was not always directed toward her therapist. As her
negative transference was understood, she let up on her husband
and Jimmie except when, to punish her therapist, she disturbed
her husband to the point where he was furious and, hating her
and psychiatry, wished often to terminate therapy.

As matters developed, it seemed important that Jimmie continue in treatment, since his inhibition against standing up for
his rights, in even a small nursery group, was marked. Furthermore, as time went on it became clear that although the father's

ambivalence toward him was far less than that of the mother, it was of such degree that he could not be depended on suitably to support the boy. The child continued, then, with his male therapist. The mother always called the child's penis his "good girl." The boy's confusion relative to this was profound, and his sense of obligation to the mother to think in terms consistent with her term long was obvious, although intellectually for a time she refrained from using the word. The major therapeutic task obviously became that of long-time dynamic therapy for the mother.

The last case which I wish to include here is a dramatic and tragic illustration of what can happen when awareness of the suitability of collaborative therapy, or the facilities to carry it on, are lacking. Before reporting the case I wish to mention briefly that not only can the destructiveness of parents and their thoughtlessly expressed fantasies weaken a child's ego integration and defenses but, also, a physician's fantasies and statements or predictions about a child can be devastating to a parent's ego defenses against destructiveness toward the child. Many end results of this mechanism are encountered.

Case 5.—The case in point was that of an identical twin, a boy three years of age, named Dick. The child had been in a frightful automobile accident when he was a year and a half old. A physician had told the parents that even if he lived, "he would be only a vegetable." The mother then wished he would die and, realizing that she always had disliked him, she felt relieved that he might die. These feelings, however, were unknown to the therapist until much later. The boy lived to become the terror of the neighborhood; he was utterly impulse ridden.

When he was brought for study, his intelligence and aptitudes were found to rate a trifle higher than those of the "well" twin. In a few play hours with him, during which he was the object of a degree of friendly, definite firmness with regard to acting out, he appeared to be a charming, active, fine little boy. The neighbors then found him to be so, but he was his old self with his mother.

The boy's problems were not organic and the parents were told that in time he would be well. It is known, however, that a neurotic parent cannot safely be robbed of hostile and vicarious gratification such as this mother was achieving through Dick's acting out, unless help is given her. This mother required assistance to resolve the need which had boiled to the surface when the surgeon substantially had given her permission to *believe* that her son was to be a psychotic vegetable. She should have had a collaborating therapist early in the picture, but one was not available just at the time and the family was planning to move away in a few months. To open up the woman's problem until after the move seemed unwise.

Actually, as events proved, it was unwise not to do so. For two weeks, her vicious attacks on the boy were interspersed with long periods of dreamy withdrawal, in which she seemed to be out of contact, even to the point of failure to feed the children, and in the course of which she was depressed and entertained suicidal thoughts. The development of these symptoms was not brought to my attention. Still, I should have foreseen their development, because I knew from long experience that the mother would be much disturbed to receive a hopeful (from the therapist's point of view) diagnosis about the boy. Such an event is as predictable as a colorimetric end point in a chemical determination.

In a few weeks the mother had broken so completely that she had to be hospitalized on a closed ward. Protected in the hospital, the mother relaxed, and study made it clear we were dealing with a highly sadistic woman. For years she had been very successful in a career and she had done fairly well with her family until the drastic diagnostic prediction about her twin son, which sanctioned her acting out through him and toward him. She had been ruthlessly treated by her father; she hated and mistrusted men, and she had been hostilely seductive toward many in her past. It became clear that hers was a malignant, hysterical personality, that she was not schizophrenic, and that she would be easily accessible to treatment, stormy as it would be. Actually this woman, before her break, had asked for some therapy if possible and probably the unfortunate break in her ego adjustment could have been averted by a second therapist.

THE COLLABORATIVE TEAM IN RESEARCH

The possibilities of the collaborative team as a research instrument have been explored only in the past twelve years. Many of us who have been interested in this matter have found that not only was the curative process catalyzed, in collaborative therapy, but that our observation of etiologic factors observed at their source of operation made for far greater scientific accuracy than we could attain by reconstruction of what might, or must, have happened. It was detailed observation of what operated in the parent-child symbiosis that led some of us, ten years ago, to question seriously many theoretical ideas such as those of "death instinct," "instinctual anxiety," "phylogenetic imbalances in opposing instinctual strengths," and so forth. Szasz, in his recent article (6), has brilliantly offered evidence from biologic sources—tissue cultures, for instance—which seems definitely to discount a death instinct. This is in line with what many of us have observed clinically and have questioned.

A group of us at the Institute for Juvenile Research, more than ten years ago, aware of the tool which social workers were sparingly, but effectively, using as a kind of collaborative psychotherapy, decided that we should study the parents as closely as the child relative to the baffling problem of so-called school phobias. Our observations eventuated in clear-cut understanding of the etiology of such neuroses in the child and the parents. This had far-reaching results and led to our use of collaborative therapy and to our research on "acting out." Reports of all of this work have been published (1, 3, 4, 5, 7, 8).

CONJECTURAL IMPLICATIONS DRAWN FROM COLLABORATIVE EXPERIENCE

Many child analysts have maintained, as did Anna Freud, that many children were not accessible to cure by analysis. The explanations for failure have never been definitive. If a child is in the course of analysis, some child analysts have maintained a parent should not be disturbed by being treated at the same time. In selected cases I have seen the necessity of doing this, however, and results have been beneficial, as is evident in this report. Accordingly, I am unimpressed with flat statements, unsupported by evidence, that the close type of collaboration of which I am writing should not be utilized.

Research in collaborative therapy has netted much advance in understanding of the dynamics of fixation. As Szasz has so correctly stated, in work with higher biologic forms such as man the investigator is not dealing with "closed systems" as he is in simple physics or chemistry; he is dealing with "open systems"; namely, with "symbioses."

Some of us who are working in child psychiatry today are observing lines of similar evidence for the etiology of psychosis. For instance, an eight-year-old daughter maintains that her mother is trying to poison her. Analysis of the mother's denial of her wish to destroy the child leads rapidly to the child's relaxation and freedom from the belief that her mother wishes to destroy her. This illustration can be multiplied over and over, but detailed careful studies of this kind of case must be made and are in progress all over the country.

Many syndromes certainly are composed of varying quantities of etiologic factors some of which are outright organic factors and some of which are emotional. These factors constitute a spectrum, one end of which is largely organic and the opposite end of which is largely emotional; between the two ends are variable mixtures of the organic and the emotional. Epilepsy, or so-called "convulsive disorders," furnish an apt illustration. Detailed studies by neurologists and psychiatrists, together with the collaboration of two or more psychotherapists if the emotional component is large, undoubtedly will furnish much more scientific evidence than is available now; such evidence is much needed. Automatically to give drugs to *all* persons with convulsive disorders, without further neurologic or psychiatric research, would lead to a dead end.

Collaborative research is as thrilling as a refined detective story, and nearly everyone who has ever been a part of a collaborative team, or engaged in group research, will bear this out. Fitting the pieces together, gathering hints as to what to watch for in the material of the two or three patients, is a fascinating experience that goes hand in hand with the gratification of realizing improvement in the patients. It is my impression that subtle observations in the home setting recurrently would enrich our understanding in ways heretofore largely unexplored. For this, psychiatric social workers experienced in intensive collaborative work are ideal members of a team. I am convinced that such home observation has been relegated too much to the category of early diagnostic exploratory studies. Possibly great secrets, therefore, have remained undisclosed. Anyone who reads many of the best detective stories can see in what infinite detail every lead is explored.

CAUTIONS ONCE MORE

Herein I have aimed to emphasize some of the benefits which I believe can be derived from the careful type of collaborative therapy that has been my experience. In closing, it seems important to reinforce cautions against certain hazards which I have suggested earlier. The closest communication between psychiatrist and psychiatric social worker must be maintained. The personal relationships between the collaborators of necessity must be kept continuously clear. More than a casual diagnostic study needs to be conducted to evaluate critically which patients would or would not be accessible to the collaborative approach. Lastly, until both collaborators are highly experienced, the psychiatrist certainly should be a highly trained and experienced member of the team, for the final responsibility, clinically and legally, is his.

BIBLIOGRAPHY

1. JOHNSON, A. M. Sanctions for superego lacunae of adolescents. In *Searchlights on Delinquency* (edited by K. R. Eissler) . New York: International Universities Press, 1949.
2. —— The etiology of fixations and symptoms. *Psychoanal. Quart.* In press.
3. —— and FALSTEIN, E. I., SZUREK, S. A., and SVENDSEN, School phobia. *Am. J. Orthopsychiat.*, 11:702-711, 1941.
4. —— and FISHBACK, D. Analysis of a disturbed adolescent girl and collaborative psychiatric treatment of the mother. *Ibid.*, 14:195-203, 1944.
5. —— and SZUREK, S. A. The genesis of antisocial acting out in children and adults. *Psychoanal. Quart.* 21, 1952.
6. SZAZ, T. S. On the psychoanalytic theory of instincts. *Psychoanal. Quart.*, 21:25-48, 1952.
7. SZUREK, S. A. Some impressions from clinical experience with delinquents. In *Searchlights on Delinquency* (edited by K. R. Eissler) . New York: International Universities Press, 1949.
8. —— JOHNSON, A., and FALSTEIN, E. Collaborative psychiatric therapy of parent-child problems. *Am. J. Orthopsychiat.*, 12:511-516, 1942.

BACKGROUND ARTICLES

ACKERMAN, N. Interpersonal disturbances in the family: a frame of reference for psychotherapy. Unpublished data.

DAWLEY, A. Trends in therapy. VI. Inter-related movement of parent and child in therapy with children. *Am. J. Orthopsychiat.*, 9:748-754, 1939.

LEVY, D. M. Critical evaluation of the present state of child psychiatry. *Am. J. Psychiat.*, 108:481-494, 1952.

SHEIMO, S. L. Concomitant treatment of mother and child: a case of mother and adolescent daughter. Unpublished data.

SZUREK, S. A. Some lessons from efforts at psychotherapy with parents. Unpublished data.

Chapter 6

THE PSYCHOANALYST'S CONTRIBUTION
TO THE FAMILY AGENCY

PETER B. NEUBAUER, M.D.

To formulate concepts and techniques of work to be applied in a field allied to one's own, means to accept a responsibility which is impossible to fulfill. It would imply that the psychiatric consultant in this instance is fully acquainted with the scope of the work of a social agency and that he is able to test his contribution as part of his work. However, as a consultant, he does not possess this knowledge. Such formulations can only emerge out of a true co-operative process based on three steps:

1. The psychoanalyst's formulation of his contribution
2. The social worker's statement of demands from the consultant in the course of their daily practice
3. The final formulation and testing emerging from a collaborative effort.

This chapter, therefore, should be considered as the first step in this process.

It is necessary to point out that psychoanalysis refers to three disciplines:

1. General psychology of human behavior
2. Method of study and research, and
3. Psychoanalysis as a method of therapy.

It is not necessary to repeat here the basic concepts and formulation of psychoanalytic psychology. We will refer to them with the assumption that they have been previously discussed and will use only those which relate to the topics chosen for discussion. As psychoanalysis moves from the study of the unconscious conflict to the role of the ego, the contribution which it can make to the field of social work becomes more and more important.

We need not discuss psychoanalysis as a method of study in this chapter. Our concern is with the formulation of techniques of treatment. Psychoanalytic psychology will help the educator, the psychologist, social worker, and anthropologist to deepen his understanding of human needs and functions, but the use of psychoanalytic therapy in allied fields must inevitably lead to confusion and malpractice. Here the consultant has a special responsibility. Everyone who knows some of the development in case work will share this concern. The role of the consultant in the social agency is to increase the skill in case work and not to introduce psychoanalytic therapy.

In order to avoid such disturbing influence, it appears advisable to maintain our clinical orientation. That is to say, our work should be based on:

1. The diagnostic evaluation of the problem
2. The outline of the treatment goal
3. The selection of methods and techniques to achieve this goal.

(1) The diagnostic evaluation will force the consultant to expand his clinical diagnostic categories and thinking into a setting which includes, as pointed out before, a variety of specific social factors. As has been expressed frequently, our diagnostic statements are traditionally oriented toward the evaluation of the pathology and insufficiently consider the balance between health and disturbance. This becomes a specifically crucial point in social agencies, and it must lead to the formulation of psychosocial diagnostic statements in which an attempt is made to balance not only disturbances with health, but also social factors and psychic reactions. As long as we are clear about this, we will avoid an orientation which confuses the field of medical "therapy" with case work "treatment."

(2) Such considerations determine the formulation of treatment

goals. Again the psychosocial balance will be kept in mind so that the goals will focus on restoring and improving the function of the individual, in spite of certain emotional disturbances, rather than on dissolving the emotional disturbance as expressed in symptoms.

Let us take the example of a twenty-six-year-old man, hospitalized with the diagnosis of schizophrenia. After discharge from the hospital, his family referred him to a family agency for help.[1] He presented problems of social and work adjustment. The intake worker could have stated that a social agency is not equipped to help people with such problems, referring to the diagnosis of schizophrenia. If the intake worker refuses to accept the modification of the schizophrenic pathology as a treatment goal, she certainly has made a correct decision. But if she considers a plan which makes a contribution to this client, in spite of this medical diagnosis, she would find many avenues of help.

After the diagnostic implications have been discussed with the psychiatric consultant—that there is no acute process at present and no evidence of destructive impulses—vocational guidance could be considered. A careful re-evaluation of the client's work capacity, according to his present status, could lead him to find a job in which the demands made on him would not be excessive. The members of his family must be guided to help him readjust, and not to push him toward too ambitious goals. If the treatment goal outlined is appropriate to the social agency's interest, it is very often surprising how much help an agency can offer to a person with a schizophrenic history, by avoiding the treatment of the "schizophrenia."

(3) Treatment methods will include not only the direct interview, utilizing the interpersonal experience, but also a modification of the environmental factors. While this, in itself, is in no way foreign to medical therapy, the training period necessary to introduce the psychiatric consultant into social work proves that we have to make a particular effort to achieve such an orientation.

So far, I have mentioned points of orientation related to the general field of social work. I have done this to clarify the differ-

1 *Editor's note:* Cf. Chapter 7, pp. 138 ff.

ence between "psychotherapy" and case work "treatment" and to set the stage for the discussion of the role of a family agency.

There is no doubt that wherever we work with children our treatment must be family oriented. Even when the child is in therapy, continuous guidance toward integration is necessary. Child guidance long ago became family guidance. Why then do we have family agencies and child guidance agencies?

This may be difficult to understand unless we consider the history of case work. What could possibly be the difference between the help given in a child guidance agency and work with children in a family agency—or the difference between work with adults in a family agency as compared with any other agency? The difference still seems to be a certain emphasis which is made, or should be made, in an agency which has accepted, as its central approach, an orientation toward the family as a unit. One could say, therefore, that in a family agency the family is not a part of the work with the child, but the child is a part of the work with the family. Such a formulation imposes upon the intake worker the careful selection of those who will be accessible, and would exclude those children where "therapy" is indicated.

The reader may have noticed the emphasis given to the differentiation between "therapy" and "treatment." Therapy is used in this chapter as an attempt to dissolve specific emotional pathology based on intrapsychic conflict, and treatment is used for those attempts in case work which should improve and aid the function of the individual in his psychosocial adjustment, whether he has specific psychic symptoms, or in spite of them.

Utilizing the clinical approach, I would like to discuss the contribution of psychoanalysis to family diagnosis.

FAMILY DIAGNOSIS

Very early in its history, psychoanalysis viewed human problems in the light of the dynamic interaction of the individual within the family. Individual pathology was seen as reflecting the family relationship. The genetic approach in analysis has proven that early childhood experiences, that is to say, the attitude of the parents to the child, are an essential factor in the normal development of character and emotional deviations. This has led directly to the understanding of the family dynamics. We have accepted this today to such a degree that we immediately translate descriptions of such symptoms as thumb sucking, as an expression of the child's difficulties, into the corresponding deviant attitude of the mother. When we speak of the separation problem of the nursery school child, we think of the inability of the mother to separate from the child. Today it is unthinkable to consider one without the other.

The formulation of the oedipus complex was the most significant and the clearest contribution to the understanding of family dynamics. Here a normal stage of development was related to the family constellation and to the dynamic interaction of the family members. The necessity of the child to find a place in relation to mother and father for the purpose of its own sexual differentiation and social adjustment became the basis for the understanding of neurotic development.

We have to remember the advantages as well as the limitations of a generally applied "family approach." Yet, it can be stated that the basis for professional interest of a family agency is really the problem which arises from the family constellation. With good reason, therefore, problems which have their origin in the pregenital phase are excluded from the services offered by such an agency. And serious character or other disturbances which stem from early traumatization will, therefore, not be a part of the problems which a family agency will accept for help.

We are impressed by the necessity to diagnose families, to find a "shorthand" which will help us categorize families as we are able to do with individuals, and to express thereby the degree of cohesion of the family, or to state that this unit may be broken into parts. There may be a category for a family in which the relationship to members of the community is more strongly developed than their relationship to each other, and the "defense mechanisms of the family" can be described and understood. We are far from having achieved this. In spite of this, the study of individual families has led to the development of an approach which is based on family dynamics.

Let us look at the family which comes to an agency for help for an eight-year-old child with a behavior problem in school. The intake study reveals that there is a brother, two years older, who has never accepted the existence of the younger one and has continuously fought with him. The mother has strong feelings of identification with the child, has overprotected him, and has thereby increased the rivalry of the older child. The father, unable to find his authority in the family, has chosen his work in order to maintain his self-esteem, and remains peripheral to the life of the family. As we consider a plan to help this child, we are actually planning to help the entire family, unless we feel that our client needs to be referred for therapy.

Such a family approach raises a number of questions. Is it necessary for us to assist all the members of the family? Is it more advisable to select one particular member for assistance in order to effect a change in this family? Should we help in directly contacting the weakest member, or should we work with the healthiest so he can help the others? If we help the father find his place, he might bind some of the conflict between the boys and release some of the closeness between mother and the younger child. The contact with the mother could expose her part in promoting the problem between the children. We could help the older boy with his jealousy. We would, of course, assume that there is enough flexibility of ego adaptation left to achieve changes through other members and that a careful diagnostic study has been made by the intake worker.

Let us take another example. Here is a family which applies for a camp experience for Mark. The traditional approach might study the development and Mark's emotional capacity to enjoy such an experience and then make a recommendation. Within a family agency such a problem must be evaluated not only in terms of the meaning of a vacation to the child, but also with a view toward the implications of such a request within the dynamics of the family. What does such a request mean to the mother? Does she suggest it in order to have rest from a burdensome child? If this is so, does Mark sense that the camp suggestion means exclusion from the family? Do the siblings feel that Mark will have an advantage and that they are deprived by having to remain at home? Or, on the contrary, will it mean to them that they are the preferred ones because they can stay at home while Mark has to leave? Does the father agree with the mother, or are there disagreements about camp, and might the professional person's recommendation be used to settle an argument instead of to harmonize family attitudes?

This is an example which demonstrates that a step forward of one family member may disturb several of the others and could, therefore, create additional disturbances. It demonstrates that in making recommendations the family agency must be oriented toward the effect of any approach on the total family and might at times exclude a procedure which may be helpful to one member of the family, if it would be inadvisable for the family as a whole.

We can say that the relations among family members attempt to gratify the needs of each individual, and the satisfaction which one individual will derive depends on another member of the family permitting this to occur. A deprivation of one family member may lead to a satisfaction of another. Therefore, professional aid to a family must be offered after a careful consideration of this balance of forces. In a family agency, the assistance offered should be one which is most constructive for most of the family members. This is another difference between clinics and social agencies.

The two examples given were chosen to relate the problems of children in the family. Where extrafamilial experience has not yet achieved its full influence, the family interaction is clearly observed. Psychoanalytic study reveals that family dynamics are still at work in the adult, but at that time of his life they are modified by the position of the individual in society. Any family study includes not only the study of children in relation to their parents, but also the parents' attitude in relation to their own childhood and their unconscious application of this to their own children. Such family studies will, therefore, encompass three generations.

I would like to stress again that the family approach implies that the capacity to interact is intact, that there is sufficient psychic mobility for such a group experience. When there is a fixed structure, a character disturbance or a neurosis, the family approach will not be able to modify these. Modification through the environment means pliability. Thus, a family agency orients itself toward ego intactness. It rests on the understanding of the conflicted and nonconflicted areas of the ego and is based on a study which shows that there is enough strength to "learn by experience." Such ego functions as judgment, planning, making choices, are utilized in the case work technique.

Diagnosis must lead to a treatment plan. The "therapist" accepts those patients who want help. If a child with specific psychopathology is presented, therapy is induced and help given, even when the parents are not yet able to understand their role in their child's difficulties.

Social work has accepted too much of the same approach. We could think that a child is presented to the case worker by the mother, so that she can take over functions which the mother is unable to carry out. Instead of accepting this as the problem presented, it might be necessary to postpone the assignment of this child with this case worker for many months, until sufficient progress has been made with the mother or with the father, so they can become a part of the treatment plan. If one member of the family improves and therefore might stimulate disturbances in others, it might at times be necessary to concentrate on the others in order to achieve a new balance of forces which will not counteract the efforts of the worker. Such an orientation necessitates a good deal of fluidity of assignment, which I think must be an essential part of a family-oriented case worker. It appears to me that such fluidity existed in the past, but that the psychiatric consultant and other influences have limited this fluidity and have made case work assignment mechanical and imitative of therapy. The assignment, for instance, of different workers to the child and to the mother, and a third worker to another member of the family, needs to be reinvestigated and, in my opinion, changed in order to achieve a family approach.[2]

A mother asks for help for her child who is a "sissy" because at the age of seven, he still clings to her. When she has to go on an errand he has to go with her or he waits at the window for her

2 *Editor's note:* Cf. Chapter 7, pp. 132 ff.

return. Study of the history and of the child and mother shows that the mother lives her life through the child, that she cannot let him "go away," because she fears he might be harmed without her protection. To initiate treatment with such a child would be premature unless sufficient help has been given to the mother to enable her to permit his independence. At times the treatment of the mother must even preceed the treatment of the child. Otherwise, his moving to new relationships will set off anxieties and fears in the mother which will counteract or interrupt treatment progress.

The placement of children in foster homes, homes for adolescents or in institutions, can only be done after all attempts are made to mobilize the family strength in order to make such a step unnecessary. To sentence a delinquent child means to pronounce sentence on a family, and to ask for placement of the child appears to be a displacement of justice. The traditional home visits, the aid which homemakers can give, the role of a nurse in a family agency, should be reinstated as a part to strengthen family function.

THE STAGES OF DEVELOPMENT

Psychoanalysis has investigated the psychic structure and the dynamics in relationship to stages of development of the individual. We have learned to understand the needs of the infant in different stages, the needs of a child in his preoedipal period, the oedipal constellation, the latency period, preadolescence and adolescence. We have learned how these stages interrelate drives for individual gratification with the demands the environment makes on us. I refer here again to the review of the general formulation of psychoanalytic psychology.[3]

Frequent studies are made to show the effect of the parents' attitudes on the child, while the effect of the child's demands on the parents is neglected. We consider the needs of the infant and the parents' capacity to fulfill these needs. We must also consider the changes which occur in the life of the mother, the shift in her activities and her personal relationships in order to fulfill these

[3] *Editor's note:* Cf. Part I.

needs of the child, as well as the effect the newborn has on the father and on other members of the family. We have to balance again the effect of the parents on the children with the effect of the children on the parents. Here the investigation of stages of development gives us more precise answers.

Let us consider a mother who is rather quiet and even-tempered, who has learned to bind impulses and demands, and has established a relationship with her husband which protects her equilibrium. Her infant is very active, reacts to noise and demands "total" attention. This sets off tensions and fears in the mother, with feelings of inadequacy. The infant is someone so different from her, and she has no way to escape this challenge. Now a struggle will start which will determine who will make the adjustment or achieve some degree of compromise. We usually say that the difficulties of the child reflect the mother's problems, and neglect the challenge which such a child presents to the mother. As a confirmation of such dynamic studies, we often learn from the history how the next child presented no problem, and we find that he was not alien to the psychic balance of the mother. The same considerations are obviously true for the acceptance or conflict which may be stimulated in the father or siblings.

The child's different activity pattern and tolerance span might function as a trigger to set off old or latent problems in the parents. It would be advisable to add to the study of "what parents do to children" the question of "what children do to parents" to complete the total dynamic interplay.

We know, for instance, in good detail, the adolescent's psychic fluidity, his defense mechanisms at work, and the demands he makes on the family. We have to study what the adolescent does to the family and what sort of disturbances he carries over to other members.

Psychoanalysis is interested in extending its study of the developmental stages. There is great interest in understanding pre-adolescence more fully to meet the need for a more successful therapy for these children. It appears to many that adolescence might deserve a subdivision, since the difference between the ages twelve to fifteen and fifteen to eighteen seems sufficiently marked. There is no detailed delineation of the adult life, which opens a fertile field for ego psychology. While previously the child had been neglected by professional studies, it seems that now the adult deserves additional attention.

The psychoanalytic consultant needs to extend his understanding of the normal as well as the pathological development of individuals fourteen to eighteen years old, as well as of those eighteen to twenty-five years old, and twenty-eight to forty-five years old. We will best understand the fluidity of the defenses at work and the demands made by society on us at different periods of life.

To what degree is the twenty-five-year-old influenced by society's expectation that now when he has achieved sufficient professional experience to support himself, he "has to make his work pay" and build a family? What can we say when we are asked to describe what we expect of a middle-aged man? Do we speak of his family responsibility, his financial security, his social status? To what degree do such considerations pose a dynamic situation which colors an individual's reactions to problems and serves to set off latent problems and bring them into the open? To what degree does financial insecurity at the age of fifty mean that life is a failure, while the same status at the age of thirty is accepted when there is expectation and hope? These are questions to be studied by ego psychology and sociology.

Psychoanalytical investigation has shown that growth does not occur in a continuous gradual curve. In the past, one accepted the biological change during puberty and spoke of three phases—childhood, puberty, and adult life. Closer study revealed that psychic changes entered into biological changes, that there are periods which follow characteristic patterns of psychic structure and dynamics. With the biological capacity to walk, to speak, to think, arrives the psychic stage of self-differentiation. With the ability to explore the world away from mother comes the need to find one's place in the family. After the age of two and a half, the child undertakes specific tasks in connection with the oedipal phase of development.

PSYCHOSOCIAL ADJUSTMENT

We have stated that the contribution which we can make to the field of social work will depend on our ability to see its function clearly. We spoke of the difference between therapy and treatment. The therapist is aware of biological and sociocultural factors, but he deals with them only as they are reflected and represented in the psychic conflict. Social work takes a different position in this regard. It is oriented toward the psychic forces which are available for the interplay between social experience and psychic reaction. This position permits the mobilization of psychic energy in the direct contact between the social worker and the client and the mobilization of social forces which can come to the aid of the client.

We have mentioned the nurse, the homemaker, foster parents, camps, homes for boys and girls and for the aged. Let us add the worker's visits to schools, his discussions with the teacher of the educational program and their subsequent effect on the school and the child.

Here is another example. A man is having difficulty on his job. He reacts to it with irritation, fatigue, sleep disturbance. The history reveals that he had never experienced such problems when he worked under conditions in which he carried out his superior's decisions. In his new job, where he was given a good deal of free choice, feelings of inadequacy were provoked. He started to complain, accepting help from the mechanism of projection, about the disorderliness of the organization, the incompetence of his boss who has poor relations with his staff. Therapy was indicated, if his pattern of functioning led him inescapably into situations where he failed, either by choosing these conditions or provoking situations to reinstate the same experience. The inflexibility of the adaptive forces would not permit a social work approach. Therapy will have to follow his pattern to the original constellation in which his need for self-fulfillment and his pathological environment made such a deviation necessary. The uncovery of the unconscious gratification, by repeating his patterns, will be essential.

What we see in our example suggests different possibilities. It will be possible to guide our client to find a place in which he can function again as he did in the past. Such plans are not so ambitious as to expect that the social worker will be able to help all people to adjust to all situations. It will aim to reinstate a balance between the psychic capacity and a given social scene.

Unless the social worker is clear about this, she will approach this client with a long-term treatment plan. The psychoanalytically oriented consultant has an important responsibility in outlining the treatment goal. By guiding the worker to uncover the unconscious conflict, he may mislead her and propose a long and inappropriate treatment procedure. The understanding of the unconscious wish for dependence on a strong parental figure, and the strong reaction when disappointed, does not necessitate a recommendation for the working through of such an unconscious conflict.

Psychoanalytic postulates in regard to the adaptive quality of the ego and the role of the defense mechanisms will permit us to evaluate the extent of the conflict, but it will also guide us to the shortest road to recovery. The study of the synthetic function of the ego becomes an important consideration for the social worker. A careful evaluation of the history of the client's functioning will offer important clues to the re-establishment of those conditions which in the past have proved to permit the most productive psychosocial balance.

It is conceivable that case work will again increase the number of short-treatment cases. It will do this now under the influence of a more scientific understanding of ego adaptation. A critical investigation of all those cases in treatment over many years, for which no working through of the conflict has been attempted or achieved, nor any real aid ever offered, will help us to select in the future those cases for which case work techniques will be most appropriate. In addition to this, a family agency which bases its interest on group dynamics will logically develop plans based on group activities. It can be predicted that group guidance and group case work will find an important place among the tools available to a family agency.

The direct contact with the client is still the basis for helping people to help themselves. Here, psychoanalytic experience has been most helpful to case work. Such terms as "transference," "insight," "interpretation," and many others, have become part of the social work vocabulary. With this the understanding of human behavior has increased, and social work practice has been profoundly influenced. To the degree that they have been incorporated into the technique of treatment without modification they have helped to confuse social work practice.

Let us consider the knowledge of "interpretation." This term connotes the therapist's attempt to bring into conscious awareness heretofore unconscious thoughts and feelings and to reveal their hidden meaning. As such, it can be nothing else but a part of psychoanalytic therapy. It would, therefore, be better not to speak of "interpretation" when we mean "clarification" for those reactions and feelings available to the ego's recognition without the analytic process.

This differentiation is of extreme importance. Only if we are clear about the distinctions in functioning can the consultant make his constructive contribution. These differences will also lead to a more careful intake study. The more we know about the success and failure of our work, the better are we able to select those problems which we can help and to refer the others.

The intake procedure reflects to a great degree the competence of the professional work. This is as true for the intake in analytic therapy as it is for case work. Clear recognition of differences should make it easier for the case worker to know whom to refer to the therapist. But it will also make it clear to the therapist when he can best avail himself of the social worker's skill.

These are some considerations which arise from the consultant's experience as an analyst in a family agency. Each point made will require further elaboration and collaboration. An attempt has been made to avoid repetition of psychoanalytic formulations and to stress new interests and possibilities. Such an attitude will lead to a more profound awareness of the responsibility of those who offer consultation and those who request it.

BIBLIOGRAPHY

1. ACKERMAN, N. W. and SOBEL, R. Family diagnosis: an approach to the pre-school child. *Am. J. Orthopsychiat.*, October, 1950.
2. ALEXANDER, F. and FRENCH, T. *Psychoanalytic Therapy*. New York: Ronald Press, 1946.
3. BLOS, P. *Adolescent Personality*. New York: D. Appleton-Century, 1941.
4. ERIKSON, E. H. *Childhood and Society*. New York: W. W. Norton & Co., 1950.
5. FREUD, A. *The Ego and the Mechanisms of Defense*. New York: International Universities Press, 1946.
6. —— and BURLINGHAM, D. *War and Children*. New York: International Universities Press, 1943.
7. —— —— —— *Infants Without Families*. New York: International Universities Press, 1944.
8. FREUD, S. *Three Contributions to the Theory of Sex*. New York: Nervous and Mentral Disease Publishing Co., 1930.
9. —— *Group Psychology and the Analysis of the Ego*. London: Hogarth Press, 1922.
10. FRIES, M. Psychosomatic relationships between mother and infant. *Psychosom. Med.*, April, 1944.
11. HAMILTON, G. *Psychotherapy in Child Guidance*. New York: Columbia University Press, 1947.
12. JONES, E. *Essays in Applied Psycho-Analysis*. London: Hogarth Press, 1932.
13. KRIS, M. The group-educational approach to child development. Presented at the 100th Anniversary Celebration of the Community Service Society, New York, 1948.
14. REGENSBERG, J. and FRIEDGOTT, A. H. Utilizing the contribution of psychiatric staff within a family agency. Presented at the Biennial Meeting of the Family Service Association of America, 1950.
15. SCHEIDLINGER, S. *Psychoanalysis and Group Behavior: A Study of Freudian Group Psychology*. New York: W. W. Norton & Co., 1952.
16. SLAVSON, S. R. *Analytic Group Psychotherapy*. New York: Columbia University Press, 1950.
17. TAFT, J. Social casework with children. *J. Soc. Work Process,* December, 1939.

Chapter 7

THE CONTRIBUTION OF PSYCHOANALYSIS TO THE CHILD GUIDANCE UNIT[1]

ABRAHAM A. FABIAN, M.D.

Child guidance, in its theory and practice, is becoming increasingly a field of applied psychoanalysis. This trend was prophesied by Freud (8) in an address to the Fifth International Psycho-Analytical Congress in 1918. Freud envisioned the establishment of community clinics staffed by analytically trained physicians, who would adapt psychoanalysis to these clinical settings. Dynamic psychotherapy, an alloy of the "pure gold of analysis with the copper of direct suggestion," he thought, would then be made as available as other medical services to those who could not afford private care. Freud also foresaw the possibility of combining psychotherapy with material support in some instances and thus anticipated the modern blending of psychotherapy with social manipulation, the teaming of efforts of psychiatrists and social workers.

HISTORICAL BACKGROUND

The child guidance movement was given its impetus in the United States by the National Committee for Mental Hygiene, which was founded in 1909, under the inspired leadership of Adolf Meyer.[2] The pioneer mental hygienists, aware of the impossibility of coping therapeutically with the overwhelming num-

[1] *Editor's note*: This chapter should be read in conjunction with and be compared to Chapters 5 and 6.
[2] See H. L. Witmer (13).

124

ber of the mentally ill, directed their energies toward prevention. Child guidance treatment of the young with incipient deviations, they reasoned, would reduce not only psychosis but criminality and other crippling social disabilities of adulthood. The inauguration of the child guidance program was also an attempt to direct attention away from custodial efforts toward prophylaxis and from the emphasis on protecting society to the understanding of the suffering individual. But primarily child guidance represented a shift of emphasis from adult psychiatry, introducing genetic considerations to child psychiatry and, therefore, paving the way for psychoanalytic concepts.

The original theoretical formulations employed in child guidance leaned heavily on constitution and heredity. The clinical procedures were largely efforts to uncover and correct faulty habit training. The practitioners relied on the use of common sense in dealing with problems, while capitalizing on talents and assets as avenues for development to offset the liabilities, so to say, in the personality balance sheet. James' pragmatic considerations were borrowed, as well as Hall's genetic theories and the clinical tools and methodology of Healy who earlier had broken ground for the scientific study of delinquency. Healy's use of a multidisciplinary diagnostic team was copied since it fitted in with the Meyerian theory of multiple causal factors in mental disorders.

In spite of the enthusiasm and vigor with which the job was undertaken in many child guidance clinics throughout the land, the original aspirations were not realized. Psychosis and criminality rates were not appreciably affected; instead of the anticipated dent in mental hospital admissions, there was a statistical increase as custodial facilities became more plentiful.

With the failure to achieve the hoped-for goals, the philosophy and operational concepts of child guidance were re-examined. Early treatment might prevent later personality disorders, but complete therapeutic coverage for children was beyond practical implementation because a relatively small percentage of disturbed children would ever be brought or could ultimately be treated. There was also the question of what constituted adequate treatment. Child guidance was a refreshing challenge to the pessimism and therapeutic nihilism engendered by Kraepelinian concepts which gripped psychiatry until well beyond the turn of this century. But the child guidance program was weighted down by static considerations and given to environmental manipulation, re-education, the correction of medical and learning defects, and the provision of recreational and social outlets. In the main the emphasis was on diagnosis; this was in line with the scientifically valid dictum that treatment would flow naturally once causal factors were established. The battery of child guidance experts which included the basic clinical team of psychiatrist, social worker, and psychologist (and at times was expanded to include pediatrician, neurologist, endocrinologist and teacher) gathered and reviewed their findings and then deliberated on a course of action. The plan that was evolved entailed doing something to the child. The child played a completely passive role, submitting to the examinations and to the manipulations which were recommended. The tangential explorative contact with the child was followed by assigning responsibilities to the parents, guardians, teachers, etc., who were advised on maneuvers in the handling of the child or were encouraged to modify their own attitudes and behavior. If the program failed to produce the desired changes the guidance clinic could retreat into the safety of the position that the recommendations were not adequately or correctly carried out.

If the child guidance therapeutic program was seriously handicapped by the superficial psychological insights which emanated from the prevailing psychiatric theories, the therapists themselves were limited by their training and experience to cope with the clinical problems which confronted them. Many of the early clinics were offshoots of state hospitals and were staffed by them. The professional personnel, psychiatrists, social workers, and psychologists, with a background of diagnosis and custodial supervision, transplanted their accustomed efforts and organizational plans to the clinics. The psychologist continued to perform his tasks as a psychometrician. The social worker, the environmental arm of the psychiatrist, collected social data from the parents, made home and school visits and later aided in arranging placements or interpreted the psychiatrist's impressions to the adults in the child's milieu. Guided by the reports of his colleagues and his own medical, neurological, and psychiatric findings, the psychiatrist arrived at a diagnosis and prescribed the corrective measures, but rarely participated in the treatment program himself beyond advising and guiding.

An additional difficulty met by the pioneers in the field was the fact that the most severely disturbed children in the community, those most likely to become the future public charges, were referred as soon as the clinic's doors were opened. The school, the court, and social agencies quickly filled the guidance clinic with their most recalcitrant cases. The guidance clinic thus was identified with the authoritative forces in the community and was fired by their aims to readjust and rehabilitate in order to reduce social nuisance. Inevitably the tendency to sermonize and moralize crept in, especially when the service rendered was chiefly diagnostic and guidance advice was prescribed. In the relatively few instances in which the diagnosis of mental deficiency or of organic brain disease could be established, the responsibility of the clinic was adequately discharged. The nuisance was removed by placement. But in the majority of cases the diagnosis clarified little and the manipulative suggestions, all too often previously tried without benefit, disappointed the referring agency that had been led to expect more help in these stubborn cases.

Many changes grew out of these unhappy experiences which challenged the basic aims, theories, and techniques of the early clinical efforts. A significant modification was the acceptance of the notion that the milder disorders of child behavior were deserving of clinical intervention. Severe deviations, incidentally, were found to be as resistive to treatment in childhood as in adulthood. With the acceptance of this change the original aim of preventing criminality and psychosis was modified and a more positive aspect of mental hygiene came to the fore as the aim of the guidance program. The optimum setting of a guidance unit, it was generally felt, was one which guaranteed autonomy. Dissociated by physical or other ties from authoritative forces in the community, the courts and their probation officers, the schools and their attendance officers, public welfare agencies and their investigators, medical and mental hospitals, the guidance clinic was free to explore and assist without exciting suspicion or arousing prejudice of being a subtle tool of these agencies. To insure adequate preparation of children and parents referred by these agencies and to encourage sound referrals from private physicians, clergymen, teachers, recreational workers, public health nurses, as well as self-referrals by enlightened parents, the child guidance clinic assumed the task of educating all of these groups in the principles of mental hygiene and the scope of its activities.

CONTRIBUTIONS OF PSYCHOANALYSIS

More profound alterations in child guidance occurred as psychoanalytic contributions to psychiatric theory found wider acceptance. Insight into the influence of unconscious factors in behavior revolutionized the prevailing concepts of child development, normal and deviant. The clinical idiom and vocabulary of child guidance which emerged reflected the impact of Freudian psychology. That behavior is purposeful, symptoms have meaning, infantile experiences are crucial to later personality development, inner conflicts are shielded by defenses which resist investigation and therapeutic change, transference effects blur interpersonal as well as therapeutic relationships and account for unreasonable reactions—all of these fundamental principles which were adopted spelled out an approach which gave depth to investigative efforts and to therapeutic intentions.

Primarily, however, psychoanalytic concepts brought into question the very foundation stones of child guidance. Like the guinea pig, which neither comes from Guinea nor is a pig, the question arose whether child guidance was also a misnomer. Should one concentrate on the child, and is guidance the optimum avenue of therapy? Dynamic formulations emphasizing intrafamilial relationships, especially the earliest one of child and mother, made one skeptical of an approach which placed the child's problem in the foreground. Since the child cannot be isolated physically from his family, and never emotionally, the dynamic unit was the family rather than the child. Shifting the therapeutic focus to the exploration of the emotional crosscurrents in a family, especially child-parent relationships, meant that the clinic would be called on to perform simultaneous multilateral therapeutic efforts. The challenge to the term guidance was equally strong. Since behavior, especially inappropriate neurotic behavior, is unconsciously motivated, it cannot simply be guided or redirected. Its unconscious connections and determinants must be uncovered.

Broadening of the scope and practice of child guidance had its repercussions in the organization and function of the clinic personnel. The clinic team was originally gathered to pool the diagnostic capacities of several disciplines. With the need to proceed beyond diagnosis, treatment responsibilities inevitably fell on all the team members. Acquaintanceship with problems of personality growth and with psychodynamics was already mandatory because diagnostic exploration also required such a background. The assumption of therapeutic responsibilities by all members of the clinical team was the next step, drawing in, in addition to the psychiatrist, at first the social worker whose experience in interview technique was an important qualification, and more recently the psychologist.

But these developments did not mean that child guidance clinics undertook the practice of analysis or even of brief analysis. Psychoanalysis has had a profound influence on many other fields including education, anthropology, and public health. A teacher who has been analyzed, who has read widely or taken courses in dynamic psychology, whose skills and resources have been enriched and whose insights have been deepened by these experiences, does not psychoanalyze her pupils. Freud is sometimes quoted to the effect that any therapy which deals with resistances and transference is psychoanalysis. But obviously the goals and techniques are the pertinent criteria in the definition of a therapy (12). In psychoanalysis, through free association and dream interpretation, one seeks to bring unconscious conflicts and fantasies to consciousness. In the psychoanalytic process a long-term view is maintained toward personality reconstruction rather than the goal of ameliorating immediate problems or symptoms. To achieve these aims, resistances must be dissolved step by step and the conflicts worked through. The development of a transference neurosis and its resolution are usual concomitants of the treatment. In child guidance at the present time, the overwhelming community pressures and the dearth of clinical facilities and personnel, dictate limited contact with patients. As a result modifications of technique, chiefly the abandonment of free association, obscures insight into inner conflicts. The unconscious fantasies cannot be adequately explored, the erotic even less than the aggressive. These limitations, incidentally, probably account for the tendency in brief forms of therapy to underestimate the importance of sexual conflicts and to emphasize the untoward effects of bottling up of hatred rather than of libido.

It is well to point out the pitfalls of equating psychoanalytic psychotherapy with psychoanalysis. The misinterpretations and abuses resulting from the free translation and adaptation of psychoanalytic principles in child rearing are well known. In an effort to prevent repressions, misguided parents have given their children unrestricted and undiscplined freedom and unwittingly contributed to the development of irreparable personality damage in them. It should be stressed that the awareness of psychodynamic principles does not give a therapist license to interpret a patient's productions outside of a controlled analytic situation even if an oedipus or castration complex seems quite apparent. More often than not, the lack of adequate material may tempt the analytically sophisticated therapist to speculate freely and then act on these speculations. Wild interpretation may be a consequence. Patients encouraged to engage in catharsis with abandon may develop anxiety which cannot be blotted up as it might be in an intensive treatment program. Therapeutic settings which encourage activity, so-called activity therapy programs, promote acting out rather than verbalization. The therapist with a fertile imagination may translate this activity into symbolic meanings which are imputed to the patient. Where the prearranged settings include amputation dolls or other emotionally laden materials which induce abreactions, the temptation to project speculations onto the patient is even greater.

Leaving cautioning aside, there remains the challenging question, "What is psychoanalytic psychotherapy?" Once psychoanalysis is modified and diluted, the number of variations in technique is limitless. The only constant factor would seem to be that the therapist is an analyst, or someone who through personal analysis and training is familiar with the objectives and methods of psychoanalysis and, therefore, is not driven to prove that the same developments and end results can be attained in brief contact with a patient as in psychoanalysis. The dynamically oriented therapist utilizes to advantage his clinical skills and his awareness of transference, countertransference, and resistance phenomena in helping his patients. He is also in a better position to establish and maintain good relationships with colleagues, board members, and to co-operate with other lay and professional affiliates in the community. The techniques at his disposal range from the manipulative and supportive to catharsis and inter- pretation in individual or group therapy. Treatment may only remotely resemble analysis and improvement often occurs with- out the uncovering and working through of conflicts. The posi- tive transference is not only the vehicle for therapy but often is exploited exclusively, especially in minor problems, and to tide over acute or transient situations. Maintaining a positive opti- mistic outlook, the therapist may successfully support parents who are being buffeted about by transitory oedipal or adolescent storms in their children. Parents who have never previously expe- rienced unconditional acceptance become amenable to suggestion in such an atmosphere. Partial insight may be sufficient to amel- iorate interpersonal and social repercussions of deep conflicts.

The Social Worker as Therapist

Adaptation of psychoanalytically oriented psychotherapy to guidance practice, and participation of the entire clinical team in the therapeutic program, raised problems of leadership, super- vision, and training. The social worker was first to be included in the expanded and modified psychotherapeutic activities; more recently the psychologist has broken the bonds which tied him to assisting with educational disabilities and he too has assumed increased therapeutic responsibilities. Let it be said that this trend is not universally accepted and in many clinics is still lag- ging. Even where nonmedical personnel carry on treatment, its scope is often narrowly defined so as to differentiate it from psychotherapy. Nevertheless, this is the trend. The clinical team, multidisciplinary in its organization, has become multifunctional in each discipline by taking on treatment tasks in addition to diagnostic functions. In the assumption of the therapeutic role, the diagnostic aptitudes were not discarded; each team member became more versatile.

Early in the history of the child guidance movement, when environmental manipulation gave way to attempts to influence the child-parent relationship, the role of the social worker was broadened. Called into the clinic from her field work explorations and manipulations, the social worker was at first assigned the task of supplementing the psychiatrist's treatment of the child by doing supportive work with the parent. Work with the parent, not yet labeled psychotherapy, was referred to as case work. Since the major therapeutic interest was concentrated on the child, the handling of the parent was considered a subsidiary task. There was no clash of spheres of activity because the psychiatrist always took on the child for treatment while the parent was always assigned to the social worker.[3] Strict adherence to this assignment plan continues in some clinics, partly out of tradition.

Supportive work with the parent is of crucial importance in stabilizing the treatment, insuring its continuation especially during stormy periods, and maintaining lines of communication at all times. For these and other more pertinent reasons in individual cases, maintaining a warm co-operative attitude on the part of the parent is necessary. A relationship at this level perhaps encompasses what is meant by case work with a parent. In any event, it is the opinion of many authorities, social workers included, that the social worker should function only within the boundaries of case work in her relationships with clients. And, the term client, incidentally, underlines case work. At a recent national conference[4] in which the status of the social worker in the child guidance clinic team was debated, the position adopted was that she should confine herself to intake, case work with parents, and community activities. Psychotherapy, the psychiatrist's

[3] *Editor's note:* Cf. Chapter 6, pp. 116 f.
[4] See G. B. Short (11).

responsibility, was considered outside of the social work domain.

The very title, psychiatric social worker, should give one pause before attempting to define rigid boundaries of performance. Within both fields, psychiatry and social work, new theories, objectives and methodologies are constantly evolving. What was acceptable from a psychiatric and social work point of view some years ago may be obsolete today. Consequently to specify the role of the psychiatric social worker according to concepts in vogue at some previous time leads to stasis. A social worker should function, not within an arbitrary set of guide lines, but rather in accordance with her own development and experience, as well as within the framework and philosophy of the agency in which she works, the degree of integration in the clinical team of which she is a part, and the acceptance of the clinic by the community in which it operates (6, 9). It is still common practice, however, to assign to the social worker only those problems which are family and socially oriented and to advise her to concern herself only with immediate reality conflicts which confront her clients.

Differentiations and delimitations of casework from psychotherapy are arbitrarily drawn and imposed on the patient in order to chart out limited fields of activity. For, there is no life situation or behavioral manifestation which is divorced from inner psychological problems. Unhappy and inadequate adjustments, marital, social and economic, are all too frequently associated with, or are products of, neurotic character distortions, ego restrictions, depressive and masochistic reactions, or other forms of psychopathology. Clinically, the dichotomy of inner and outer, psychological and social, is as artificial as the rigid separation of the diagnostic from the therapeutic function.

Another scheme of limiting psychotherapeutic intervention is the attempt to narrow clinical problems by concentrating on a single etiological factor. According to one theory, all difficulties stem from anxiety due to birth separation. A school of thought that partially derives from this theory stresses the child-parent relationship as the root of all psychological difficulties and the prime area for all therapeutic measures. The protagonists of this monolithic etiological theory, spending their therapeutic energies in resolving child-parent dependency relationships, work under considerable handicaps. If the child-parent relationship becomes the keystone of childhood psychopathology, little room is left for endogenous hereditary and constitutional factors. Moreover, it overlooks the possibility that the poor relationship may itself be a secondary phenomenon. The clinician is at a serious disadvantage if he steadfastly blinds himself to the possibility of the existence of a grave disorder, an incipient psychosis, epilepsy or an organic disturbance such as a postencephalitic reaction in a child, which keeps the parent in turmoil. Those who concentrate exclusively on child-parent relationships develop a tendency to regard parents as the malefactors of childhood neurosis. Inevitably, prejudicial attitudes creep into the clinical contacts with parents and overt or covert pressures are applied to effect changes in attitude toward the children. Often a moralizing note becomes unmistakable and occasionally shaming or scolding is advocated as a justifiable maneuver.

The obvious advantage of applying a constricted etiological theory is that it charts out a safe area of operations for the therapist and sets limitations so that deeper involvement is avoided. Through the simplification which results, procedures can be routinized. Therapy becomes a process of a fixed number of interviews with a set plan of attack and termination that can be precisely anticipated. The training of therapists is also facilitated because it is virtually by cathechism.

It can be said that in the elevation of the clinical importance of one causative factor, there is truth to the claim, even if it is only a partial truth. The earliest phase of the child-parent relationship is of crucial importance to subsequent individuation, reality testing, and the development of ties to love objects. Behavior and defensive patterns are etched in during early infancy which later appear with inexorable repetitiveness. In situations or relationships which are so structured as to be reminiscent of earlier life experiences these inappropriate and ineffectual responses are compulsively evoked. But emphasis on the child-parent relationship, as an all inclusive theory of etiology, has questionable validity. It is static. It overlooks, for example, the dynamic implications of regressive behavior, the importance of the coincidence of a traumatic experience and a particular phase of development, and the effect of one phase of development upon subsequent ones.

Ellen C. was destructive and abusive to all things, animate and inanimate. She cursed and fumed, smashed furniture, tore up plants by their roots, bit puppy dogs, and behaved aggressively toward her younger sibling and her parents. Ellen became very disturbed at the age of three years, when her mother went to the hospital for an operation. Ellen developed severe diarrhea which resulted in rectal prolapse for which she was treated by injections of caustic solutions that produced anal constriction. For several years thereafter Ellen's bowel movements were induced by cathartics and enemata. The disturbed child-parent relationship in this case was a single facet of a complex interplay of dynamic forces and traumatizing fixating experiences.

George G. was a shy, little boy with many phobias, and bizarre reactions of withdrawal, sudden explosions of temper, intense jealous reactions and the habit of eating his nasal secretions and the roots of hairs which he so persistently plucked from his head that he developed bald spots. During George's infancy his mother reacted with a mild depression to a frustrating life situation. Although she had related herself minimally to the child prior to her reactive depression, she now clung to him in a frantic way. After her recovery she turned George back completely to his nurse. Subsequently, after the mother received intensive psychotherapy she sought to improve her relationship with her son. By this time George evinced serious symptoms suggesting grave psychopathology. His most violent tempers were directed at his mother, who, despite her adequate adjustment in all other areas, could not tolerate his attacks. The therapy of the existing child-parent relationship would have been a futile chase after an anachronism.

THE PSYCHOANALYTICALLY ORIENTED CHILD GUIDANCE CLINIC PROGRAM

The primary function of the child guidance clinic is to provide outpatient treatment facilities for families in which there are emotionally disturbed children. Among the many factors which shape the treatment program are: (1) the length of time the clinic has been in operation in the community; (2) the training, maturity, and other positive personality qualifications of the staff members, and the degree of integration which the clinic team has achieved; and (3) the preparation and orientation of the clinic board of directors, of the local citizens, the personnel in schools, courts, hospitals and social agencies, clergymen, private medical practitioners, and other professional affiliates. Adequate financial support of the clinic, mutual respect and co-operation in professional relationships, and sound referral policies on the part of those utilizing the clinic as a resource, are the clinic's foundation stones.

The proper discharge of the central function of treatment is not the sum of the clinic's activities. Diagnostic screening, always a preliminary to embarking on a treatment program, may be offered as a limited consultation service or in conjunction with counseling. In addition the clinic may have an active training program for guidance personnel, a research program and withal serve as a mental hygiene beacon in the community.

DIAGNOSTIC SCREENING

The patient's first contact with the clinic is generally with the intake worker. The social worker, because of her experience in assessing social as well as psychological pathology, and her familiarity with other agencies, and the recreational, welfare and institutional resources in the community usually performs this pre-diagnostic screening job. Intake screening requires considerable skill in interviewing to deal with the heightened reactions of anxiety, hostility, guilt, and jealousy, which are often encountered in the initial contact with the applicant. To cope with these reactions and yet explore the problem sufficiently so as to see its general outlines is an art which is perfected only by experience. The neophyte assigned to do intake screening in a routine way may not be sensitive to those situations where probing is inadvisable and had best be postponed. If exploration is permissible, delineation of the pathology, if only in the most tentative terms, may permit screening out of (1) low-grade mental defectives, (2) children with severe organic brain disorders, and (3) families beset with overwhelming socioeconomic pressures or tangled marital difficulties which temporarily reduce the possibility of amelioration of the problems through psychotherapy. Referral for med-

ical aid, institutional placement, welfare or family agency requires an acquaintanceship with the intake policies and other
practices of these organizations and skill in preparing the applicant for the other service because of the disappointment reactions
and feelings of rejection which are frequently aroused by referrals. If inquiry into economic status reveals the ability to afford
private care, referral is indicated; where the need to get treatment free or at low clinic rates is part of a neurotic problem,
such a referral may meet formidable resistances.

Ultimately, intake screening should include an investigation
of those factors in the circumstances of the referral, the life situations and the personalities of the parents or guardians which
might interfere with receptivity of treatment. Parents who have
been pressured into coming to the clinic by the school, court or
hospital, may arrive in a tense, belligerent mood and defy the
clinic to find abnormalities in their children. Their rationalizations and projections of blame are often unsurmountable barriers. Social repercussions of overt disorders in children, such as
stuttering and tics, may bring parents who want relief, whether it
be by magic or punitive measures, but not through psychotherapeutic investigations. The nuisance caused by a child's enuresis,
soiling, persistent vomiting, feeding or sleep disturbances, excessive clinging or tenacious phobias may produce such intrafamilial
tensions that child guidance is sought. But, here also, the clinical
indications for treatment may not coincide with acceptance of
long-term treatment plans. The objections raised may be that
treatment will interfere with school attendance or with music
lessons. The stigma of treatment is often raised. Resistance of the
other parent or of an influential relative may compromise treatment. The lack of receptivity, however, does not always rule out
the possibility of treatment. Its existence must be ascertained so
that difficulties will be anticipated and resistances can be met and
neutralized in the preliminary phase of treatment.

Those cases which filter through the intake screen, children
and parents, are then examined by the psychologist and psychiatrist. At the staff conference, the test and interview data are
pooled. The tentative diagnostic and prognostic impressions and

the formulation of treatment plans are the conjoint efforts of the three disciplines represented in the clinical team.

The standard nosological classifications of childhood disorders, static and descriptive, are incongruities in a dynamically oriented clinical setting. There is some justification, however, for using the categories of mental deficiency, organic brain disease, borderline and frank psychosis, not to eliminate these children from therapeutic consideration, for which diagnostic labels are often used, but to essay therapy on a limited basis.[5] Where the therapeutic program does not have a sound clinical groundwork and where these grave clinical conditions are not diagnosed, treatment may be pursued with unwarranted optimism.

There remains the preponderant group of children seen in child guidance clinics whose problems fall outside of the categories of severe psychopathology. Most of them are cryptically classified as primary behavior disorders, others are descriptively labeled conduct disorders. Etiological considerations are implied in some terms which have received currency in child guidance parlance, such as, the rejected child, the overindulged child, the hostile mother, etc. Although these terms are more pretentious, they are also descriptive entities which beg the question of etiology. Even the classification of disorders into preoedipal and oedipal types is too concrete and literal a translation of dynamic theory into clinical practice. While anxiety states, phobias, and incipient obsessional patterns sometimes crystallize out and persist (7), the symptoms are often mixed and rapidly shifting. For practical purposes one may differentiate children whose conflicts are internalized and go on to develop symptoms and those who act out their conflicts (3). However, all classifications of childhood problems, if they ignore familial, and particularly maternal psychopathology, focus on fragments while obscuring the total gestalt, even if they give peace to the statistician.

Rather than diagnostic categories, Anna Freud's (7) criteria for the indications for child analysis, adapted to clinic use, are valuable aids in sorting out those children who deserve treatment. Unlike the adult neurotic whose suffering and interfer-

5 *Editor's note:* For a concurring opinion, cf. Chapter 6, pp. 111 ff.

ence with his sexual adjustment and capacity to work bring him into treatment, the child usually denies his symptoms and resists treatment. Nor can interference or arrest in libidinal development be a criterion for treatment, because the fantasies which give the clues to these developmental levels cannot be uncovered in initial diagnostic contacts. In assessing childhood neurosis, the crucial question is not one of weighing symptoms or inhibitions but of determining the degree to which these difficulties interfere with the child's further development. The ego functions of reality testing, memory building, synthesis of conflicting strivings and emotions, and motility control are the maturational clues. Disturbances in these functions which are severe and *chronic* are indications for therapeutic intervention.

THERAPY

Abbreviated forms of therapy make great demands on intuitiveness, resourcefulness and flexibility. The therapist must have at his command a variety of approaches and modifications, and be able to work with individuals or groups. He must be willing to sacrifice idealistic therapeutic ambitions for practical results, deep and penetrative investigations for more superficial inquiries, and long-term extensive alterations, for more immediate adjustments. The patient's needs, capacities, receptivity, and life situation will dictate the type of treatment rather than the therapist's standardized method into which the patient must be fitted.

Neurotic entanglements of child with parent, and other family members, calls for multiple therapeutic efforts. Rigid therapeutic assignments, which force social workers to see parents only, may hamstring the clinical team.[6] A social worker may be highly competent and well trained in therapy with children or adolescents. In general, the treatment challenge should be met by the most skillful therapist available. The choice of therapist by fixed rule is as inadvisable as the application of a fixed therapeutic technique. Treatment should be molded to the patient's needs rather than to a hierarchial scheme or a therapist's limitations.

6 *Editor's note:* Cf. Chapter 6, pp. 116 ff.

Therapy, especially in the initial phase, is a continuation of the diagnostic effort. In fact throughout the clinic contact there can be no clear-cut separation of diagnostic from therapeutic procedures. Dynamic therapy is always explorative and, therefore, diagnostic in intent. The uncovering process which is at the heart of the psychoanalytically oriented treatment program has no fixed objectives. The patient, child or adult, must be inducted into the technique of finding clues which will give meaning to the disturbed behavior. While the setting for child work must include play materials which provide opportunities for playing out fantasies, the ultimate aim in working with all patients is to further the inquiry by verbal communications, except for those cases which are handled supportively rather than through exploration of conflicts.

Although wherever indicated, the aim of treatment is exploration, a prolonged period of preparation may be necessary before treatment can be begun. In children the resistances may be unusually tenacious. Either because symptoms are denied or used aggressively against the parent, or for some other secondary gain, the child may for a long time spend the clinic time in uncommunicative play. If absence from school is arranged in order to allow for the treatment session, and the child is having school difficulties or is suffering from a learning disability which is causing him to feel inadequate or embarrassed by his poor school performance, the resistive child will welcome therapy as an escape from an obnoxious situation, but will permit no penetration of his defenses. Parents who are ambivalent about treatment, and early in the treatment this is generally true, often have to be eased into or smuggled into treatment. There are those parents who never go beyond the point of giving factual accounts of their children's misbehavior for which they request advice in the handling or reassurance that they have behaved properly.

With Parents

The therapy with the parent is conducted at different levels of intensity but in all cases the aim is to establish sufficiently good contact to overcome feelings of shame and stigmatization, to soothe the narcissistic wound of failure as a parent, to dampen the jealousy of and competition with the child's therapist, and to neutralize guilt feelings. A supportive, reassuring attitude is maintained in order to prevent interruption of treatment which is especially prone to occur early in the program. Maintaining good contact with the parent is also imperative during those very resistive phases in the child's treatment when one cannot rely upon the child for sufficient ego strength to insure continuation. During times when the child's rebelliousness and defiant acting out charges the atmosphere in the family, only a strong bond with the parents will sustain the treatment. Furthermore, work with the parent provides the therapist with information on the current happenings, as well as historical data, so necessary for the reconstruction of the child's profile; the importance of the delineation of the infantile neurosis in psychoanalytic theory is well known. Parents also may report dreams and fantasies which children may forget or be unwilling to reveal in their own sessions. For all these reasons a strong, positive transference on the part of the parent is of the essence in child guidance work.

In some instances work with the parent never goes beyond these boundaries. This is true in the supportive contacts with intellectually limited parents, those who are making a borderline adjustment to reality and others who have had previous psychotic breaks and are now making marginal adjustments. It might seem that such parents are not suitable candidates for child guidance therapy. However, the child guidance clinic has a responsibility to the community, more particularly to the children of these limited and sick parents who often are in desperate need of psychotherapeutic aid, or at least of some emotional insulation from these parents when placement is impossible or is strongly contested. Aside from supportive efforts, direct manipulation and assistance in budgeting, providing adequate housing, arranging for a job, for medical care and for convalescence, represent the goal-limited lines of therapy with these parents. There are among these parents, who are seriously handicapped or disturbed, those who demand more intensive therapy. Clinical insight and prudence would militate against acceding to these requests.

Where there is no apparent contraindication to exploration one can proceed cautiously. It is well to emphasize that explorative therapy of the parent is not undertaken in lieu of the basic positive relationship outlined above which aids and supports the treatment of the child, but rather is in addition to it. To list the problems encountered in the therapy of parents would be tantamount to calling the roll of the psychopathological disorders of adults. Suffice it to say, that in the treatment of parents in a child guidance setting the objectives are limited. Reference should be made to those instances in which a parent brings the child to the clinic for treatment as a substitute or opening wedge for her own treatment. Although efforts at improving neurotic life adjustments of some parents are often successful, neuroses are rarely cured. Treatment of the parent is imperative in those cases where the progress of the child would be limited or halted unless changes in parental attitudes were achieved.

Mrs. S. who suffered from a moderately severe cardiac condition had endangered her life twice, when, against the advice of her physicians, she went through pregnancies. Both times she was disappointed. Both times she had prayed for a girl, who would then nurse her as she had nursed her own mother through prolonged invalidism. To Mrs. S., her boys, aged four and seven years, who suffered from many neurotic symptoms, were useless; their hyperactivity drained her limited physical resources. In her handling of her older boy during his infancy she rarely fondled him and often left him to cry it out. Later, he became aware of his mother's preoccupation with the dangers of complications from tooth decay and extractions which frightened her away from dental care; he too developed a severe phobia in relation to the dentist. Mrs. S. spoke about her problems in individual and group therapy sessions. In the second year of treatment Mrs. S. began to modify her attitudes toward her older son. Embracing the child was at first a strange and artificial experience which she forced herself to carry out. Gradually she "learned to love him" and to support him when he was attacked and otherwise needed her help. Although she did not feel that she would ever stop leaning on people for advice and help, she came to feel that she could help her sons to grow up unafraid.

A child may be completely bound to the parent by repeated

seductions. Therapy of the parent may loosen the symbiotic relationship.

Mrs. G. brought her nine-year-old daughter because the child was becoming rebellious and defiant. The child revealed that the mother cared for her and watched over her as if she were an infant, wiping her after she had defecated and supervising her every activity. It was possible to maintain Mrs. G. in treatment long enough to permit the child to win her independence.

Where the child represents the parent's crutch or cure, the parent will fiercely resist changes which spell any rift in the relationship.

Mrs. P. complained that her nine-year-old son had many fears, of injuries, of riding in trains and elevators, and would not go to school unless she accompanied him. In his interviews, the boy disclosed that his mother's fears coincided with his own and forthrightly stated that unless she were helped he saw little likelihood that he would improve.

Mrs. P. as an adolescent suffered from anxiety states which crystallized into an agoraphobia after her marriage. Her doctor advised a pregnancy as a cure, and a cure it was because until her son was six years old she was able to negotiate the streets by wheeling him about in a carriage. His enrollment in school, which was mandatory, reopened her problem. Her solution was to get volunteer work at his school and to accompany her son to and from it. During treatment, when the boy was making heroic efforts to cope with his fears, his mother's desperate attempts to keep him dependent on her would appear despite her conscious desires to liberate him.

The meaning of the child's symptoms to the parent may become apparent, but the possibility of uncovering through child guidance therapy the underlying libidinal implications is less likely. One may extrapolate from psychoanalytic experience and speculate that a boy represents a penis to his mother, that his separation from her constitutes a castrating experience for her, or that in another case the child is symbolically equated with feces by his mother, but in the absence of corroborative material, these remain speculations. Hostile attitudes are more easily explored in brief therapy. Displacement of the mother's hostility from her husband to her child is often encountered.

John Y., a five-year-old boy, was brutally treated by his mother. Mrs. Y. was deeply disappointed in her husband because he flunked out of dental school a year after she married him. Her bitterness grew as she watched her more fortunate friends go on to lives of financial ease, while she struggled along on her husband's limited salary from his menial job. To remind her husband of the injustice he had done her, she kept his dental texts prominently displayed in her living room. John tied her to this failure whom she despised.

In some cases, the simple displacement of hostility yields to more intensive investigation and deeper connections come to light. In these instances, antagonism to the husband and marital strife are antedated by a hostile relationship to father or brother. The choice of the husband and the subsequent wrangling represent the persistence and repetition of the neurotic struggle.

One might classify the therapy of parents according to the age range of the children they bring to the clinic. Variations in technique are dictated by the special problems connected with the child's level of development. (1) The preschool child's problem is generally more amenable to environmental influence. Since the mother is, and to a large extent creates, the child's environment, she should be treated as intensively as the clinic's program will permit. Group treatment of the mothers of preschool children is a particularly valuable method.[7] It permits the inclusion and simultaneous diagnostic observation of several women. Some mothers profit from the interchange of opinions in the group which dilutes anxiety and guilt feelings. Others, with more severe neurotic problems, are transferred to individual therapy. (2) Oedipal struggles in children may light up unresolved conflicts in parents. Treatment of the parent is akin to a holding action until the child's clamor abates. (3) The therapy of the child in the latency period presents many obstacles, among which the paucity of material obtained from the child is outstanding. Contact with the parent is especially helpful to the

[7] Cf. A. A. Fabian, J. E. Crampton and M. A. Holden (4).

child's therapist who otherwise might be in the dark as to occurrences in the child's immediate life situation. (4) Therapy of the adolescent as a rule proceeds without benefit of parallel work with the parent, mainly because of the adolescent's strong objection to any contact with the parent. Where the child will permit the parent to participate in the treatment program, the therapists are buffeted by pleas from both sides for judgments in their favor.

Child guidance treatment of the parent has always been largely treatment of the mother. In the case of some children, work with the father may be just as urgent. The child may even be brought by the mother in the hope that the clinic will exert pressure on or draw in the sick father for treatment. In order to round out the child guidance program, therefore, provisions must be made to work with fathers. Some clinics arrange evening sessions for fathers who cannot attend during the day. Group therapy with fathers is also a valuable adjunct in their treatment.

Therapy of Children

The fact that in the sequential arrangement in this review the treatment of the parent takes precedence over the treatment of the child is by design, and is meant to emphasize the relative importance of work with parents in a child guidance setting. Movement in the child is almost always predicated on effective work with the parent when child and parent are locked in a pathological bond. Although the symptoms in both are frequently mirror images, the underlying mechanisms may differ.

Anna C., an eight-year-old girl, suffered from a persistent cough for which no organic basis could be discovered. Her mother, while asymptomatic at the time of intake, subsequently developed a cough which she said recurred intermittently. Mrs. C.'s cough and previous symptoms of globus hystericus were linked with fellatio and biting fantasies. Anna's cough, on the other hand, was an expression of her identification with her beautiful mother whom she imitated and sought to emulate in all ways.

Preschool children can be treated in a group in a setting which resembles a nursery. There are, however, many features which distinguish it from a nursery. (1) The leader, often referred to by the children as teacher or mother, is a trained therapist. It is her task to create and maintain an atmosphere of benevolent support, impartial handling and judicious but definite limitations. Her observations, because of her background and experience, are valuable diagnostically to spot those children who need supplementary or exclusively individual therapy. (2) The children are carefully screened by physical, psychological, and psychiatric examinations to rule out those with organic or intellectual defects, as well as those with marked separation anxiety. (3) The group is kept small, four or five children at the most are included.

Individual treatment of children through preadolescence is usually conducted in a playroom. The therapy of infantilized children with severe anxiety and phobias must be initiated in the presence of the parent until weaning is achieved. Although play materials, paints, crayons, and clay are provided, neither the play nor the creative efforts are directly interpreted in order to avoid interference with the child's sublimations. The central aim is to establish a strong, positive bond, to win the child's confidence so as to get verbalization of the problem for which treatment is pursued and to introduce the child to methods of exploring the problems. Role play is encouraged as well as reporting of fantasies and dreams. Interpretations are used sparingly after the establishment of a positive relationship.

The experienced therapist has greater facility in establishing rapport with children; special abilities with certain age groups or problems may even lead to specialization. But limited therapeutic contact in child guidance clinics may interfere with the ease and speed with which a positive relationship can be forged. It is particularly difficult to win over severely traumatized children who have been rejected and unloved, those who are born out of wedlock or are the products of unhappy, loveless marriages. An impermeable shell surrounds children referred from foster homes or institutions where they were placed because of illness, death, psychosis or imprisonment of their parents or because they have been seriously neglected, abused or abandoned. Similarly, children with severe neurotic problems, the schizoid, borderline and frankly psychotic, are difficult to reach even with more intensive types of therapy. But, if therapeutic ambitions are not so importunate as to prevent acceptance of limited goals, child guidance contact with many of these children can be profitable for them. Aichhorn's (1) philosophy and techniques are guides and inspirations in these thorny cases.

For Francis, aged fifteen, freedom while on probation from the court for a sexual assault on a child was conditional upon attendance at the guidance clinic. For over a year he was sullen and resentful in manner and warded off all attempts at verbal contact. On his birthday the therapist presented him with a gift. Apparently caught off guard, Francis became tearful and bewildered and remonstrated with the therapist. He later confessed that he had never received a gift and that his birthdays always passed unnoticed by his family. This experience was the opening wedge in effective treatment. Although many vicissitudes were encountered later in the treatment, the relationship with the therapist sustained the boy in his sometimes faltering efforts to escape the delinquent pattern.

In the average case, that is, where the physical, social, and psychological pathology is not overwhelming, a positive relationship develops more rapidly. Reassurance and partial insight may be given through interpretations which are not necessarily in depth.

Albert, an eight-year-old phobic boy who was very concerned about bodily injury, accompanied his therapist on a shopping tour. At a busy traffic intersection, Albert halted and paled. The therapist, taking his hand, told him that the fear was understandable, that when he grew up he would be able to manage to cross by himself, but that now, if he stayed close he would be perfectly safe in making the crossing. Albert relaxed and was in good spirits during the remainder of the trip.

The Limitations of Therapy

The limitations of child guidance therapy are those of any limited ambulatory form of therapy. Severe psychopathology and therapeutic negativism ordinarily will not yield to abbreviated techniques. Even the most careful screening will not detect the presence of serious disturbances or overpowering resistances to treatment. The lack of receptivity on the part of the parent may be known and failure anticipated and yet treatment may be instituted on the chance that the child may be helped. In some cases there may be eagerness to give full co-operation but the parental problem blocks progress.

Paul N., a seven-year-old boy, the older of two children, was brought because of his temper outbursts and stubbornness. There had been a child who preceded Paul. This first child developed what appeared to be a mild respiratory infection. Routine treatment was given but the tragic sequel was that within twenty-four hours the infant was dead. The two children who followed had unusual susceptibility to respiratory diseases; both had had pneumonia several times according to the mother. The children were so well trained that if they sneezed they would yell out reassurance to the mother that it was "only the first sneeze." Mrs. N. was always saving the children and had to continue to do so.

Direction of Therapy

It is not possible to predict the course and ultimate outcome of psychotherapy. More serious pathology than is apparent on the surface may become evident as treatment proceeds. Psychosis or the threat of an imminent break with reality may develop. Somatic complications, or psychosomatic symptoms requiring medical consultations may have to be dealt with. Because of the psychiatric, medical and legal implications, a psychotherapeutic program should have psychiatric direction and supervision. From the inception of the movement, child guidance clinics have co-ordinated the efforts of three professional disciplines under phychiatric direction.

Qualifications of the Therapist

Academic training in dynamic theory and psychopathology and on-the-job training in a clinic, which provides sound and continuous supervision, qualify the therapist. New staff members, even those with considerable experience need a period of indoctrination in the problems, policies, and techniques which are unique to the particular setting. Integration into the clinical team is a slow process of personality dovetailing. Personal warmth, optimism, intuitiveness and flexibility and ease in interpersonal relationships are definite advantages in a therapist. There has been considerable debate on the question of personal psychoanalysis as a requirement for guidance clinic therapists. Because child guidance therapy is generally psychoanalytically oriented, such preparation would seem valuable. For proper conduct in the handling of transferences in therapy and in interprofessional relationships, personal analysis is desirable but is not mandatory for the gifted individual. However, therapy should be supervised by an analytically trained member of the staff, not only to give dynamic direction but also to guard against wild analysis and the overcompensating tendency to ignore realistic and practical measures for complex analytic considerations.

Supervision of Therapy

The knotty question of supervision[8] has been vigorously debated in the social work field for decades. The difficulties and confusions are in part the products of the attempt to confine the problems arising in supervision to the conscious level. Where there has been some appreciation of the unconscious forces at work in the interpersonal supervisory relationship, as in all other relationships, in terms of transference and countertransference, supervisors have sometimes tried to deal with these problems directly. Complications are especially likely to occur when the supervisor strays from the supervisory job into attempts at analyzing the student. Such probing is as objectionable and dangerous as any form of wild analysis.

There are other problems arising in the supervisory relationship. In passing one may mention briefly the supervisor who has a need to maintain control and cannot permit his student to grow and to develop independently and one who is unable to impart information because it represents a loss of power for him and a diminution of his own position. Supervision provides opportunities to give vent to sadistic impulses and to humiliate the novitiate. The student, who is being supervised, may also be stymied by inner conflicts and neurotic character difficulties. The student may possess a passive, dependent attitude which prevents

8 *Editor's note*: Cf. Chapter 5.

him from assuming responsibility, or he may be in a constant state of rebelliousness and unable to accept direction. The learning experience not only reflects the personalities of the supervisor and the student, but is also colored by the material under discussion by them which may set off latent anxieties in either one. Mention should also be made of the problems arising in team conferences of the therapists when countertransferences clash or rank is pulled. Personal analysis is a partial answer to some of these problems.

TRAINING

Neither medical schools, psychiatric institutions, schools of social work, or academic faculties of psychology prepare their students completely for child guidance work. Preparation for child guidance is postgraduate training for qualified psychologists, social workers, and psychiatrists. The problem of training personnel is, therefore, the responsibility of the child guidance clinics. The American Association of Psychiatric Clinics for Children was recently organized to set up and maintain standards of training and to give accreditation to those clinics which can provide such training. Ultimately, the training of personnel is another contribution by the clinic to the community in that it helps meet the tremendous need for more clinical services.

RESEARCH

Research to test new techniques, to modify and apply dynamic approaches, and to test the limitations of methods is also the province of child guidance clinics. Therapeutic instruments can be forged and tested only where they are being used. To widen the boundaries of clinic service, analytically oriented group therapy (4) is finding increasing acceptance, and attention is being given to the possibility of providing ambulatory treatment for some psychotic children (5), and the large group of children with borderline or dull intelligence who are generally the outcasts of therapy programs. Learning disability as a symptom of an underlying emotional disorder is being given its proper emphasis in child guidance research (2).

EDUCATION AND PROPHYLAXIS

The value of the child guidance clinic to the community is no longer a debatable issue; demonstration clinics and pilot projects are things of the past. Wherever a clinic is set up, nevertheless, it must establish a place for itself in the family of the community agencies. An area of operation must be defined and efforts made to win over those individuals and organizations that deal with children. To chop out a sphere of influence aggressively, is to forsake co-operation. On the other hand it is necessary to avoid becoming the dumping ground for the hopeless cases in the community.

The child guidance clinic can function as the spearhead of the mental hygiene movement in the community. This responsibility is even greater in a community which has otherwise limited social service, welfare, and psychiatric resources. Orientation of teachers, public health nurses, school psychologists, and other professional personnel in a mental hygiene point of view is an important clinic function, since these people are the community's first line of defense. It may be possible for them to intervene effectively in many situations on the level of their own practices, and thus reduce the number of patients; it will also sharpen the criteria which warrant referral to the clinic. There is some question, however, as to whether orientation can be achieved by lecturing; seminars and workshops may be more fruitful. By the same token, there is a swing away from single lectures to the laity which often provoke latent anxieties and guilt and create waves of self-referral beyond the capacity of the clinics.

The answer to lengthening waiting lists is not to be found only in expansion of clinic services. Prophylaxis is important. Improvement in institutional care of infants and children, promulgation of mental hygiene principles in well-baby clinics, screening of candidates for teachers' colleges, and teaching in medical, nursing and social work schools, are some important areas in which clinic personnel can make contributions or where clinics can press for improvements.

Finally, mental hygiene begins at home. It should pervade the clinic. Mutual respect, support, sharing, and professional co-operation are the keynotes of a well-integrated clinic team.

BIBLIOGRAPHY

1. AICHHORN, A. *Wayward Youth.* New York: Viking Press, 1945.
2. FABIAN, A. A. Clinical and experimental studies of school children who are retarded in reading. *Quart. J. Child Behavior,* 3:15, 1951.
3. —— and BENDER, L. Head injury in children: predisposing factors. *Am. J. Orthopsychiat.,* 17:68, 1947.
4. —— CRAMPTON, J. E. and HOLDEN, M. A. Parallel group treatment of pre-school children and their mothers. *Int. J. Group Psychotherapy,* 1:37, 1951.
5. —— and HOLDEN, M. A. Treatment of childhood schizophrenia in a child guidance clinic. *Am. J. Orthopsychiat.,* 21:571, 1951.
6. FRENCH, L. M. *Psychiatric Social Work.* New York: Commonwealth Fund, 1940.
7. FREUD, A. Indications for child analysis. In *The Psychoanalytic Study of the Child,* 1:127, 1945. New York: International Universities Press.
8. FREUD, S. Turning in the ways of psychoanalytic therapy. In *Collected Papers,* 2:392. London: Hogarth Press, 1924.
9. JOSSELYN, I. M. Psychosocial development of children. *Family Service Association of America,* 1948.
10. PEARSON, G. H. J. *Emotional Disorders of Children.* New York: W. W. Norton & Co., 1949.
11. SHORT, G. B. Psychiatric social work in the child guidance clinic. *Proceedings of the Dartmouth Conference, American Association of Psychiatric Social Workers,* 1950.
12. STONE, L. Psychoanalysis and brief psychotherapy. *Psychoanal. Quart.,* 20:215, 1951.
13. WITMER, H. L. *Psychiatric Clinics for Children.* New York: Commonwealth Fund, 1940.

Chapter 8

FOSTER HOME PLACEMENT

LILLIAN K. KAPLAN, M.D.

The work of the analyst in foster home placement has been especially useful in three areas—education, diagnosis and treatment.

As educator the analyst works on a consultative basis to further the case worker's understanding of the psychodynamics involved in the interpersonal reactions. It is the lifeline in all placement to maintain the equilibrium between the relationships of the child with his own family and the foster family. This can be accomplished by watching for the dangerous elements which make for unhappiness in any living situation, and which are prone to develop in the process of adjusting to separation from one's own family and living with a foster family. These danger signals are, the element of rivalry which is inherent in the situation, the element of loyalty with its secondary by-product of denial which may lead to serious emotional conflict, and, last but not least, the defense mechanism which manifests itself by a need to depreciate oneself in order to feel wanted.

In the second area of usefulness, the analyst, as diagnostician, aims for much the same result as in the first—a greater knowledge and understanding of psychoanalytic concepts of the personality functioning. In the third and final area, the psychoanalyst's skill is utilized in the treatment of children. Here co-operation of psychoanalyst and case worker may help all concerned to achieve the desired result of a more adequate state of mental health.

In the not too distant past, when a child lost his parents or his parents could not care for him adequately, the only solution thought possible, particularly with very young children, was the institution. Here children were cared for in virtual isolation until ready for display and adoption; those a little older were put out to service. Orphanage directors, on the whole, tried to excel by giving the children meticulous care in matters of health, food, and religious training. Some of the more enlightened directors even tried to provide individual clothing. Although the standards were high, however, two factors essential for the development of a balanced personality were of necessity missing—the child's feeling that he was an important part of the life around him, and the fact that his interpersonal relationships lacked the vitality of love.

When dynamic psychology in the late nineteenth century began to emphasize the importance of interpersonal relationships, the large orphanage began to give way to foster home placements. A growth in the understanding of these relationships made it clear that living in a home as part of a family was essential for the child's emotional maturation, and the foster home grew in popularity as a more desirable method for providing certain of the conditions necessary for the psychological development of the child.

This newer point of view holds that if a child is sent to an institution for the first time at an age of eleven, twelve, or thirteen, he has some backlog of experience and some beginning of a self-system, whether good or bad. The infant has no such measuring rod, no inner reserves on which to draw. The child at birth is a "bundle of propensities" entirely dependent on those who care for him. He must learn to become a social being through imitation, by introjecting the environment to arrive at some kind of identification. The external world is a threatening and dangerous stranger to the infant, but he may learn to accept and deal with this world if he has the good fortune to have understanding and responsive adults around him, men as well as women.

As a result of the growth of these dynamic concepts, the placement of children in foster homes is now one of the most important functions of the child-caring agency, whether arranged as a temporary measure or as a long-term, nonadoptive plan. The foster child is different from other children in that he is separated from his parents by circumstances over which he has no control. However, he is fortunate to have the aid of people who have been trained to understand his problems, people who are aware of his great need to feel part of some whole, and who will help him to "belong." The best possible psychological as well as the best physical comforts are provided in foster home placement.

The psychoanalyst stands ready to help theory evolve into practice, and works with the staff for insight into the personality patterns which may have developed prior to placement, deciding which of these patterns are adaptable to foster home living and what kind of personality in the foster parent will strengthen the more positive patterns.

The social worker, who studies the quality of the existing emotional climate in the prospective foster home, and who acts in a supervisory capacity to the child, foster family and family afterwards, brings psychoanalytic as well as case work experience into the placement situation.

When the child has been placed in a foster home, the analyst may then be most useful in helping the case worker to establish a relationship which will benefit the child and bring real satisfaction to parent and foster parent. Beyond functioning as a diagnostician of the child's problems, the analyst can help the social worker to understand behavior from the psychodynamic point of view, so that the whole pattern of interpersonal relationships—child, parent, foster parent, and social worker—may be more effective because there is a deeper understanding of the segments.

By this co-operation a well-balanced and adequate solution may be achieved. The collaboration of the professional workers on the clinic teams becomes the medium through which it is possible to maintain a connection between the inner problems of the child and the reality of adult feelings toward which the child needs to grow and develop. Because of the child's dependency neither his problem nor its resolution may be considered outside the frame of the feelings, actions and attitudes of the significant adult figures upon whom the responsibility for the child's care rests.

The need to place a child in a foster home may be the outcome of some disturbance in the physical or mental health of the parents. From this would come their inability to cope with or tolerate the physical or psychological difficulties presented by the child. However, it must be emphasized that there is a distinction between a temporary disturbance, or maladjustment, and a prolonged or permanent personality disturbance of a serious nature.

A mother who is experiencing an unusually nerve-racking menopause can be helped to accept it as a transient phenomenon and to deal with family problems more satisfactorily. The child, too, can be guided to adopt a more thoughtful and considerate point of view. A father who is having a particularly difficult time in his business may not control his irritability, but that does not make him unfit for the role of being a parent. Family relationships can remain intact in such circumstances, and the children will learn that they must adapt themselves to what may seem a less than desirable world. To shield a child from these relatively normal experiences would be doing him a disservice.

The psychoanalyst is able to determine when the personality disturbances of a parent pass the margin of safety, and can work with the social worker to protect the mental and physical health of the child. For example, when a history of frank psychosis is revealed, placement becomes a necessity. A child of eight, who thought one morning that "Mummy was having one of her spells again, only worse this time," and then went into the next room to find that her mother had committed suicide, still broods over it, and is bedeviled by the obsession that she will follow her mother's pattern. This same child, placed before the tragedy in a sane, healthy home with reasonably "normal" adults, would have had a different outlook today.

If the parent is a drug addict or an alcoholic, and sufficiently guilt-ridden to ask for placement of his child, the request should be met as it will be constructive to both parent and child. The child who has not been exposed too long to this kind of frustration may be helped to find roots through identification with the mothering and fathering foster parents and will lose his feeling of being different from more fortunate children. The parent, freed from day-to-day care and conscious of the responsibility he has shifted to the agency and to a foster family, may become more accessible to help himself, find some of the reasons for his difficulties, and thus reach a better adjustment through understanding.

Anne, aged nine, would lie awake nights awaiting and dreading the sound of her father's footsteps. She was afraid her father would injure her mother on one of his drunken sprees. She is now twelve years old and is learning to love and trust her father, who has been cured of alcoholism through the help of a well-known child care agency. Nevertheless, it is a continuous ordeal for both, particularly at those times when the girl dreams that her father has come home drunk and only she is there to protect her mother.

In the case of the hypochondriac, the case worker need be concerned when the condition assumes pathological proportions. When this happens the whole atmosphere at home has become destructive for the child, as well as for the parent who often augments his suffering by imagining that the child makes him worse. This disease process in a progressed stage will keep a parent from assuming sufficient responsibility for his child.

Another category of children who must be placed with people other than their parents includes those with antisocial behavior which the parents cannot control.

Joseph at thirteen has been called a "thoroughly bad boy." He is markedly egocentric and has violent tantrums when he cannot have his own way. He is dishonest, deceitful, untrustworthy. He takes delight in causing mental or physical suffering. He is insolent, but preserves a show of manners when he thinks it will get him something he wants. If he is denied anything he will wreck his room or the rooms of others.

The psychoanalyst was consulted about Joseph when the boy was eight years old and advised treatment at once. The parents were sure he would outgrow his behavior.[1] Their method of treatment was to indulge him beyond reason. When Joseph was thirteen he was seen by the analyst again, at which time the personality had deteriorated to the point where institutional care

1 *Editor's note:* See Chapter 11.

was advised. The stage now is set for Joseph to develop a pathological character disorder. While placement in a foster home
when he was eight would have helped, its effectiveness at this
point is dubious.

Once a child actually is placed in a foster home it is the foster
parents who should take the initiative in establishing the relationships. The foster home is a substitute for the real home, and
it should bring the child that sense of security, understanding
and love that he had a right to expect from his real parents.

Foster parents are no rare specimens of human beings. People
who can permit development in a child without expecting grati-
tude, homage, thanks, subservience and conformity at all times,
but who, on the contrary, can guide, aid and abet independent
thinking and experience without being threatened themselves,
are the ideal foster parents. This makes possible the development
of a person who has the ability to respect himself as well as others.

Since foster parents are not a rare species, it follows that they
are fallible. They will make mistakes and sometimes may find it
very difficult to meet some of the problems which arise. To help
direct and channel their efforts into a constructive program the
social worker and the psychoanalyst must work together. It is important that the psychoanalyst and the social worker discuss the
child's background with them in order to enlist the co-operation
of the foster parents in the proposed program. The foster parents
should be familiarized with the child's history as well as his
behavior patterns, and they should have some idea of what may
be expected in the near future in terms of the child's behavior
and development. In this way pressures and tensions can be
anticipated and tempered.

It is of primary importance that the personalities of the child
and the new adults in his life should match, either in a complementary or in a supplementary fashion.

Jerry's mother had been a beautiful girl with a feeble and
childish mind. At fifteen she was a streetwalker, and Jerry was
the result of one of her casual encounters—which one she did not
know. She was picked up and committed to a mental institution,
and the baby, not yet a year old, was sent to an orphanage.

During the next fourteen years Jerry's life was a succession of institutions and foster homes. Each experience made him feel more unwanted, more shut within himself, less articulate. At one time he asked about his parents and was told that he had been abandoned. Undoubtedly it seemed the kindest answer to the woman who gave it, but it was the wrong answer for Jerry. Not only was he unwanted by other people, but the very mother who bore him had not cared to keep him. Foster parents still wanted to try him for he had inherited his mother's good looks, but in just a short time Jerry would be returned as "unresponsive and stupid."

At fifteen Jerry was placed in the home of a family with three teen-aged children. Although ordinarily suspicious because of his past experiences, Jerry turned to the mother instinctively because he felt that she wanted him. The father was kind, but, even in the case of his own children, left family matters to his wife. The children reflected their mother's attitude, but had the good sense not to push matters. For three years the woman filled Jerry's life with patient love and understanding. She had no reproaches for his illiteracy; she just seemed to like him as he was. Gradually he began to feel that life was good and that he might have a place in it. At eighteen, Jerry looked for a job and found a place as a helper to a linoleum layer. Each morning his foster mother would write in large letters the signs of the buses he would take in proper order, and show him how he should reverse them to come home.

Into Jerry's life came the desire to learn. No night school would do, for Jerry had an I.Q. of 68 and would learn more slowly than a class would be expected to advance. A retired school teacher in the neighborhood had watched his progress with interest and offered to teach Jerry how to read. He is working valiantly, and there is hope that a latent intelligence is wakening which is greater than that which has been credited to him. Jerry now has a chance to be a much more substantial person than could have been imagined in his childhood.

One of the important requirements of the foster home is that the foster parents should not be too divergent from the child in mental capacity. It would be well-nigh impossible for a child with an I.Q. in the 70-90 range to fit into the family of a college professor unless they were unusually perceptive and could make their thinking fit the needs of a slow child. Otherwise, the lack of contact would leave the child even more bewildered and hurt, and the disappointment of the foster parents and child would make any normal, constructive relationship impossible. On the other hand, placement of a precocious child in the home of foster parents of average intelligence might prove to be an equally frustrating experience for all concerned.

Although foster parents sometimes think they can be happy in their family relationship despite the child's lack of mental brilliance, the situation is always fraught with danger.

Sonia was a delightfully pretty child of four with winsome ways and apparent brightness. The agency warned the prospective foster parents, a brilliant writer and his wife, that the tests had shown Sonia to be of rather limited intelligence, and that it was a risk to suppose she could attain the standard set in their home. But the child's attractiveness won, and the couple took her, hoping to adopt her later.

Within four years strain developed. While the mother loved Sonia and wished to adopt her despite her limitations, the father found that he lived in a state of irritation. He was constantly comparing Sonia's school record, her remarks at home, and her comprehension of conversations with the achievements of neighboring children of the same age. He fought the idea of adoption, although he conceded that they must look after Sonia as she had a claim on them. A compromise was reached, and Sonia remains as their ward. The father, who was undoubtedly sensitive about having the child bear his name, has learned to be more patient with her, and the family is reasonably happy. But what a different story it would have been if Sonia had been as bright as she appeared.

Differences in cultural and economic standards are considered in placement in order to avoid possible conflict for the child and his own parents during the period of their separation as well as on reunion. Foster parents are sometimes impatient with the agency when this matter comes up, especially those who feel that they have material advantages to offer. It is difficult for them to realize that when the child becomes accustomed to these advantages he may be scornful of his own people.

It is a tribute to the strength and flexibility in human beings that many are able to tolerate constant deprivation and still maintain their mental health. Conversely, it goes without saying that economic security is no guarantee of emotional security. Although a long-time experience of frustration and deprivation of privileges may well create a feeling of inferiority, insecurity and smoldering anger.

It is imperative to avoid repetition in the foster home of any pathological pattern which may have existed in the child's own home. If the new environment presents but a repetition of the old difficulties, the old whinings, reproaches and guilt feelings, it would be better to leave the child where he is.

The desire to be a good parent or foster parent does not always make one. However, if the agency has to choose between a foster parent with a skillful manner in handling children, and one relatively awkward but genuinely fond of children and eager to have them around, the odds are in favor of the second, who can more easily become a means of positive identification for the child.

On the whole, a better adjustment is possible if the positive features of the child's own home can be duplicated in the foster home. A similarity of emotional functioning is helpful; a child brought up in a family where emotional control is the standard might find it hard to live in a family where sentiment continually overflows. While children need affection, all of them do not enjoy similar expressions of it.

After the child has been placed in a foster home, there must be a period of getting to know each other for both the child and the new parents. If the foster home has been well chosen, the social worker need not call until child and parent have come to know each other better. However, in cases where a timid, unhappy child has made friends with the social worker during his visits to the agency prior to placement, the child may need the assurance of a familiar face. The social worker visits the foster home to see if the relationship is developing constructively.

The psychoanalyst, via the case work staff, can brief the foster parents on the expected problems related to growth and development such as biting, toilet training, masturbation. The case worker with this additional insight into the dynamics of growth and possible deviations is better able to cope with the fears, anxieties and taboos of both sets of parents. Between the ages of one and one half and two, for example, a child is expected to bite. The psychoanalyst can help to decide when this symptom exists in excess and is cause for alarm. He may consult with the social worker to find out whether the foster mother still feeds the youngster prepared baby food, or she may want to know whether the child has ever been abruptly stopped from biting, etc.

A child may be masturbating at the age of three. Rather than let her restrain the child, the mother can be helped to understand that this is a continuation of an exploration process, and the social worker can evaluate the foster mother's anxieties in terms of what the neighbors will think, what taboos she associates with masturbation, and why!

Toilet training is yet another case where understanding of the child's levels of maturation is urgent. During the first decades of the twentieth century nurses would begin to toilet-train infants as young as three months, and an occasional accident was considered catastrophic. Today it is common knowledge that sphincter control is not established until much later, that a child cannot be toilet-trained before the age when control is possible, and that age variations are the rule rather than the exception.

In analyzing and interpreting behavior the psychoanalyst stresses mainly the feeling tone, rather than hard-and-fast rules. If a mother theoretically accepts a child's bed-wetting, but really feels the child is a nuisance, the child will begin to sense this. It is not always what the parent says to the child as much as how she says it.

On the other end of the scale, the foster mother must be helped to understand that, if the child feels secure in the mother's love, frustration can be of great value in the growth process. Until the child is one and one half or two most of his demands are met. During the first six months of his life his capacity to perceive is limited, and he needs protection.[2] The mother must guess his every wish and also must provide all stimuli for development. This picture changes during the second half of the first year when the child becomes more independent and steps forth for himself. Correspondingly, the restrictions on the part of society gradually increase.

As the child grows older his cry does not always bring his mother to his side. We try to help him learn that he can wait.

[2] *Editor's note*: See Chapters 3 and 9.

This is how he realizes that there are other people in the world, and that they too have needs, and gradually he becomes able to give up immediate satisfaction for later gratification. With this type of insight the foster mother is able to understand that the child's demands are sometimes too great, that denying him immediate gratification should not necessarily make her feel guilty or that she is not a "good" mother. It is important to remember that there is no such thing as a child in the abstract. Every child is different from every other, and each individual child needs to be helped to make an adjustment to the world in which he lives.

In the case of the foster child, separation from his parents is a difficult thing, but it may be one of the steps in the maturation process. At the age of two, when the child's life is largely governed by the pleasure-pain principle, his reaction to separation may be violent. If the child kicks and screams when faced with the separation, the case worker can help the foster parent to understand that the child does not possess a severely disturbed personality, but that he is following an exaggerated normal pattern which will subside within a few days.

It must be stressed that in many cases of foster home placement the physical separation has already been preceded by a psychological separation. A child of overprotective parents may strongly resist going to school; in treatment, he may reveal a "nobody-can-make-me" attitude to the analyst. Separation at this time would be a positive goal in the child's development.

While it is true that the child experiences shock when exposed to separation without being adequately prepared, it is not the fact of the separation that is harmful so much as the form. The parents should prepare the child for the impending separation without misrepresentation. Most children are realists and will be able to cope with this separation if they understand it.

The treatment of the disturbed foster child has been seen as an over-all problem of more than average difficulty because of the hierarchy of adult relationships which surround the foster child. In the normal family the child is faced with the oedipal situation. This is not a fantastic sexual concoction, but rather every child's problem of his love relationships with both parents and his acceptance of them in their different and proper roles as

mother and father, man and woman. In the foster home config-
uration, however, there is a different triangular problem—the
foster family, the child's own family, and the child. In addition
to interpreting the behavior of the child, the analyst may be
obliged to help the social worker interpret the behavior of the
parents to the foster family.

If the child's mother is a streetwalker, the analyst will attempt
to help the social worker understand and interpret to the foster
family the motivation of the mother's difficulty. The analyst may
point out the etiology of loneliness, or whatever personal difficulty may exist. Similarly, if the child's mother has a mental illness which manifests itself by withdrawal and detachment rather
than in rages or violent scenes, the foster family may conclude
that she is condescending or that she treats them with disdain.
The social worker and the analyst who represent the agency in
the individual situations, wield an enormous influence in channeling the various relationships constructively. There is no such
thing as a perfect parent, but the placement workers can do the
best possible within the limitations of their facilities.

One case of successful placement involved a seventeen-year-old
girl whose mother was known to be Jewish and whose father was
oriental, although the workers had no way of ascertaining this
except by the girl's physical features. She is living with a foster
family which has been helped to accept her apparent difference
from other people, and she, herself, has been helped to adjust
her own feelings in relation to this problem.

In another case, a boy of eleven came into placement from a
home in which the mother was mentally ill and had manipulated
both the father and the child by blaming them for her illness.
The mother had always used a ruse to make the child do what
she wanted. Instead of simply asking him to pick up his toys, she
would promise a visit or an excursion of some sort which would
never materialize.

Since the mother had promised that he could come home
"when he was a good boy," the child tried hard to make himself
inconspicuous in the foster home. He withdrew, became quiet,
docile and subservient in the home, but would give vent to impulsive behavior at school. He became the school clown. He
would sit in the principal's office with his feet out the window,
and so on. When the boy came into placement he was already

accustomed to thinking and feeling a certain way. He had established a method of dealing with his real father and mother, and it was difficult for him to recognize or trust the differences he experienced with a new set of adults. The boy had an I.Q. of 135, and, therefore, could not be regarded as a limited child.

When the psychoanalyst obtained a detailed history of the mother from the case worker it was discovered that the early stages of the illness had appeared when the mother was sixteen. The father, a dependent and passive person, also had been very insecure and intensely guilt-ridden, since he, too, was unaware that the mother had been mentally ill prior to her marriage. Because he did not want to irritate his wife, he complied with all of her demands, which only exaggerated the illness. Once this documentation was available, the case worker and the analyst worked with a maternal uncle who was interested in the boy. The uncle told the child about the history of the mother's illness, and explained that it had manifested itself long before he had been born.

A better relationship was then established between the boy and his father, who was helped to feel less guilty, and who no longer felt compelled to meet every demand of his wife. As the boy saw his father assert himself, he, too, was able to feel freer in relation to his mother. When he saw a change in his own family, he was able to trust the behavior of the foster family, and was strengthened in his ability to be spontaneous in his own behavior and his responses to people generally.

The psychiatrist does not see cases in which the professional skills of the child-placing agency and the help of the foster parents have been used constructively. Moreover, he does not see the child whose parents have actually supported the movement into placement. The children he sees have failed to form or to use constructive relationships with either agency or foster parent. They have presented serious emotional disturbances and behavior problems such as truancy, stealing, lying, enuresis, tics, psychosomatic disorders, or severe temper tantrums, and have not responded favorably to offers of case work help. In such cases psychoanalytic treatment is considered as a catalytic agent, speeding up and making possible meaningful new relationships and new experiences.

When a child is under psychoanalytic treatment the analyst at times has to bring the foster parents to a realization that some of their behavior is not for the good of the child. If possible, it is better for the psychoanalyst to do this rather than the social worker since the relation of the foster mother or father to the analyst is necessarily a little less personal.

Mrs. H. was a kindly person. She had experienced frustrations which had given her certain false values, and since she was nearing the menopause, these patterns had become exaggerated. Mrs. H. had a compulsive need to impress the neighbors, which she expressed by giving her foster child unsuitable, ostentatious play things. In this case the analyst took several interviews to show Mrs. H. her faulty attitude. Finally Mrs. H. brought out old, loved toys for the child she had taken into her home, toys he was not afraid of injuring and which were far more desirable than the shiny new toys bought to impress the neighbors.

One of the facts to be considered in placement is that the child always "brings" his own parents with him. Sometimes he does so consciously, dwelling upon the manner in which his mother did this or his father did that. At times this does no harm, although it may make the process of integration in the foster home somewhat slower. In other cases the child carries along a feeling of guilt, thinking he may be responsible for the separation. Here the case worker may be able to help the foster parents to cope with the manifold manifestations resulting from the child's sense of guilt, while the child may be guided in using the positive strengths of his personality.

In addition, the social worker must be able to help the foster parents deal with the problems that arise when the child's own parents visit him. Seeing them again may bring back memories of all the troubles he had at home. Often, however, the troubles have faded into the background, and the child wants his own parents. He finds it difficult to let them go and wants to go with them. The parents, too, find it hard to say "good-bye," and their farewells are unduly prolonged. Frequently the visit of the parents means another adjustment in the new environment for the child. Here, too, the social worker can help the triangular relationship. The foster parents can be helped by understanding and by identification with the problem created for them, the child helped in resolving his struggle against placement, the parent guided in dealing with his feeling of guilt and fear of losing control with respect to his child.

When a child lives in a foster home for a long time, the relationship settles into something which is very similar to a real parent-child bond. However, there still is need for the parent and child to feel that the members of the placement agency are counsellors and friends. Numerous problems arise—an increase in spending allowance, girl or boy friends, evening curfew, and many more disturbing circumstances which require attention. The foster parents feel more secure in their decision if they have discussed it with the social worker. The child feels that, if all agree, there must be a good reason.

One of the most important functions of the social worker as well as the psychoanalyst is to let the foster parent know that she is doing a good piece of work. A child can only express appreciation by a demonstration of affection. The social worker, with a word of praise, can do much to encourage the foster parent to continue the good work. Praise is never thrown away, although it may seem to be "gilding the lily."

It would be hard indeed to overestimate the satisfactions of a foster parent who has been the right one for the child, and who can see the results of her labors. For example, Mrs. K. was an earnest, sincere woman of European background. Her sons were in the Army and she felt the insistent need to do a good deed, a *Mitzvah,* as she called it. (*Mitzvah* is a word that embodies what we mean by "the milk of human kindness." It may mean visiting the sick, cooking for those who are in difficulty, or helping a young and inexperienced mother.) Perhaps when her *Mitzvah* was fulfilled, she felt, it would be remembered and her sons given special protection—a belief in the active power of Good over and beyond mere superstition.

Mrs. K. was extremely successful in her role of foster mother, and the therapist, who was at one point involved in treatment of her foster child, complimented her upon her achievement. The response was, "Thank you, but you really didn't have to tell me. I knew it." The therapist could not resist asking, "How do you know? What makes you so sure?"

"When our boy first came to us," said Mrs. K., "he asked,

168   LILLIAN K. KAPLAN

'What shall I call you?' 'Oh,' I said, 'Call me Sophie, or Auntie,
or Mother—or nothing.' When he fought in the street with the
other boys I could hear him say, 'I'll tell my Mother!' But when
he came in he called me nothing at all. This went on for a year.
Then one day he came in and, not seeing me, yelled, 'Mom!'
When he stopped calling me nothing and started calling me
Mother, I knew something had happened."

BIBLIOGRAPHY

1. BOWLBY, J. *Maternal Care and Mental Health.* New York: Columbia University Press, 1951.
2. CONKLIN, E. S. The foster-child fantasy. *Am. J. Psychol.,* 31, 1920.
3. FREUD, A. and BURLINGHAM, D. *Infants Without Families.* New York: International Universities Press, 1944.
4. FREUD, S. Three contributions to the theory of sex. In *The Basic Writings of Sigmund Freud.* New York: Modern Library, 1938.
5. FRIES, M. E. The child's ego development and the training of adults in his environment. *The Psychoanalytic Study of the Child,* 2. New York: International Universities Press, 1946.
6. ROSE, J. A. and POLLACK, J. C. Psychotherapy with the foster child. *Child Welfare,* June, 1949.
7. SPITZ, R. A. Three first steps in growing up. *Child Study,* Winter, 1950-51.
8. WOLF, K. There is no one way. *Child Study.* Winter, 1951-52.

Chapter 9

APPLICATION OF PSYCHOANALYTIC CONCEPTS TO ADOPTION AGENCY PRACTICE

VIOLA W. BERNARD, M.D.

Adoption, as an ingenious psychosocial invention can offer one of the finest and happiest adaptive solutions to the desperately frustrated needs of parentless children, childless parents, and those who cannot be parents to the children they have borne. Such are the human intricacies of this process of family formation on the basis of nurture rather than nature that sometimes the participants fail rather than fulfill each other and themselves. Adoption agencies represent the community's stake in providing skilled professional services toward implementing and safeguarding this remarkable human experience. Ways and means of carrying out such services logically evolve in relation to the growth of understanding of the clients served. As psychoanalytic concepts have enlarged and deepened general understanding of human nature, they naturally are of special significance to a field so closely concerned with areas specifically related to major psychoanalytic contributions, such as child development, psychosexual conflicts, dynamics of family relationships and the role of unconscious motivation and emotions in behavior and symptom formation.

For purposes of this discussion the potential application of psychoanalytic concepts to adoption practice may be viewed from two main standpoints, i.e., the more general and the more specific. As to the first certain psychological principles, originally

derived from psychoanalysis, have become the general property
of modern thought and are integrated into all social welfare and
social case work theory. In this way they influence all adoption
practice despite the great unevenness prevailing in this field
throughout the country. One instance of the more general relatedness of modern psychological insight to current practice
concerns the struggle to replace independent adoption by qualified professional adoptive agency service. The greatest number
of adoptions annually in this country are still those arranged
outside of authorized agencies—the so-called independent adoptions (30). As is well known, there are two main types of non-
agency adoption; the first, baby selling, or the "black market"
type, exploits human need and suffering for financial profit. On
an immediate level, at least, elimination of this evil seems more
a matter for legislation and enforcement than psychoanalytically
oriented agency practice. The other type of independent adoptions are those placements arranged for by well-intentioned intermediaries—most often friends, doctors, lawyers, relatives or
nurses. Many of these manifestly benevolent intermediaries sadly,
if sincerely, underestimate the complexity of their task and
overestimate their own fitness for it with sometimes lucky, often
tragic results. Many act on an "ignorance is bliss" approach
whereby, for instance, an unconscious omnipotence fantasy may
be gratified, all too often at the expense of the actual long-term
welfare of the apparent immediate beneficiaries, the principal
parties to the adoption. Although the methods of changing the
present community acceptance of this well-meant independent
adoption practice lie outside the province of the agencies' main
service functions, the psychodynamic insights developed by professional adoptive workers provide impetus and clinically tested
rationale for the necessary educational, legislative and community organizational programs. Furthermore, to succeed at all, or
even justify success, such reforms must be supported by the professional adoption field in the form of constant improvement of
services that actually carry out the best of what is known so far.
Instances of destructive personally biased judgmental attitudes
by professional personnel, or inflexible agency procedures detri-
mental to the needs of the clients may violate the current body

of relevant knowledge as much or more than some of the non-agency adoptions, and thus handicap the desirable efforts toward professionalizing this work.

When approaching some of the more specific and detailed applications of psychoanalytic principles to case work in adoption, the existent unevenness of quality and diversity of method, already referred to, make it difficult to present material of uniform applicability. There is a high degree of variation in almost every aspect of agency structure and function in adoption, from state to state, within sections of the same state, and even within the same community. Detailed considerations of psychoanalytic application in adoption agencies cannot be undertaken without due recognition of these differences, and had best be directed to certain broad areas of function and types of case work regardless of the many particular ways agencies limit or structure their specific areas of responsibility. Naturally, many of these variations affect the nature, extent and feasibility of attempts to integrate psychoanalytic concepts. Among such variables may be included: qualifications of case workers in terms of professional training, experience and personality attributes; size of case loads per worker; quality and quantity of supervision; availability and orientation of psychiatric and psychological consultation; existence and nature of inservice training programs; degree of lay control over professional practice, and the social philosophy of those in control of general policy.

In general, social work participates in adoption by serving children to be adopted, both infants and older children, natural parents, and prospective adoptive couples, whether or not this is all undertaken by a single agency or divided among several whose quality of interagency collaboration is of the greatest importance to effective service. Although all these sets of clients will be considered separately for purposes of discussion, and are often served by separate agencies—children's agencies, unmarried mothers' shelters, etc.—it is well to keep remembering how enmeshed these different clients' emotional needs are with each other, and how the professional worker has an over-all responsibility of balancing the sometimes conflicting psychological needs and interests of all three, rather than overidentifying with any one at too great expense of another. This case work task of balancing clients' needs will be referred to again, but it is obvious that unobjective attitudes of "pro-unmarried motherism and anti-adoptive couplehood," or the reverse, while frequently operative in independent adoption, can lead to psychologically destructive outcomes. Resolution of the sometimes terrible difficulties inherent in this balancing task is helped by the generally accepted priority to the children's needs in case of otherwise deadlocked conflict of interest. Another general principle for all the clients is that adoption is experienced progressively through a series of gradual stages, rather than as any single event, such as the signing of papers and physical relinquishment by natural parents, or the moment of the child's actual entrance into an adoptive home. Accordingly, our focus will center on certain crucial steps along the way in this process by the participants, and on the twofold clinical functions—diagnostic and therapeutic—whereby professional services strive to safeguard and promote the maximum emotional well being of all concerned. Assuming, then, a general working knowledge of agency practices on the part of the reader, let us turn to some psychodynamic considerations in the course of work with each of these clients.

Services to children for adoption include: provision of temporary care between legal relinquishment by natural parents and adoptive placement; use of the temporary care interval to prepare the children for placement and to help some of them overcome bad effects of experiences prior to admission by the agency; as complete a diagnostic evaluation as possible in order to plan most appropriately; selection of an adoptive home; placement of the child with his new parents; periodic supervision of the new family until legal adoption is consummated six months to a year after placement.

The adoptive situation differs in so many ways for the infant and older child that it seems necessary to discuss some aspects separately. The infant, much more frequently sought by prospective adoptive couples, profits by the resulting greater selectivity the agency can exercise on his behalf in choosing his family. Once legally relinquished by his natural parents, the infant depends on the agency for temporary care until he is placed for adoption, and during this interval he is studied as totally as possible to confirm his adoptability, in general, and to assess his special attributes, in particular, in order to place him at the optimum time in the optimum adoptive home. A child's adoptability (and this refers to older children as well as infants) is reduced by the degree and kind of physical, mental and emotional pathology he may present, as well as by the amount and nature of pathology in his family background, and sometimes by the composition of his racial heredity. Although diagnostic study may conclude that a particular child is "able to contribute to and benefit from family life"—as Miss Hallinan (13) defines adoptability—the term often denotes a social reality rather than a clinical condition since it depends so largely on the placeability which in turn is caused by many factors extrinsic to the child, i.e., the desires, capacities and fears of adoptive parents and the home-finding zeal and skill of the agency. A salutary trend is under way toward reducing the numbers of children considered unadoptable by agencies. More children who need it can thus benefit by family life and fewer of these be driven into risky black market or private adoption. Growing experience (32) is validating the success of placements that agencies formerly feared making. Many progressive agencies no longer rule out a child as unadoptable on the basis of pathologically hereditary background alone, but decide the question on the basis of the child himself, sometimes prolonging the period of his observation under care. Better selectivity and case work with adoptive parents probably help account for these improved results.

Diagnostic, prophylactic and therapeutic responsibilities of the agency come into play during this period of temporary care between surrender and adoptive placement. Of the infants, some are newborns, straight from the hospital; others are a few weeks or a few months older, some of whom have experienced a traumatizing succession of being shifted about between different places and people, or other forms of stress, before coming to the agency. The care they receive represents a vital contribution to their future psychological development, according to psychoanalytic assumptions and corroborating research. It simultaneously provides an opportunity for continuous clinical observation of each baby's behavior as the principal diagnostic method, to be supplemented by psychological and pediatric examinations and, in some selected instances, by psychiatric examination as well. Because of the importance to infant development of warm, relaxed human contact and adequate stimulation, temporary foster care seems far preferable to group care. Considerable attention should be given to selecting and working with the foster mothers, and it follows, from what has already been said, that the criteria of their selection should be heavily weighted in the direction of personal attributes that can fulfill "the rights of infants" (26) by affectionate flexible mothering. Experience by the worker with the maturational sequences of infancy and her insight into the behavioral language of infancy helps her differentiate normal individual reactions from signals of disturbance calling for remedial action. Such action might take the form of helping the foster mother change some of her ways of handling the baby or even changing foster mothers. Fluctuations and aberrations in feeding behavior, for instance, are recognized as delicate barometers of the infant's condition. Anna Freud (12) has recently added to the sizable psychoanalytic literature around this topic by a theoretical contribution in which she differentiates three main ways in which the function of eating is open to disturbance: organic feeding disturbances, nonorganic disturbances of the instinctive process itself, and neurotic feeding disturbances.

There is a promising trend in psychoanalytic studies of child development toward combining more data from direct observation of infants and children with the information gained from analytic therapy of adults by reconstructions of their childhood in the context of their full life history. Direct observations have obvious methodological advantages for studying the preverbal period of the first year of life and from such investigations by Ribble, Fries, Spitz, Anna Freud, and others, adoption agencies may hope to gain much needed data of specific relevance in meeting their responsibilities and growth-promoting opportunities around temporary preadoptive foster home care and permanent adoptive placement. Thus, Fries (19), investigating factors in psychic development in a group of children she studied from birth to adolescence, offers supporting evidence—elaborated in detail—for the interacting influential roles of constitution, habit training and parental emotional stability on the personality outcome of her original infant group. In his researches into "Psychogenic Diseases in Infancy" Spitz (29) seeks to classify certain damaging consequences to infants during their first year according to causally insufficient or emotionally unhealthy forms of mothering. Correspondences between the types of disturbances and types of mothering are differentiated as to course and outcome in relation to chronological phases of ego development within the first year of life. In the light of these and many other studies, adoption for parentless infants by "good" parents seems even more than ever the most logical preventive therapy for what can be most devastating psychogenic illnesses, i.e., maternal deprivation and "mal-mothering" of infancy.

Rich potentialities for research on child development are inherent in adoption agency work because of such favorable features as an unusual degree of control over environmental conditions, access to subjects and to history data, etc. Adoption agencies in turn urgently need the findings from such research and are in a special position to apply them toward the furtherance of mental health. A psychological investigation by Leitch and Escalona (18) illustrates the research possibilities of the adoption agency setting. In response to a "felt need to integrate our basic theoretical concepts with observable aspects of infantile experience," Leitch and Escalona studied reactions to stress of 112 infants under the temporary boarding home care of a Kansas adoption agency by psychological testing, observational procedures, interviews with boarding mothers and agency staff. Tension level changes were studied by observing changes in posture, motility, amount of activity, readiness to startle, respiration, circulation, purposive use of objectives, social responsiveness and attention span. "Extraordinary variability in the kind of situation which aroused tension in different infants were noted."

Predictions play such a vital role in the agency's selective decisions that lead to the merging into a family of a particular child and of a particular couple that the bases of predictions must be constantly tested and improved. Many questions as yet far from settled beset the adoptive worker daily. What influences on the infant's future development may be expected from familial incidence of psychosis in his background? What sort of character development can be expected of him later in the light of what kinds of early experiences—especially as to parents and parent substitutes, physical health and habit training? How may his scores on infant psychological tests reflect his ultimate intelligence and how will this be affected by the kind of adoptive placement chosen for him?

Follow-ups of carefully studied placements are greatly needed for the validation of assumptions underlying practice that bear on these and many other questions. One attempt in this direction by Ruth Brenner and Ruth Hartley (4), in consultation with Dr. David M. Levy, evaluated the placement outcome of fifty children who were tested psychologically before and after placement. Agency predictions were compared with case work evaluation of the degree of success in family formation. This will be referred to again when we discuss agency work with adoptive couples. The psychological data "suggests that the value of infant psychological tests for prediction at three months, and even at fifteen or sixteen months, has been grossly overestimated by social workers. In order to obtain a test score which would in any individual case make accurate prediction of intellectual expectancy possible, it would be necessary to wait for testing until the child is four years of age."

This leads us into an important question in which the adoption workers are showing considerable current interest and experimentation, i.e., how long after relinquishment should agencies keep babies under care before placing in adoptive homes, or put another way, at how young an age is it sound practice to place infants for adoption. There is a growing tendency toward revising previous policies in the direction of earlier placements which is indeed in keeping with psychoanalytic principles.

Escalona's study (10) of the use of infant tests for predictive purposes suggests promising possibilities that bear on this question. Seventy-two infants under the care of child placement agencies, including adoption agencies, were tested and retested after intervals varying from six months to several years. She stresses a shift in aim of infant testing corresponding to a changed view of intelligence from that of an already present potential awaiting realization during the maturation process to that of "a fluctuating function, a delicate interaction of many forces and structural conditions—as one among many functions of variables." She points out that the test response "is not something located within the infant being tested but a process of interaction between the infant organism and the immediate environment, i.e., the testing situation." Therefore, "to the extent that the test scores obtained in infancy are regarded as predicting intelligence in later life as measured by subsequent intelligence tests—to that extent we are making a prediction not only about the subject but also about some aspects of the subject's environment at a later time." This coincides with the concepts that shaped the design of the Brenner-Hartley study in which the predictions of the subject's environment at a later time were made in respect to methods and criteria in choosing the infant's adoptive parents and assisting them in the early placement period. As stressed by Brenner, this newer view justifies and requires modification from the more traditional and almost exclusive emphasis on the adoptable child to dynamically oriented case work with prospective adoptive parents, even though the child remains the agency's primary client. Escalona's results lead her to expect that the validity of infant testing can be improved during the first half year of life by using the test situation as a framework for more comprehensive diagnosis of the infant's total functioning.

Another kind of data is germane to this question of the most desirable age for adoptive placement of infants. According to Spitz (27, 28) in several articles describing his psychoanalytic researches by direct observations of infants, most babies under six months are not yet capable of relating to the mother figure as a specific individual.[1] Vital as the mothering experience is for the infant in the first half year, Spitz finds that its emerging ego development and capacity for object love has not advanced beyond

1 *Editor's note:* Cf. Chapters 3 and 4.

its reacting to the maternal figure in terms of the satisfying or unsatisfying situation of which she is the central part. Her exact individuality therefore cannot be affectively perceived as such, so she is interchangeable as a person as far as the infant is concerned, just so that the mothering experience retains continuity and need satisfaction. After six months or so the baby's ability perceptively to discriminate has progressed so that his mother as a specific individual becomes all important to him. She serves in fact as a sort of external ego for him in view of his own helplessness and he may experience separation anxiety and even mourning reactions if he loses her. Strangers, recognized as such, are now reacted to with a certain degree of anxiety. To the extent that these observations by Spitz accurately reflect the timing of events in psychic development during the first year they would strongly support the desirability of adoptive placement before six months of age so that the mother-child relationship can be established with the permanent mother, and separation from the boarding mother effected while these are still essentially interchangeable for him emotionally.

The principle of balancing the interwoven needs and interests of natural parents, adoptive parents and adoptive children, mentioned earlier, is central to decisions around adoptive placements early in infancy. The Brenner-Hartley report reviews some of the thinking of this writer on the subject as of 1946 (4, p. 131). Selectivity as to such placements and some of the criteria to be considered were stressed. These included the natural parents' capacity and timing in reaching a final decision about surrender; the completeness of available family history for the baby and its degree of freedom from hereditary pathology; the prenatal obstetrical and birth history of the infant and its physical health as established by medical examinations; the capacity of adoptive parents knowingly to assume some added risks in terms of the child's development, as well as the natural parents' possible change of plan. The great advantages to adoptive parents and babies of very early placement and the growing body of successful experience with such placements since 1946 warrant our making them in greater numbers. As Fairweather (11) points out in "Early Placement and Adoption" agencies may well have overstressed the protection they could offer prospective adoptive couples against the development of physical or mental abnormalities beyond the predictive accuracy of medical and psychological procedures in infancy, since to give complete assurance of normal development "we should have to place adults, not children." (One might add that the process of holding the children for later testing under conditions of parental deprivation adversely influences the very attributes to be tested.)

Fairweather suggests instead that the case work services provided by the agencies constitute their main advantage over independent adoption from the standpoint of protection. Thus, those natural parents who are helped by case work are less likely to reverse their final decisions than those who feel that they were forced into signing or surrender by inner or outer pressure. The length of time the natural parent may need to reach a final decision to surrender and her capacity consistently to maintain the decision, once made, depends on many factors but among these the level of her emotional maturity, degree of ambivalence about surrender, and the quality of case work service available to her, and her accessibility to it are most important in considering the early adoptive placement of their infants. Oman reports (22) a study of one hundred mothers who had applied to the State Charities Aid Association for adoptive placement of their infants from the standpoint of their use of time before actually signing surrenders. Although ninety-six were certain they wanted adoption when they applied for it, over half of them—over 60 per cent— changed their plans entirely or wavered. About one half of these finally did decide on adoption, the majority reaching that decision between the fourth and sixth month after the baby's birth. The 40 mothers who maintained their initial decision were thought to have derived emotional benefit from the waiting period between their seeking adoptive placement for their child and the actual surrender. Since Oman omits details, however, about the case work use of the interval between the baby's birth and surrender, it is not possible to evaluate whether equally sound final decisions might have been reachable sooner by more intensive or skillful case work help to these mothers. Fairweather reports on the successful adoptive outcome of seventy-one babies placed by her agency at three months or younger; twenty-one such placements made in one year (1947) were evaluated four years later by psychologists and case workers. The adjustment of all the children seemed healthy. When these were compared with a group of children placed at six months to two years, the adjustments for children and adoptive parents of these older placements were found to be slower and more difficult. Fairweather's conclusion that this difference in adjustment was due to the time of placement is somewhat open to question in view of the innumerable determinants of adjustment not taken into account by her study.

As to the prospective adoptive parents, it is true we seek for early adoption those who can best handle the added risks and who desire a parental experience with an infant who resembles a newborn of their own as closely as possible; yet these couples gain by the reduction of risks of another sort. I refer to the arousal of parental responsiveness, especially maternal, to the very young, totally dependent infant. Emotional risks to the adoptive placement from the parental side of the equation may stem from anxieties, inhibitions and conflicts in assuming the parental role frequently intensified for this group by their inner reactions to their long-standing incapacity for childbearing. Actual satisfying experience with their baby as near its beginning as possible can be of great protective value for the future child-parent relationship. In view of the potential advantages of early placement, when not contraindicated clinically, it is evident that agency procedures should work toward eliminating delays due to administrative rather than clinical reasons. Understanding what is at stake psychologically can give impetus to correcting the detention of babies in preadoptive boarding homes, for instance, because of staff delays in completing adoptive home studies.

In the adoptive placement of older children, the child must be planned with and not just planned for, as in the case of infants. Naturally, case work must cover a very wide range in meeting the needs of these children so differing in age, past experiences and current level of their total functioning. In general the work falls into the two broad categories of toddlers and older children. Because so many adoptive applicants prefer infants, suitable homes are harder to find. This difficulty is aggravated by the relatively higher incidence of some degree of disturbance in many of these children, particularly the older group, reflective of earlier deprivation and mishandling. These disturbances may be expressed in reduced ability to relate in appealing fashion to prospective adoptive applicants, so that the results of rejection bring about further rejection or, the child may require considerable case work help while in the agency's foster home before he can utilize the emotional nourishment offered him by permanent parents. Parallel to the direct case work preparation of the child for adoption— sometimes aided by psychiatric consultation—careful and sensitive interpretation of his behavior and needs to adoptive applicants, in advance of the first meeting, and thereafter throughout the gradualized steps of placement may be decisive for his placeability and the ongoing happiness of the newly formed family. Hallinan (14) describes some of the psychosocial implications of adoptions of older children, emphasizes the obligations of agencies to effect these, and reports successful outcomes for them.

All the social case work techniques and theoretical concepts underlying them of high quality child placement practice apply to this aspect of adoption work and need not be reviewed here. In addition, however, certain distinctive elements in adoptive placement need special consideration, notably the finality and permanence sought in adoption and its "real" rather than substitutive family membership which differs qualitatively from temporary foster placement. Establishment of a positive relationship between the child and case worker provides the most potent means of helping him in his truly great undertaking—the letting go of his immediate familiar world and the moving into acceptance of a new life with a "mommy and daddy for always." By this relationship the worker serves the child as a firm supportive bridge during his frightening and confusing transitions. She provides continuity between the shifting relationships he is losing and gaining, and on the foundation of the trust she can engender and the anxieties she can relieve, the child can tolerate those immediate painful feelings she may need to stimulate for the sake of his ultimate welfare. Specifically, the case worker must help the preadoptive child clarify, in ways compatible with his age level and individuality, his understanding and feelings about his past, present and future. What does he remember of his natural parents (or parent substitutes), and how does he understand their nonavailability to him now? Disregarding and disallowing his memories and feelings on that score can incapacitate him from moving ahead emotionally through a partial loss of his sense of self, and by burdening him with excessive unresolved frustrated longings, fears, resentments, and guilt. For instance, does he feel deserted and betrayed and, as Wires (31) has suggested, does he feel himself guilty of desertion and disloyalty to his earlier ties if he yields to the temptation of giving himself to the new adoptive family? The child needs help too with his comprehension and feelings about the necessity to leave his immediately preadoptive environment. McCleery (20) states, "He needs to know this definitely or he can feel, in a sense, kidnapped. . . . The worker must have the courage to face the truth with him without evasion, even if it involves pain" throughout the whole process to "free a child from the clinging hands of the past, and to equip him to go on to a more constructive happy future." Rainer (24) emphasizing the same principle of helping the child towards an understanding of previous separations as prerequisite to his acceptance of adoption writes, "Reaching this understanding often comes as a painful experience for the child. He may have feelings of personal worthlessness or questions about rejective experiences. He may be having difficulty in facing reality factors. . . . As these are brought out and the worker accepts his feelings and then helps him to clarify these in relation to his own worth as a person, he can move into new experiences." She adds that the difficulty of such tasks for children old enough consciously to experience the loss of their own parents should stimulate the preventive effort of helping parents reach as early a decision as clinically feasible regarding adoptive placement for their children.

The social worker's task may be seen as helping the preadoptive child survive an undue succession of prematurely ruptured attachments to parental figures with minimum hardship and psychological damage while repairing, conserving and fostering his capacity for healthy attachment to new parents. Appropriate reassurance based on understanding the child's language, behavioral and symptomatic as well as verbal, entails repetition, consistency and honesty by the worker. Enlisting and permitting maximum participation by the child in the adoptive planning and placement is generally recognized as a most desirable reassurance against his anxiety-laden sense of helplessness as a passive pawn at the mercy of all-powerful unpredictable grownups. Sensitive timing of the various stages of adoption attuned to the particular child's inner pace is a vital ingredient of reassurance; destructive anxiety can mount when certain steps of the process are too prolonged, such as between a child's relating to prospective parents and his actual placement with them; by the same token, however, panic may stem from feeling rushed and stampeded so that a more graduated spacing and slowing down is the most effective reassurance. Another general principle along this line with preadoptive children consists of consolidating each step along the way of new environments and new relationships by converting a previous unknown into a positively experienced known which can then furnish continuity as the next unfamiliar element is introduced.

Psychodynamic insight and concepts of personality development underlying these principles and procedures for direct work with children for adoption so that theoretical substantiation in general may be found abundantly in the literature. It may be of some interest to single out, however, one ingredient of personality recently discussed by Erikson (9) because of its particular applicability to our topic. Erikson regards the inner institution of "ego identity" as crucial to healthy personality and defines it as "a sense of identity, continuity and distinctiveness . . . . a sense of who one is, of knowing where one belongs, of knowing what one wants to do . . . . a sense accrued throughout the stages of childhood that there is continuity and sameness and meaning to one's life history." Ego identity, as something both conscious and unconscious, is normally established at the end of adolescence, according to Erikson, and sufferers from impaired or insufficient ego identity cannot "integrate all the various steps of their previous ego development, nor achieve a sense of belonging from their status in their society." By contrast, healthy ego identity entails "feeling that his past has a meaning in terms of his future but also from the feeling that the future has a meaning in terms of his past." It is obvious that the typical life history of a child adopted later than infancy, with its lack of continuity between successive, unrelated experiences and relationships—natural parents, institutions, foster homes and adoptive homes—is especially inconducive to healthy establishment of ego identity in Erikson's sense. Such a series of changing worlds for the young child opposes his accrual of feeling identical with himself. Correspondingly, however, this specific impairment may be greatly minimized and corrected by the case worker's therapeutic opportunities as discussed above, particularly as to continuity, meaningful relatedness to past and future, and the restoration of trust.

In the same paper Erikson relates the earliest stages of identity development to the young infant's gradually established sense of trust through repeated reassuring experiences of inner need satisfaction by an outer human world whose warmth and love can be believed in. Erikson views "a sense of basic trust in existence" as the earliest criterion of healthy infant personality. He regards the trust-mistrust conflict as the first nuclear conflict whose outcome depends a great deal on the very early child care and training. To support his view of trust formation as "a basic problem of social interaction," Erikson cites the "continuous retesting of the alternation of basic trust and basic mistrust" in regressive psychopathological conditions. This alternation pattern is extremely familiar to those working with children for adoption. The preadoptive vicissitudes so often experienced by these children are indeed inimical to this basic sense of trust and much of the adoptive case worker's skill and patience is directed toward its maximum repair and belated building. Whatever the case worker can accomplish and initiate along these lines before placement can hopefully be greatly extended and strengthened for the child after he becomes part of his adoptive family. Finding the kind of parents with whom this can take place, therefore, and giving them enabling support and direction constitutes the crucial indirect help to the child for which the direct preplacement work with him is a prerequisite.

The writer's main experience with adoption has been gained as psychiatric consultant to the Free Synagogue Child Adoption Committee so that the following case example illustrating some of the foregoing is selected from that agency with due recognition, as already noted, of the many prevailing differences in practice among agencies.

Jimmy was two years eleven months old when he started with us and he was placed in his adoptive home eight months later at three years seven months. Let us look more closely at some of what happened to him, in him and with him during those eight months of intensive and decisive experience.

Jimmy had been placed as a foundling of three months in an infant's institution where he remained for a year. He was admitted there in good physical condition and his health was essentially good throughout his stay. At sixteen months he was transferred to a foster home agency and placed in a three-baby temporary foster home. Adoption plans could not be considered pending clarification of the child's parenthood by the Department of Welfare. Jimmy remained in the foster home until his transfer at almost three years to the adoption agency's foster home. When referred to the Child Adoption Committee available history from the two previous agencies indicated that his adjustment at the infant's institution was felt to be very good. The foster home had not fully met his needs with the result that "he is quite fearful of strangers, although he responds to the affection of people he knows and tends to demand excessive attention and to react with temper outbursts overreadily when frustrated. Intellectually Jimmy seems to be developing normally although when he was nearly two the psychologist could not administer a standard test because he was so upset and showed so much resistance. Motor development is good but language is retarded. Jimmy has a slight convergent squint which is barely noticeable and an open bite which is noticeable but rather cute." As an interesting sidelight, a different worker describing the child's appearance around the same time states that "the open bite detracts from his appearance to some extent." (This neatly illustrates the factor of worker's subjectivity in appraising physical defects. Although very minor in this instance it can assume importance. Thus workers often worry about the negative effect on prospective adoptive parents of telling them about a child's defect lest this will cause the couple to reject the child. Sometimes these workers fail to realize how much their own subjective negative attitude toward a certain attribute may tip the scales for the clients, nor how the subjectivity of the latter, if left free of influence by the worker, may actually value or ignore the so-called defect. Furthermore, the negative or positive value placed on such a specific physical attribute of the child by worker or prospective adoptive parent may vary with other less conscious feelings of like or dislike toward the child of which the judgment about his appearance is a displacement. It may not be irrelevant, for instance, that the worker describing Jimmy's overbite as unattractive at her first meeting had undergone an extremely trying session with him at the doctor's office where he had screamed in fear and anger from the moment of entering the building, ignoring her overtures. On the other hand, I overheard the worker who finally consummated Jimmy's adoptive placement in a general glow of mutual affection, refer to this same overbite many months later as "very cute and attractive.")

In outline, the casework with Jimmy proceeded as follows: Seven weeks after his first meeting with Mrs. K. at the Child Adoption Committee's office, brought by Miss P., his worker at the foster home agency, Jimmy left the foster home where he had lived for the past year and a half of his three-year-old life and was taken by Mrs. K. to a CAC foster home. This occurred at their fourth meeting. The objectives of this first four-session phase of case work included the separation from his foster mother whom he called "mommy" and preparation for the new foster mother and her family, referred to by Mrs. K. as "Aunt Marie" to help him better distinguish the difference in relationship between his temporary foster mother and a real "mommy," a term to be reserved for the adoptive mother. During this first phase a shift was accomplished whereby his initial clinging to Miss P., his former worker, and fear of Mrs. K., the stranger, was very gradually reversed so that he could increasingly let go of Miss P. and relate positively to Mrs. K. He was given repeated opportunities to test out and find out what Mrs. K. was like. In fact, he dramatized this by minutely exploring her face with his hands, a reaction he was to repeat with new foster parents and at the first meeting with his adoptive parents. His advances were encouraged and his retreatings respected. Through blocks and a doll house he was told about Aunt Marie's family and details of her house, such as just where he would sleep, etc. His smashing of blocks and avoidance of listening about Aunt Marie were recognized and accepted as his protest against the change, but after reassurance, candy, enjoyable play, cuddling and obvious acceptance of him and his feelings, the theme would be reopened with diminishing protest and increasing interest. At the next to the last session before the actual transfer, the child was obviously relieved by reassurance he would go back home that day and only next time to Aunt Marie's. The respite of "more time" can often avert trauma. On the day of transfer he cried on leaving Miss P. and was not cheered by the new clothes he had previously welcomed. Diagnostically this may be taken as a favorable indication of capacity to relate; the pain was mitigated by his ability to accept comforting from Mrs. K. on the basis of the rapport previously established. He wet his pants en route which was well handled by Mrs. K. and by Aunt Marie on arrival through Mrs. K.'s help. Symptomatic enuresis recurred from time to time during the eight months under CAC care, almost always specifically traceable either to separation anxiety and resultant hostility or to testing out the tolerance of new parent figures after an initial period of "good" behavior.

The second case work phase occupied the next five months and included ten visits by the case worker, as well as many additional telephone contacts between case worker and foster mother. The objectives were multiple. Jimmy and his new foster family took to each other extremely well. The worker's first task was to re-establish her positive relationship with Jimmy in view of his greater ambivalence for fear her visits might mean her taking him away again from his new found family with Aunt Marie. Thus, he was enuretic in the home for the first time the night before her expected visit and he only kissed her as she was leaving. By her second visit, however, he apparently responded to the reassuring outcome of the previous time by offering a warm welcome. The worker's visits provided an opportunity for assessing his adjustment as a guide to his readiness for adoption. She could also get to know him better for greater discernment in selecting the adoptive home most suitable for him. By keeping in touch with Jimmy and the foster family, Mrs. K. could interpret his behavior to the foster mother and make suggestions as needed that prevented and relieved difficulties and promoted constructive and satisfying experiences. Thus, when Jimmy's initial honeymoon was over and he became disobedient and negativistic towards the foster mother, telling her to "shut up," Mrs. K.'s explanations to the foster mother dissipated the latter's incipient hostility and replaced it with justified pride in Jimmy's progress as illustrated by the improvement in speech. He now spoke in full sentences instead of isolated words, although his pronunciation was still unclear. After about two months Mrs. K. began more open preparatory discussion about finding Jimmy an adoptive home, although some clarification had been attempted ever since the outset of contact. Thus, he had begun to call his foster mother "mommy" and Mrs. K. records: "I said to Jimmy that Aunt Marie was not his mommy, that I was looking for a mommy and daddy for him and that when I found a mommy and daddy I thought Jimmy would like we could then go and visit them and then come back to Aunt Marie's, and if Jimmy did like this mommy and daddy we could go back there again and he could stay there forever. Jimmy said that he did not want to visit anybody and I said that we were not going now, that I was only looking for them and when I found them perhaps he will then want to go to visit. Jimmy looked at me questioningly and then smiled at me and nodded his head." At another session, by which time Jimmy had finally come to calling the foster mother Aunt Marie, worker reports: "I said to Jimmy that I knew he liked it here and he would want to stay. I also told him that Aunt Marie liked him but that she and Uncle Peter were not his mommy and daddy and they kept him and looked after him and liked him, but I wanted him to have a mommy and daddy so that he could stay with them all the time, and therefore we may have to go to visit them. Jimmy said 'No' and busied himself instead of listening to me. I kept on repeating the sentences in very simple words and then Jimmy again, as once before, looked up at me and smiled." During this period Jimmy was developing very well, physically and socially. Some increase in bed wetting and temper outbursts became apparent and some limitation of concentration span troubled Mrs. K. Despite the worker's interpretive and guidance efforts the foster mother, more accustomed to younger children, did not handle the boy's growing aggressiveness too well. This probably contributed somewhat to his symptoms just mentioned, but another source no doubt was the anxiety provoked by the case worker through her repeated preparations for adoptive placement to which Jimmy reacted with renewed separation anxiety, clinging to his immediate known world—that of the foster family. In the long run, however, it was felt better for Jimmy to endure this deliberately incurred anxiety, with much in the relation with Mrs. K. to sustain and gratify him, than to expose him to worse emotional consequences through repressed conflicts, emotional unpreparedness and a sense of nonparticipation in his own life plan. However, it was felt important to avoid protracted anxiety through delay in adoptive placement once Jimmy was felt to be ready for it.

Psychiatric consultation had been sought for prognostic evaluation of his residual symptoms which, in addition to those mentioned, included car sickness, fear of the bogeyman, and fear of being bitten by animals, as well as a tendency to bite other people himself. Despite unknowns in Jimmy's early history and his subsequent shifts, prognosis was considered reasonably favorable. Psychological examination revealed a score of average intelligence with evidence to suggest higher potential. Since the test was undertaken when the child was physically under par with a head cold, the likelihood of his actual ability exceeding the score is the greater.

By the end of what I have called the second phase of case work Mrs. K. took Jimmy to the CAC office from the foster home (entailing a train ride since the foster home is in a suburb and the office in New York City). Jimmy was prepared for this trip well in advance and had come to look forward to it, but only after he had actually clamped his hand over Mrs. K.'s mouth when she began to talk again about a new family. He recognized the CAC office and the toys he played with during his first few interviews with considerable pleasure and sense of continuity. "A man and a lady" dropped in while he was playing there and he accepted them as a matter of course. Actually they were prospective adoptive parents viewing the child for possible adoption. According to her promise, Mrs. K. journeyed back with Jimmy to the foster home, thereby emphasizing her trustworthiness to him. The couple did not wish to proceed further with Jimmy due to their persistent preference for a much younger child, but the trip seemed to liberate Jimmy somehow, perhaps through successful facing and surviving some thing he had dreaded.

The last month of Jimmy's care by the CAC may be regarded as phase three of his case work and was carried out by another worker, Mrs. S., because Mrs. K. had to leave the agency. Mrs. K. prepared Jimmy for this change and explained her departure to him. The youngster took this transfer very well, partly due to the skill of the new worker, partly because of Mrs. K.'s handling of the shift, and to a large extent, I think, because he really grasped that Mrs. K., Mrs. S., and the CAC office which he had just revisited, were all part of the same supportive team, one member of which could therefore somewhat represent another on his behalf, so that the legacy of good feeling built up through the months with Mrs. K. was available to Mrs. S. In any event, Mrs. S. telescoped the over-all time of phase three by seeing Jimmy very intensively. No doubt this played a role too in his responsiveness to her, since Mrs. K. had visited him much less frequently and for shorter periods. Mrs. S. saw Jimmy four times within five days, spending a morning or afternoon with him each time on pleasurable outings. Mrs. S. reports: "I told him I was the lady Mrs. K. had told him about and that I was coming to see him instead of Mrs. K., etc. He nodded his head in acceptance. As time went on in my contacts, I told him that I was going to find a mommy and daddy for him. He didn't like to hear this. Interestingly enough though, during this week when I was seeing so much of Jimmy he never once wet the bed. At times when I was reading to him, or if I hugged him, he would pick up my hand and bite me. He also gave me a few 'socks.' He related easily and loved the attention he was given by me. He expressed many fears such as of a bogeyman, was afraid to pick up a book that had fallen off the

porch because 'rats would come out and bite me.' I brought him
a circus book one day and while he liked the story, he was afraid
each animal pictured would bite him."

On the fourth outing within the five day period, Mrs. S. told
him that she would be coming to see him again three days from
then and would bring some friends with her, a man and a lady.
He nodded assent to this. Mrs. S. meanwhile had discussed Jimmy
with Mr. and Mrs. N. who were extremely eager to see him as
soon as possible. In the words of Mrs. S., "Jimmy was a little
shy in the beginning but he soon warmed up to Mr. and Mrs. N.,
the toys they brought helping in this. He was intrigued with Mr.
N.'s green car and he wanted a ride, so we went to the park I
had taken him to before [again the stress on the familiar]. He
bit Mr. and Mrs. N. a few times, for which I had prepared them."
After the visit Mrs. S. was in touch with the N.'s. At first Mrs. N.
had a little reservation because of Jimmy's poor speech, but three
days later she had come to think of the speech difficulty as an
insecurity symptom and with Mr. N. felt very positive and comfortable about Jimmy as their son. They visited Jimmy again,
giving him a holster with two guns and a cowboy hat which he
had greatly longed for. Once he got them he wouldn't take them
off and even slept with them. After this visit Mrs. N. was positive
she wanted Jimmy and felt she had exaggerated the speech difficulty before and now was easily able to understand him. (Note
earlier comments about subjective correspondence between liking
the child and liking his "defects.") Mrs. S. and the N.'s visited
Jimmy for the third time on the following day, on which occasion
the N.'s took him out in the green car which Jimmy liked very
much. He seemed quite comfortable in leaving with them, without Mrs. S., although when he returned he wanted to know where
she was to tell her about what they had done.

"I spoke to Jimmy about the N.'s and he told me he liked them.
I told him they didn't have any little boy but wanted one very
much, that they would like to have him for their little boy if he
would like this. He shook his head 'Yes' and then hid his face
in my lap. I told him about their house in the country, the ride
in the car to get there, the bed he would sleep in, etc. and he
listened very carefully." Mrs. S. had arranged with the N.'s for
Jimmy's placement with them for the very next day, feeling that
readiness had been established and prolongation would be more
anxiety-provoking for Jimmy.

When Mrs. S. and the N.'s arrived Jimmy was dressed in his
cowboy equipment, with clothes and toys packed, eagerly awaiting their arrival. He had continued dry at night throughout this
period of meetings with the N.'s. "We played a while in the house
and finally Mr. and Mrs. N. asked Jimmy if he was ready to go

with them, and he ran for his things, ran out to the car and was all ready to go. He waved good-bye to us very gayly and seemed very comfortable in going off with Mr. and Mrs. N."

Phase three of case work with Jimmy, then, was concentrated within a nine-day period starting with Mrs. S.'s first visit and concluding with adoptive placement. Both the acceleration of the last period of work and the patient, slow-going pace of the earlier months seem clinically helpful in terms of the child's progress. Excerpts from Mrs. N.'s letters to Mrs. S. right after Jimmy joined them and during the next few months convey the flavor of the postplacement experience and attest to the agency's effective selectivity of adoptive parents and case work with them preparatory to actual placement, which constitute an all-important service to Jimmy and other Jimmies.

Five days after placement Mrs. N. wrote, "Jimmy is going through the various stages of adjustment much faster than expected. He called us mommy and daddy from the moment we arrived. When we take a walk or go visiting we have to know 'where my house is' [need for reassurance—V.W.B.]. We have some difficulty changing clothes and so far pajamas have not been worn. He hasn't had a bath but does clean up quite well. [Is he afraid if he takes off his clothes to take a bath or change to pajamas that he will be unprotected and defenseless, or perhaps does he fear the loss of his new clothes if he let go of them?— V.W.B.] He had a few mild temper outbursts lasting about five minutes when he got very tired because a rabbit trap was set up for twenty minutes and no rabbit would come to it. If too many of his friends (three) should come at once to the house, he shuts the door of his room so that 'they can't take my toys.' For a day or two he didn't like me and wouldn't share his daddy with me. His resentment and hostilities are taken out on old logs and rocks and pieces of lumber, and less frequently on us. His doll shares some of it. And tonight he got a plastic Shmoo about his size which bounces back when you punch it. He enjoys that immensely. He often asks to be told a story. The greatest thrill we got was when he saw his daddy the first evening after the day's absence. Words could not express his joy at the reunion." A few days later Mrs. N.'s letter reported a victorious bath, less frequent and less intense biting, and a let-up on his initial excessive and exclusive appetite for sweets. By the following month Mrs. N.'s letter indicates that Jimmy is sharing his toys more easily because he seems much less afraid that he will lose them. His temper outbursts are less frequent and more controlled. "His fear of a bogeyman is actually a fear of the dark. We have tried to help him overcome it, but that will take more time." Although preferring to wipe out every reminder of life other than that in their present family, Mrs. N. overcomes her disinclination of speaking with Jimmy about Mrs. S. because she can see the value of a more realistic continuity for Jimmy and, grateful to the agency, she accepts its continued interest and responsibility for the next months prior to legal adoption. Mrs. N. reports that Jimmy loves to hear about all his relatives "those he has seen as well as those he hasn't seen. He brags to the other children about his grandmas, grandpa, cousins, etc." [Is not this an expression of hunger for belongingness on the part of a child who never had any relatives at all?—V.W.B.] When the family moved to the city for the winter from the country where Jimmy first joined them and spent his first months, the N.'s recognized and understood renewed expressions of anxiety. Another move might mean a dreaded separation as in the past. The N.'s decided to tell him the story of his adoption. "We call it the 'Jimmy Story.' He enjoyed the story very much, especially when details were mentioned that he remembered . . . . he has been wearing pajamas for the last ten days or so."

Four months after placement Mrs. S. reports: "He bites his nails once in a while, but not as often as he did in the beginning. He was afraid of the animals when the N.'s took him to the zoo so they haven't repeated this though he seems to be less afraid of dogs now and loves kittens and cats. He no longer gets car sick. Temper tantrums occur on occasion when Jimmy is very frustrated, but they are much milder and less frequent. He is happy, loves to help around the house, and has moved the hands on the clock to where they should be when Mr. N. comes home in order to make his daddy come home sooner. He plays very well with other children, speaks as distinctly as is normal for a child his age, and no longer bites people. His concentration span is excellent and he can entertain himself with his toys for long periods of time."

Several references have been made already to case work with prospective adoptive parents in terms of the agency's responsibility to them as clients in their own right, and in relation to the children's welfare by optimum selective home finding. A most desirable trend has been under way for some time in a number of adoption agencies toward more and better case work with adoptive applicants. It is to be hoped that the field in general will increasingly make the necessary adjustments in administration, personnel and staff qualifications to further extend this development. This trend, concerned as it is with unconscious motivations, attitudes and conflicts, is probably due in large measure to the general integration of psychoanalytic concepts into case work from which it certainly derives much of its rationale and method. Gains in psychological insight also account for a parallel shift in the weighting of factors sought in "desirable" adoptive homes. Emotional capacities for parenthood rather than economic advantages per se, for instance, are considered more important and, of course, are harder to ascertain.

Several important aspects of case work with adoptive parents as developed in the agency with which I am connected have been well described in articles by Brown (5), Michaels (21), and Brenner (3), so that it would seem needlessly repetitious to review this in detail. In general, case work with this type of client attempts several functions. Selective assessment, of course, is the main one entailing diagnostic skills of a high order. However, in line with the well known principle that diagnosis and therapy are to some extent inseparable processes, a case worker can help as well as appraise. It is true that these clients come to the agency seeking a child, not therapy, so the help must be within the context of the adoption situation. Adoption for these couples may be viewed as a gradual sequential process. The case worker enters into this process at several stages along the way, her functions varying somewhat with each. Only some of those who embark on this sequence with the agency actually reach their original goal of adoption. They may withdraw themselves or be refused a child by the agency at any of the successive steps, although every effort should be made toward disqualification as early in the progression as clinically possible in order to minimize false hopes and resultant greater trauma.

What then are we looking for in adoptive parents and how should we look for it? In this subtle complex realm of parental potential there can be no simple checklist of qualifying and disqualifying items, nor any single rule of thumb method for differentiating, on behalf of the children for whom the agency is responsible, those who may be most or least suited for successful adoptive parenthood. We can neither ignore our responsibility to use existent knowledge and skills toward such appraisals, nor delude ourselves into a sense of infallibility regarding our judgments in areas where so much remains unknown or controversial.

In general, we seek couples whose relationship with each other is mutually satisfying but which will be enhanced, rather than upset, by the addition of a child. We seek couples whose conscious and unconscious motivations to adopt are relatively free of neurotic conflict and compatible with warm, mature love for the child as an individual in his own right. We seek couples who have come to terms enough with their feelings about their childlessness to accept adoption in lieu of biological parenthood with maximum comfort and minimum fear, shame or resentment. In short, we seek couples who are on good adult terms with themselves and each other, who are ready for adoption psychologically and situationally, and whose desire for children stems from emotionally healthy needs and capacities. And not infrequently, in the course of searching for those attributes through case work interviews, opportunities arise whereby the case worker can use her skill and insight therapeutically—still within the adoptive context—so that inhibiting anxieties or self-doubts may be relieved and latent capacities released sufficiently to make a decisive difference in a couple's ability to move into adoption successfully.

From the outset of contact another way the worker assists is by furnishing realistic information about adoption since applicants usually approach the agency with a varying number of misconceptions and false expectations. The client's reactions and use of this data at the initial interview, or any subsequent stage, not only has value for him by way of preparation for adoption experience, but may offer diagnostic indications of such relevant personality factors as flexibility and the degree of realistic dominance over the irrational elements in his mental life. It is not infrequent that such factual confrontation results in couples discovering for themselves that they cannot really accept a child other than their own, or that they are in much less agreement about wanting a child than either had let the other, or sometimes even himself, know until then. The value of maladjustment prevention by self-withdrawal for such couples is obvious, as well as for the child they might have obtained and probably would have, had they sought independent adoption.

The reasons for the couple's childlessness, what it means and has meant to the husband and wife, and how it affects their feelings toward themselves, each other, and their motivation to adopt should be carefully explored. Naturally, we try to reach behind the clients' conscious attitudes, cognizant of the deep feelings and conflicts entailed, and the profound psychic interconnections between reproductive incapacity and the total personality. The question of whether the impaired fertility afflicts the husband, wife, or both, is of considerable psychodynamic significance. Likewise, the psychological implications of absolute sterility, as in hysterectomy, for example, are different than for relative infertility. As part of intake procedure, our agency routinely requests a confidential letter from the couple's physician stating the cause or causes of childlessness, its treatability, and the prognosis for future childbearing.

Psychogenic sterility, or more accurately, functional infertility, may be symptomatic of unconscious neurotic conflicts closely related in these clients to repressed motives, anxieties and fantasies underlying the conscious wish to adopt. Studies so far have been mainly limited to female psychogenic sterility. Hypotheses as to the specific physiological mechanisms involved are still speculative but the clinical experience of many of us supports Kroger and Freed's (17) statement: "Psychogenic sterility should receive more attention from clinicians because it is now recognized that emotional conflicts can produce dysfunctions in the generative organs." Psychosomatic researches by Therese Benedek (1) have pointed to interconnections between ovarian hormonal cycles and emotional manifestations; she elaborates some of the implications of these findings in a recent discussion of infertility in women as a psychosomatic defense (in the absence of causative organic pathology). "The term 'defense' is defined as an unconscious function of the ego to protect the self—the total personality—against the dangers originating within the organism; in this case the physiologic processes of the procreative functions." According to Benedek, the monthly hormonal preparation for pregnancy of the sexual cycle is paralleled by an emotional preparation which by monthly repetition normally fosters psychosexual maturation. In certain neurotic and immature women, however, this inner process is reacted to with fear and each monthly repetition builds up defenses against the repressed irra-tionally dreaded dangers until actual protective inability to conceive is "achieved." This should not be misconstrued to mean that all women seeking adoption with somatically unexplained infertility fit into this category and should be denied adoption. As already stressed, our evaluations cannot be made on the basis of a single factor. Repeated patterns and clusters rather than isolated instances are necessary in personality appraisal. Alertness to possibilities, however, sharpens perception of clues that may then be substantiated or refuted by further evidence.

Without wishing to attach undue importance to the topic of infertility in adoptive work, it might be of interest to pursue this discussion somewhat further. It is common knowledge that pre-viously "sterile" women sometimes conceive shortly after adopt-ing a child, or even during some stage of the adoption process. Systematic investigation and establishment of causal connections is still lacking essentially.[2] Kroger and Freed (17), referring to a study by Hanson and Rock (American Journal of Obstetrics and Gynecology, Vol. 59, pp. 311-319, 1950) state: "Hanson and Rock questioned a group of 202 women and found that adoption can-not be considered a reliable cure for sterility. Their study is inter-esting but we doubt the reliability of questionnaire material." Orr (23) has reported the case of a woman who became pregnant following the decision to adopt. He had analyzed both this pa-tient and her husband. Conception had been previously unsuc-cessful, despite medical treatment for both husband and wife. Orr suggests how the psychodynamic realignment entailed in this woman's preparation for the adoptive baby might have in-fluenced conception. The concomitant somatic treatment received by husband and wife does not refute psychic causality in this case but renders it less conclusive. Helene Deutsch (8) devotes a chap-ter to psychogenic sterility in women and describes five specific types from her psychoanalytic experience, stating that she con-siders unconscious fear as the most frequent cause of such steril-ity. In another valuable chapter on adoptive mothers discussed from the psychoanalytic standpoint, Deutsch mentions three cases of women who became pregnant in connection with adop-

[2] Female Functional Infertility and Adoption, Viola W. Bernard, in work.

tion, the first when about to adopt, the second less than a year after adopting a baby, and the third—the only one of the three whom Deutsch analyzed herself—during the first year of her adoptive motherhood. Deutsch suggests some psychodynamic explanations. Knight (16) also refers briefly to functional sterility, citing instances of childless women who sought adoption when convinced of the impossibility of conception and who became pregnant after adopting a child. He theorizes that unconscious opposition to childbearing possibly responsible for the functional sterility "was somehow overcome by the experience of adoption and taking care of a child."

Data from adoptive mothers studied by the writer is in general agreement with Knight, Deutsch, Orr, and Benedek. An extremely interesting instance of the reciprocal possibilities between clinical service and research inherent in adoption work in general, and the problem of functional infertility in particular, occurred a few years ago. Jacobson (15) has contributed the first detailed psychoanalytic case report in the literature of a case of sterility cured by psychoanalytic treatment. Conception occurred during the eighth month of analysis and the pregnancy and delivery were normal. The patient, a married woman in her mid-thirties, had been amenorrheic since the age of sixteen after two years of normal periods. Her sterility, thought due to ovarian deficiency, had remained medically refractory throughout the ten years of her marriage, despite strenuous conscious efforts to become pregnant. There had been no medical treatment other than psychoanalysis for an appreciable time, however, since the sterility was regarded as organically irreversible on the basis of a biopsy report of atrophic endometrium.

The patient's need and suitability for analysis had been first recognized by this writer as psychiatric consultant to the adoption agency from which the patient and her husband were then seeking a baby. Although, as well put by Michaels (21), psychiatric referral of adoptive applicants by the agency is most often unwise, even when psychopathology becomes evident, this patient was among the exceptions for whom it was indicated. The patient dramatically demonstrated unconscious fear and opposition to the motherhood she had sought so desperately by develop-

ing acute anxiety, depression and bodily symptoms when her
conscious wish for the adoptive baby was realized. The baby who
had been placed with the couple showed signs of reactive stress
and the agency, acting on its responsibility for the child, replaced
it in a more favorable home. Referred to as Mrs. A., this initial
phase of the case history supplementing Jacobson's report may
be found in a paper by the writer (2). In view of how much
preparatory psychiatric help this patient needed in order to
accept referral, it seems more than likely that progressive illness
rather than the gratifying therapeutic result would have eventuated for this woman without the agency's intervention. The psychiatrist's activity included several direct interviews, as well as
continuous consultation with the case worker. Although scarcely
typical of day-to-day agency function, the case illustrates how
analytically oriented case work with the adoptive parents can
prevent or reduce serious future maladjustment for the child, as
well as for the parents.

The main function of adoption work, of course, is the very
positive one of helping to dispel the deep frustration of barren
couples and homeless children by family formation. Concomitant
prevention of greater frustrations by ill-advised adoptions is less
rewarding and more arduous, but essential. Experience has
proven repeatedly, for instance, that couples should not adopt
while either or both are suffering from depression, for their own
sakes' and the child's. Ignorant of this, many couples—urged on
by their sympathetic, well-meaning friends—desperately turn to
adoption in reaction to recent tragic bereavement such as the
death of a child. The same misguided hope to cure depression by
adoption may be seen in some mood disturbances related to
sterility. In either case, the decision about adoption should await
recovery from the depression, for placement during it is in clinical violation of everything known about the psychopathology
of depression, popular misconceptions to the contrary, and leads
to added rather than lessened misery. Recently bereaved parents
adopting a "replacement child" cannot help but relate to him
with rejection and ambivalence. His value for them as a substitute for the deceased child entails rejection of him in his own
right; hostility for surviving and displacing their own child is

almost inevitable, often complicated by guilt feelings toward the latter should they let themselves love the newcomer for himself. Stampeded by great pressure from the community and their own compassion, workers have been misled into rushing such emergency placements through, often waiving the ascertainment of history data and precrisis personality which might even have been disqualifying had adoptive application preceded the occurrence of tragedy. Of course it is true that most adoptions, for the parents, are attempts to substitute for their own children that could not be born or who could not survive. But this adjustment through substitution works out far better when the adopted child is felt as replacing the otherwise lost opportunity to experience family life and parental role, rather than as a replacement of a specific child.

Adoptive placement is also contraindicated while a couple is emotionally preoccupied by insistent craving for conception and is in the midst of active medical measures to achieve it. This does not mean that the agency should unrealistically expect couples to eradicate a longing for biologic parenthood from which, after all, the soundest urge toward adoption derives its force. What *is* meant, however, is illustrated by a couple seen recently who pleaded for an adoptive baby at the same time as they frantically intensified efforts to achieve conception by every method at once, including hypnotism and artificial insemination. They should be dissuaded from considering adoption until, should they ultimately fail to achieve the much preferred natural pregnancy, they can accomplish the inner adaptation whereby rechanneling of their needs and yearnings permits preponderant fulfillment rather than frustration by adoption; otherwise they cannot help but resent adoption as a narcissistic defeat and the adopted child as a symbol of that defeat. Insufficiently resolved conflicts about their fertility can impair the adoptive parents' relation to their child in many subtle ways. Some such parents find it too difficult to tell the child about his adoption, even though doing so is generally recognized as best for the child. Not infrequently their disinclination, rationalized as kindness to the youngster, is rooted in retained, acute feelings of shame and guilty anxiety about infertility so that "telling" about adoption means revealing too painful a defect. For such parents the adopted child may be valued far less for himself than as a narcissistic compensation for a persistent sense of narcissistic injury. The child inevitably disappoints such a parent whose expectations are irrationally high, whereupon adoption provides an all-too-ready rationalization for rejection, i.e., "He's not really my child."

Hopefully, reference to some of these frequently seen hazards will not give rise to false pessimism about adoption. The case of Jimmy and Mr. and Mrs. N., presented earlier, typifies the brighter aspects. Results of placement outcome for the fifty children followed up by Brenner and Hartley (4) were on the whole very encouraging. Retrospective study of mistakes in the cases of the relatively less successful outcomes have already led to improved practice. In order continually to improve the bases for predictions in this field, more such detailed follow-up studies are desirable, preferably with larger samples. Brenner's discussion of the characteristics of the fifty couples in relation to the placement outcome is of particular interest in this matter of adoptive parent selection, although one might have wished it possible to have included data as to how the child's inborn tendencies and reactions to preadoptive experience influenced parental attitudes, in turn so crucial for the child's adjustment. In the same study David M. Levy developed a rating scale for adoptive homes in an attempt to provide a standard scheme for observation as a research tool for further investigations. Levy selected six areas of the parent-child relationship which he thought reflected conditions which contribute to children's growth and emotional security. These are "affection, admiration and criticism, ease or tension, patience and indulgence, freedom and time spent by the parents with the child." These six qualities were rated by case work observations on a six-point scale ranging from "insufficient" to "excessive," and a scoring system was worked out based on low desirability for both extremes. The method admittedly involved qualitative judgment in evaluating what was too little or too much in each of the parent-child areas. However, Levy set up definitions as guides and reports that three independent clinicians experienced in adoption work—a social worker, psychiatrist, and psychologist—used the scale and came out with the same answers. As a further check, the best and worst homes, as evaluated by the social worker, were found to have been picked up by the six-item scale. Despite a number of sizable limitations recognized by the authors, the instrument is to be welcomed as a promising methodological advance for extending research.

For adoptive parents the first sight of the child suggested to them by the agency is a profound and culminating experience. For an older child, the same is true although he is usually protected against possible rejection by the couple's seeing him before he meets them as possible parents. We have already viewed the child's side of the experience through the story of Jimmy and Mr. and Mrs. N. Some of the implications for the prospective parents were described by the writer (2) some years ago. The first meeting represents a major stage in facing the actuality of parenthood. As the adoption thus materializes into reality many couples find the realization and happiness they had anticipated. Occasionally, however, latent conflicts with marked anxiety and rejection of the child are aroused, in contrast to previous manifest attitudes. Although always distressing for the client, these reactions may or may not prove serious. The case worker and couple need to re-evaluate the wisdom of adoption for them and here again the case worker's insight and help can be decisive in enabling some to move on comfortably to adoption and others to face their previously unrecognized deep-seated opposition to adoption in order that they may withdraw with minimum trauma. Certain common patterns as well as significant differences in the underlying conflicts and conflict solutions were described.

Insight derived from psychoanalytic principles enlarges the adoption worker's view of her own role and personality dynamics in relation to her professional work. While this is true for all social worker-client interactions, the specifics of what is at stake for her triple clientele—adoptive couple, natural parents, and children—and the vital way these bear on her own basic experience are especially acute and profound in the adoption field. Realization of the psychological cruciality of the relatively final family relationships the worker helps bring about or prevent, and of her personal emotional resonance to the fundamental urges, frustrations, conflicts and gratifications with which she daily deals, heightens her sense of responsibility, with resultant satisfactions and anxieties as well. Relief from such anxieties may understandably be sought by some workers' need to blind themselves to their own subjectivity and to the psychological requirements of their clients, instead of the more desirable, though taxing course of maximum awareness and thereby maximum effectiveness and safety for themselves and their clients.

Aside from professional training and acquired case work skills, adoption work makes high demands in terms of personal stability and maturity. Unconscious conflicts and attitudes linked to the worker's own early family relationships, psychosexual development, and experiences or lack of them as wife and mother are under constantly bombarding stimuli inherent in the case material. A certain amount of the worker's psychic energy goes into the continuous task of self-scrutiny and disengaging the client and herself from what can otherwise be her unconsciously rationalized expression of hidden needs deceptively distorting her desired objectivity. Because the emotional substance of adoption is so powerful for all concerned, touching on the deepest human longings, deprivations and fears, the social worker participating in these profound and intricate human processes may experience reinforcement of constructive sublimations and adaptations or intensification of neurotic propensities, depending on the many variables of individual personality functioning. As Clothier (6) states: "Whatever the inner need may be that leads the social worker into her profession, that need is the motivating force or energy which makes her usefulness possible. Like any elemental force or power the inner need that seeks solution can operate socially or destructively."

Naturally the specific ways in which adoption workers may project their own unconscious feelings into their jobs are innumerable. Extremes of sympathy or hostility toward any one of the sets of clients may be regarded as warning signals of possible inner involvement calling for self-exploration. A few rather frequently occurring patterns might be mentioned as illustrative. Overpunitive and condemning reactions, overt or disguised, toward the unmarried mother may stem from unconscious envy of the latter's "sexual freedom" and/or chilbearing achievement based on a sense of personal thwarting. Or, the unmarried mother may represent a threat to the outcome of a worker's inner battle between conscience and forbidden impulse so that by invoking social penalties on the externalized transgressor self—the unmarried mother—the worker may unconsciously seek this roundabout way to strengthen her own inner defenses. On the other hand, depending on the balance of inner conflicting forces, the unmarried mother may unconsciously stand for a different aspect of self, in arousing the worker's vehement championing in terms of self-rescue and exoneration. Particularly strong and deep-rooted personal feelings may be set off by the unwed mother's decision about keeping or surrendering her child for adoption. Is the worker unconsciously tempted to rob the unwed mother of her baby? In fearing this form of baby-snatching in herself, must she overcompensate by denying needed appropriate help toward clinically indicated adoption in the name of "passive technique?" Or perhaps her hostility, through identifying with the baby, is mainly due to remobilization of early abandonment terrors.

The worker's childhood feelings toward parents often exert an understandable regressive influence on her reactions to adoptive parents and may combine with an overidentification with the child to be placed. The possibilities of unconscious childish fantasy fulfillment, wishful as well as fearful, add to the inner pressure under which the worker labors. Can any parents be perfect enough? Or, swinging over to her inner view of the parents' view, can any child be perfect enough? Are parents figures to be compulsively obeyed or defied, looked up to or looked down on, or competed with? Do the unconscious implications of power in the worker's role and the residual fantasies of omnipotence over those early omnipotent figures—parents—significantly intrude on the realistic current situations? On behalf of the child for adoption, is the fear of possible rejection too great to risk placement? How do the worker's own feelings about the children she herself mothers, or wants to mother, or does not want to mother, affect her unconscious feelings of envy or vicarious gratification in helping relieve the adoptive parents' childlessness. Brenner (3), in fact, suggests that the lag in application of "sound psychiatric case work principles for evaluating adoptive parents . . . . is partly the result of our unconscious fear of examining our own feelings about parents."

Certainly the multiple and often conflicting professional loyalties, as Clothier (6) has stressed, which the case worker in this field strives to harmonize, are unusually great. Instead of a single client's problem, the adoption worker serves the needs of several, i.e., natural parents, adoptive parents, and children for adoption. Although the child traditionally is regarded as the primary client, whose needs are paramount, our knowledge of the interdependence of family relationships leads toward maximum consideration for all concerned as in line with the best interests of the child. As McCleery (20) has properly stressed, the agency, through supervision and administration, can contribute significantly to helping the worker "find a way of handling his anxieties so that they will not be passed on to the children or the parents."

Although the natural parents constitute another major group of adoption agency clients, as already mentioned, they will not be discussed further in this presentation. Most of them, though not all, are unmarried mothers and space does not permit doing justice to the wealth of clinical data concerning them. Furthermore, their needs are so multiple (medical, financial, case work, shelter care, etc.) that the adoption agency should be but one, and by no means the central resource of interrelated community services offering comprehensive coverage.

A final phase of case work function on behalf of adoptive parents and children is that of supervision prior to legal adoption. The term "supervision" reflects the child-protective aspect but not the casework function. A term less suggestive of old-style authoritative snooping would seem preferable and in line with professional progress. The case worker visits the newly formed family periodically during the first six months or year after placement, her functions differing somewhat in an infant placement from that of an older child. For the latter, relationship with the child as well as the parents is of importance. Most children are apt to react to her with ambivalence. On the one hand the worker, granted a good preadoption relationship, represents continuity, familiarity and security for the child. Adjusting as he must to a whole new world, her visits can signify her continued protective support and interest. On the negative side, however, the child may see the worker as a "taking away" person because of her role in his previous separations from natural parents or foster homes. Her visit therefore may threaten the treasured permanence of his new-found home. With understanding reassurance, most workers can sufficiently minimize the anxiety to salvage her security value for him. Some ambivalence toward the worker is almost always felt by the adoptive parents as well. A good preadoptive relationship is usual, heightened by very warm feelings in reaction to obtaining the long-desired child. On the other hand, the worker represents an obstacle to the healthy and desired process of becoming a self-contained independent family unit. The agency's legal right to remove the child, if deemed necessary for its welfare, is also a source of some anxiety. With careful preadoptive selection and preparation recourse to this power of removal is seldom necessary, but on occasion it is invoked, as in the case of Mrs. A., the mother described earlier, who was referred for analytic treatment and later bore her own child. An up-to-date discussion of the purposes and methods of supervision is to be found in a report of interagency meetings in New York City (25). As regards the case work function, the group agreed as to the value of help related specifically to the adoption situation. They were not in total accord as to the desirability of case work service for the less specifically adoptive aspects of family life. It seems to me, however, that no hard and fast distinction can be made between the adoptive aspects of the couple's reactions and the feelings and attitudes referable to their newness as parents. Overapprehensiveness and feelings of ineptness are common to many parents with their first baby. The new adoptive couple's anxieties around their inexperience as parents and from the special circumstance of adoption seem inseparably blended. The visiting case worker can often greatly relieve difficulties. Certainly many of these couples seek, welcome, and constructively utilize the case worker's support and guidance during these initial months, despite the degree of ambivalence already noted. Naturally there are others with different needs and resources for whom minimum postplacement agency contact is best. In my opinion the mental health potentialities of this aspect of adoptive case work have not been sufficiently explored or developed. This is due in large part to budgetary limitations. A promising innovation is being considered of offering parental guidance, individually or in groups, to adoptive couples at some period *after* they have legally adopted.

After legal adoption, contact with the agency is terminated. Through the years a certain number of parents and children return for specific assistance. Thus, a couple may bring their adolescent youngster who has come to want more information about his origins than the parents can satisfy. The worker differentiates her handling of this request in terms of her appraisal of the motives and feelings behind it for parents and youngster, as well as the quality of family relationships. The child's wish need not be symptomatic of any serious discontent and the worker, while protecting the natural parents' anonymity, may furnish some nonidentifying details. These, plus the parents' understanding willingness in coming, the physical tangibility of the agency, and the worker's helping attitude may meet such a youngster's need for connection with his past—an expression of his sense of ego identity formation so important in adolescence[3] as quoted above from Erikson. Occasionally we see tragically pathological distortions of this constellation. These very disturbed young people who had been adopted in early childhood develop an all-consuming, obsessing need to locate their biologic parents who in fantasy, or even delusion, have become the idealized good parents in contrast to the adoptive "bad" parents with whom they are usually no longer in contact. The insecurities of war precipitated a number of these acute reactions among young men particularly when facing the prospect of overseas shipment to the dangerous unknown world. The personal histories of those cases known to me invariably revealed glaringly unsuitable adoptive placements. These sick youths acted out in overt form the family romance fantasy described as universal by Otto Rank and considered of special importance in the psychology of adopted children by

[3] *Editor's note:* Cf. Chapter 10, p. 223.

several psychoanalysts, including Clothier (7) and Deutsch (8). When feeling disappointed or frustrated by their parents, all children are prone to imagine at some point in their lives that these disappointing parents are not their real parents, but through mysterious circumstances had found or somehow acquired them as infants. Their true parents were idealized paragons and some day the child will regain his wonderful rightful heritage and be free of these horrid, worthless people who call themselves his mother and father. Dynamically the fantasy is thought to evolve as a child's means of coping with his usual ambivalence conflicts. Two sets of parents permits his assignment of all bad feelings to one set, and all good feelings to the other, thus dealing with the problem of simultaneous love and hate toward the same parents. Normally this fantasy plays a minor and fleeting role in the child's mental life, but Deutsch, Clothier and others have shown through analysis how the coinciding with reality in adoption renders this fantasy of more compelling and central significance in the psychodynamics of the adopted child. His adoptive parents really did mysteriously find him as a baby, born of unknown parents, and thus reality seems to confirm his fantasies and thereby strengthens them, in contrast to the non-adopted child's use of reality to neutralize fantasy. Clothier emphasizes the role this plays in the symptomatology of emotionally disturbed adoptive children.

Since the child turns to the unknown fantasied parents, facilitated by the reality of adoption in reaction to feeling angry and hurt by his real-life adoptive parents, it follows that the most potent antidote to excessive and persistent pathological recourse to this escapist fantasy is a healthy, secure, satisfying relationship between the child and his adoptive parents. These are truly his real parents, as defined by cumulative experience of living together as a family. In emotionally healthy adoption—which includes of course a normal degree of mutual frustration, anxiety and hostility—the child's involvement with his biological parents remains within bounds. The extent to which case work along dynamic lines can foster this goal has been extensively described.

Perhaps some readers have become impatient by now with what may appear to them as needless exaggeration of the psychological complexity of adoption and the precautions advocated. This attitude may be bolstered by knowing of some apparently happy adoptions accomplished much more simply, either through independent adoption or social agencies with minimal case work. The personal qualifications for adoptive parents and for case workers may seem perfectionistic and the intensive psychological work with unmarried mothers and preadoptive children a lot of fancy nonsense. By way of reply, psychoanalysis provides a microscope whereby otherwise invisible psychic structures and processes come into view. A description of pond water in accordance with structures and movement observed in a drop under the microscope can sound unbelievable to one accustomed to water, but not to microscopes. Although hit-and-miss methods of adoptive placements sometimes do turn out well, reliance on knowledge rather than luck promises better control over the outcomes by adding to the successes and reducing the failures.

BIBLIOGRAPHY

1. BENEDEK, T. Infertility as a psychosomatic defense. *Fertility and Sterility*, 3, November-December, 1952.
2. BERNARD, V. W. First sight of the child by prospective parents as a crucial phase in adoption. *Am. J. Orthopsychiat.*, 15, 1945.
3. BRENNER, R. F. The selection of adoptive parents: a casework responsibility. *Child Welfare*, December, 1946.
4. —— and HARTLEY, R. *A Follow-Up Study of Adoptive Families.* New York: Child Adoption Research Committee, 1951.
5. BROWN, F. G. What do we seek in adoptive parents. *Soc. Casework*, April, 1951.
6. CLOTHIER, F. The social worker in the field of adoption. *Ment. Hyg.*, 24, 1940.
7. —— The psychology of the adopted child. *Ment. Hyg.*, 27, 1943.
8. DEUTSCH, H. *The Psychology of Women.* New York: Grune & Stratton, 1945.
9. ERIKSON, E. H. Growth and crises of the healthy personality. *Symposium on the Healthy Personality.* New York: Josiah Macy, Jr. Foundation, 1950.
10. ESCALONA, S. The use of infant tests for predictive purposes. *Bull. Menninger Clinic*, 14, 1950.
11. FAIRWEATHER, M. E. Early placement in adoption. *Child Welfare*, 31, 1952.
12. FREUD, A. The psychoanalytic study of infantile feeding disturbances. *The Psychoanalytic Study of the Child*, 2:119, 1947. New York: International Universities Press.

13. HALLINAN, H. W. Who are the children available for adoption? *J. Soc. Casework*, 32, 1951.
14. —— Adoption for older children. *Soc. Casework*, 33, 1952.
15. JACOBSON, E. A case of sterility. *Psychoanal. Quart.*, 15, 1946.
16. KNIGHT, R. P. Some problems involved in selecting and rearing adopted children. *Bull. Menninger Clinic*, 5, 1941.
17. KROGER, W. S. and FREED, S. C. *Psychosomatic Gynecology*. Philadelphia: W. B. Saunders Company, 1951.
18. LEITCH, M. and ESCALONA, S. K. The reaction of infants to stress: a report on clinical findings. *The Psychoanalytic Study of the Child*, 3/4:121, 1949. New York: International Universities Press.
19. MALCOVE, L. Margaret E. Fries' research in problems of infancy and childhood: a survey. *The Psychoanalytic Study of the Child*, 1:405, 1945. New York: International Universities Press.
20. MCCLEERY, S. The adoption worker's role and his personality in the professional adoption process. *Child Welfare*, October, 1952.
21. MICHAELS, R. Casework considerations in rejecting the adoption application. *J. Soc. Casework*, 18, 1947.
22. OMAN, H. G. Giving up a baby. *The Survey*, January, 1952.
23. ORR, D. W. Pregnancy following the decision to adopt. *Psychosom. Med.*, 3, 1941.
24. RAINER, L. Helping the child and the adoptive parents in the initial placement. *Child Welfare*, November, 1951.
25. REPORT OF THE INTER-AGENCY DISCUSSION GROUP OF NEW YORK CITY. The process of supervision in adoptive placements. *Child Welfare*, November, 1952.
26. RIBBLE, M. A. *The Rights of Infants*. New York: Columbia University Press, 1943.
27. SPITZ, R. A. Emotional growth in the first year. *Child Study*, Spring, 1947.
28. —— Relevancy of direct infant observation. *The Psychoanalytic Study of the Child*, 5:66, 1950. New York: International Universities Press.
29. —— The psychogenic diseases in infancy: an attempt at their etiological classification. *The Psychoanalytic Study of the Child*, 6:255, 1951. New York: International Universities Press.
30. THAYER, S. W. Moppets on the market: the problem of unregulated adoptions. *Yale Law J.*, March, 1950.
31. WIRES, E. M. Placement for adoption—a total separation? *J. Soc. Casework*, July, 1949.
32. WOLKOMIR, B. They are adoptable. *Better Times*, Welfare Council of New York City, January 31, 1947.

Chapter 10

THE CONTRIBUTION OF PSYCHOANALYSIS TO THE TREATMENT OF ADOLESCENTS

PETER BLOS, Ph.D.

An outline of the treatment of adolescents presents the problem of relating the technique of therapeutic intervention to the maturational stage of puberty. Such an attempt needs to be prefaced by an exposition of the specific psychodynamics of this stage against which personality assessment as well as therapeutic practice has to be gauged. It seems essential, then, for those working with adolescents to have a conceptual framework of this developmental stage in mind in order to understand and use meaningfully the clinical material of a given case as well as to evaluate what happens in treatment.

THEORY OF ADOLESCENCE

Adolescence and Childhood

Puberty is that period of human development when sexual maturation is brought to its final conclusion. Due to hormonal activity during this stage bodily changes occur and at the same time instinctual demands become intensified. We call adolescence the sum total of all attempts at adjustment to this developmental stage of puberty, to the new set of inner and outer conditions which confront the individual (4, 5). This period follows the relative calm of the latency period; during this phase of childhood new capacities and skills, mentally and physically, developed in terms of sublimated endeavors. In addition, the child

210

widened his social relations beyond the intimate life within the family (7). Anna Freud has summarized these changes which overtake the child while entering latency by saying: "Complete dependence on the parents ceases and identifications begin to take the place of object love" (13). These new acquisitions are valuable assets for the imminent confrontation with puberty. However, the intensification of the instinctual drive during adolescence represents, initially at least, only a quantitative rise and brings to life all modes of gratification which have ever played a role in the past; namely, during the years of psychosexual development in infancy and early childhood (13). The bizarreness and the regressive character of adolescent behavior is due to the infantile admixture in the struggle to regain or to retain a psychic equilibrium which has been jolted by the emergence of puberty. The significant emotional needs and conflicts of early childhood are recapitulated before new solutions with a qualitatively different instinctual aim (genitality) are found. Due to these facts adolescence has been called a second edition of childhood, both periods having in common that "a relatively strong id confronts a relatively weak ego" (13). Whatever personality disturbance is observed in adolescene it has to be borne in mind that the pregenital phases of sexual organization are still at work to assert themselves and to interfere with the progression to maturity. The gradual advancement during adolescence toward the central position of genital, heterosexual orientation is but the continuation of a development which was brought to a temporary standstill after the oedipal phase and represents what has been referred to as the biphasic sexual development in man (14).

Preadolescence

The preparatory phase of adolescence when pubertal changes of sexual maturation have not yet made or are just beginning to make their appearance is called preadolescence. During this phase the quantitative increase in instinctual pressure leads to an indiscriminate cathexis of all those libidinal and aggressive modes of gratification which have served each child well during the early years of his life. The resurgence of pregenitality which characterizes preadolescence brings an end to the latency period and leaves the child more difficult to reach, to control, and to teach. What education has accomplished over the years in terms of instinct control and social conformity seems doomed to rapid disintegration. Besides an increase in diffuse motility (restlessness, fidgetiness) we observe oral greediness, sadistic activities, and phallic exhibitionistic games. We witness the reawakening of coprophilic pleasures as expressed in the "foul" language of this age, the disregard of cleanliness, the fascination of odors, and the skillful production of onomatopoetic noises. These activities are accompanied by fantasies, mainly of phallic nature, embodied in the images of adventurers, of the Captain Marvels of all breeds, of pilot heroes in fighter planes and rocket ships. The eruptions of instinctual demands are met by a disapproving superego which normally is well established at this age. In this conflict the ego resorts to many well-known solutions; defenses such as repression, reaction formation, displacement, and others are reinstated or re-enforced. They account for the development of skills and interests which carry peer approval and peer prestige, and for the many overcompensatory actions, for the multitude of compulsive behavior and obsessional thinking in order to bind anxiety. One novel solution in the service of instinct gratification makes its appearance at this time. This new device to circumvent the superego conflict stems from the social maturation during latency and is now used to unburden the feeling of guilt onto the group in general, or more specifically onto the leader as the instigator of acts of transgression (31). This group phenomenon of projected guilt feelings might be a reason for the increasing significance of group or gang affiliation during this stage. Naturally, these defenses are not always commensurate to the onslaught of instinctual demands; fears, phobias, and nervous habits make their appearance as transitory symptoms.

Two typical modes of prepubertal behavior in boys and girls throw light on the central conflict of the two sexes at this stage. The boy behaves hostilely to girls, he belittles them and avoids them; in their company he brags, boasts, and teases, he shows off and exaggerates; in essence, he denies his anxiety rather than attempts to establish a relationship. The castration anxiety which brought the oedipal phase to its decline is raising its ugly head again and forces the boy into the exclusive company of his own sex ("homosexual phase" of preadolescence.) In the girl this phase is characterized by a "thrust of activity" (8), when play acting and tomboyishness reach their height.[1] In this demonstrative denial of femininity we discern the unresolved childhood conflict of penis envy. This is the central motivating conflict of the prepubertal girl, a conflict which finds a temporary suspension so dramatic at this time when phallic fantasies have their last fling before femininity will assert itself.

Object Relation

The pivotal problem of adolescence is the problem of object relations. In fact, the outcome of this theme which undergoes many variations over the years will ultimately determine the genuine or spurious attainment of adulthood. The child's need to be loved fuses gradually with a need to love; the need to receive arouses its counterpart, the need to give; the passive role of being controlled becomes gradually and partly replaced by the child's urge for active control of the outside world. The polarity of active and passive aims re-emerges again as a crucial issue during adolescence. Before a reconciliation and mature balance is reached the extreme positions of all-active or all-passive, or more often an oscillation between both, will usually mark adolescent behavior for some time. The earliest passive dependency on the mother possesses a most alluring attraction for the adolescent of both sexes. The stronger this passive need makes itself felt, for instance in the overindulged or in the severely deprived child, the more violent becomes the defense against it by rebellious and hostile fantasies and actions; if extreme, they resemble infantile rage. This conflict, obviously, can also lead to a demanding, clinging attitude or to the renunciation of instinctual desires altogether. In fact, most often a blending of all these attempts at solving the dependency problem is observable. This seems particularly critical for the girl who has

[1] Studies of the physical growth in girls has shown that during the years preceding sexual maturation (age nine to twelve) the growth rate (weight, height) is accelerated. This fact offers a physiological correlate to the events as described (35).

to submit during her adolescent years to personal restrictions
and social controls which are enforced by the mother. The frequently severe daughter-mother conflict in adolescence is due to
the girl's fight against her infantile dependency needs and, in
addition, to her oedipal rivalry with the mother. This two-
pronged conflict reflects the girl's shift from the mother as the
original love object to the father to whom she turns with the
advent of the genital phase. The intensity of hostile emotions
concentrating on the mother can best be understood as due to
the reactivation of earlier events in the emotional life of the girl.

The oedipal conflict is normally resolved by identification
with the parent of the same sex and by the erection of a superego
more rigid and critical than in its earlier phases. The rather
stabilized period of latency lasts until the relationship to the
parent becomes upset by the recrudescence of the oedipal strivings in adolescence and throws the maturing child into the conflict of incestuous desires. The thinly disguised masturbation
fantasies of boys in which maternal figures play a dominant role
illustrate this well. The severance of the emotional ties to the
parent—which is to say, the withdrawal of cathexis from the
parent as well as from the internalized parent, namely, the superego—has far-reaching consequences for the psychic equilibrium
of the adolescent. A wave of repression sets in. "Ideas which were
tolerable enough to consciousness up to puberty—for instance,
the desire for the pleasure of parental caresses—now become repressed forever" (24). The adolescent becomes most self-conscious
about any physical contact with the parent. Whenever the incestuous impulses are acted out—always complemented by the
parents' seductive involvement—any attempt at socialization of
the adolescent has become futile because the direct gratification
of infantile wishes has made expendable both the identification
with the parent and the formation of an ego ideal as an inhibiting and guiding principle.

The adolescent's relation to his siblings should not be over-
looked among the intrafamilial changes in relationships. We
witness a new flare-up of old rivalry and jealousy, of destructive
fantasies and sexual play. In addition, the libidinous attachment
between brother and sister reaches such heights of devotion,

comradeship or sensuality that a latent incestuous relationship is often easily recognized. The same feelings lead frequently to reactive hostility and rejection.

Narcissism

During the time when instinctual drives gain in intensity and assume genital focus the withdrawal of cathexis from the parent has repercussions which will be summed up in the following remarks. The separation from the parent leaves the adolescent with the feeling of being a stranger in the family, which has lost for him its old belongingness and closeness; he lives as in separateness and exile. Object libido which has been retracted has the consequence that narcissism is markedly increased. The adolescent's concentration on his beliefs, feelings, thoughts, interests, opinions, likes and dislikes, briefly, the increasing libidinal cathexis of all personal processes ("Nobody ever felt the way I do") result in an overevaluation of the self and in a temporary impairment of the reality testing capacity. This is usually referred to as the self-absorption, the self-centeredness, the self-love of the adolescent. The defense against incestuous impulses takes the form of narcissistic isolation, of a "delibidinization of the outside world," which Anna Freud has described, emphasizing its similarity to an incipient psychosis (13).

It is only to be expected that increased narcissism leads to a revival of autoerotism with its genital focus on masturbation (27, 32). As a transitory activity to heterosexuality, masturbation is an almost universal experience. The danger for the boy lies in the passive quality of gratification which easily becomes an always present pacifier for any tension whatsoever, a state of affairs which will reduce alloplastic activity to a minimum. Every achievement becomes modeled along these lines and is expected to come as easily as masturbatory satisfaction. The danger for the girl lies in the arrestment of feminine development, which is to say, in the clitoral fixation and the concomitant phallic orientation. The ensuing unstable body image is reflected in attitudes of shifting interests, in mood swings and in fantasies not always clearly delineated from reality. Characterologically, this constellation is expressed in various forms of misrepresentations, in overambitiousness, and in waves of ecstatic activity which easily and unexpectedly fades into boredom, discouragement and discontent.

The sophistication of modern adolescents with reference to masturbation, who "know it is normal" and therefore do not experience conscious guilt feelings, is often misleading. It is not the masturbatory act but the accompanying incestuous fantasy which arouses defensive aggression, unconscious feelings of guilt, self-blame and failure.

To illustrate this point I like to mention a bright young man of eighteen who came to my attention because he was distracted, tense, and was failing in his academic work. At home he had difficulties with his mother, with whom he was constantly engaged in provocative and aggressive arguments. The father had died when the boy was five. The son now accused his mother of not having brought him up properly. The patient masturbated freely and frequently without any conscious feelings of guilt. In his masturbation fantasy an older woman would admire him and be pleased with his performance. The attachment to the mother became soon the central theme of therapy and resulted in a lessening of the incestuous bond. Following this development a change in the patient's masturbation fantasy occurred; a girl friend became his partner in heterosexual play. Concurrently, the patient's exhibitionistic behavior in the home, such as walking naked through the apartment, was given up and the violent scenes between mother and son abated. His social life became more lively and his studies improved by leaps and bounds. During this time the relationship between mother and son had become more distant and cool. The mother was inconsolably distressed over this change and giving vent to her feelings she revealed her own involvement in the adolescent struggle of her son. With the progressive detachment from the mother, masturbation became less compulsive. Nonincestuous heterosexuality opened the way to alloplasticity and the free use of intelligence.

The separation from the parent carries one last blow to the narcissism of the child. The parent becomes irrevocably divested of the exaggerated power and admirable greatness from which the child derived so much of his self-esteem. The parent is now seen in the drab proportion of reality with all the weakness and shoddiness of any mortal. This disillusionment no doubt deprives the adolescent of a major source of narcissistic gratification and, therefore, it is resisted by devious means. The first blow of this nature occurred during early childhood and was answered by the so-called "family romance" (14); the second blow gives rise to fantasies of personally won greatness, fame and success. One fantasy is a restitution projected into the past, the other into the future; the latter one might be called more realistic because the future is more open to alloplastic alterations than the past. Whenever these fantasies are modified and subjected to reality testing they form the basis for realistic achievement; otherwise they deteriorate into lasting daydreams condemning any real success to a mere shadow of those cherished fantasies which are but a reflection of an unsuccessful separation from the parent. For illustration I am citing the case of a fifteen-year-old boy. He wanted to become a famous movie actor in utter disregard of his complete unfitness for such a career. This boy was given up by his mother for adoption at the age of four and the mother had since disappeared from the child's life. In his fantasy he became the movie star, seen all over the country, and eventually by his mother who would recognize him on the screen. Due to his fame they would be reunited and his wealth would provide a luxurious life for the mother who, he was told, was so poor that she had to give away her child to people who could afford to raise it. Fantasies, more or less undisguised, play a vital part in the emotional life of the adolescent and they hold the clue to symptoms which may seem incomprehensible and often bizarre.

Ambivalence

A second consequence of the withdrawal of cathexis from the parent is the defusion of instincts. This process accounts for the emotional inconsistency and unreliability of the adolescent, for the simultaneous existence of love and hate, affection and aggression directed toward the same person. This phenomenon is called ambivalence. Before the young child establishes a stable relationship to the parent aggressive and libidinal strivings co-exist undisturbed side by side. Under the growing influence of the superego the ambivalent relationship becomes conflictuous. By the various defenses, such as repression, reaction formation and displacement, relationships acquire a different quality, namely, they become more uniform and enduring, more reliable and tempered. In adolescence this process is partly undone and a new compromise has to be achieved.

The most unsettling consequence of this state of affairs is seen in the changing influence of the superego which loses its reliability and automatic function in terms of instinct control and inhibition generally. "The ego alienates itself from the superego" (13) with the consequence that the ego ceases to clamor for the approving affection ("feeling pleased with oneself") of the inner voice called conscience. The severance actions from the parent extend into a rebellious fight against superego domination. In fact, the superego is often treated like the historical prototype in the outside world, as illustrated by a girl of eighteen who started to have sexual relations during which she thought with self-pitying satisfaction how her parents would disapprove of her action. The desire to hurt her parents was stronger than any feeling for her partner. In many asocial acts we can see how the emancipation from the parent is fought out in the realm of the superego, and in minor infractions we see the same tendency in the constant resistance to regulations as to time, place, manner, good taste, etc. In the void which is created by the estrangement at the same time from his parent and his superego the adolescent avidly clings to transient identifications ("appersonations") which lack the quality of object relations but rather serve as models whose qualities can be borrowed (13). This state of things lasts until new object relations have become genuine and the ego has developed faculties and achievements from which it derives enough legitimate narcissistic gratification to do without the libidinal dependency on the superego or the parental images for the maintenance of self-esteem. At this stage, in fact, parental and family standards are, with modification, to be sure, reinstated in the ego ideal of the maturing offspring and, thereby, the continuum between generations is assured.

The Ego at Puberty

While it is a fact that the adolescent recapitulates the conflicts and libidinal positions of early childhood, it is only partly true. The adolescent onslaught of the instinctual life encounters conditions in the individual radically different from those of early childhood: intelligence has developed, judgment and logical thinking have advanced, social understanding and altruistic love have made their appearance, physical stature and biological maturity equal more or less that of the parent and, last but not least, the synthesizing capacity of the ego has become infinitely more resourceful and complex. As Jones (24) has pointed out, these advances in ego development, including the changes in body image, must be kept in mind while assessing the recapitulation of early life which takes place so dramatically during adolescence. The child's early problems centered around the controls of the sphincters and of motility generally ("control over volitional motor outflow") while in adolescence the problem has become mainly one of the "acquirement of control over emotional outflow" (24).

In this crisis the ego takes advantage of all its resources and puts to use again those defenses which have served well in earlier life. Anna Freud has described the operation of the defense mechanisms during puberty in such clarity and her work is so well known to everybody concerned with adolescence that only a cursory reference seems in order in this exposition (13).

The danger for healthy personality development during adolescence lies in the extremes of either uncontrolled instinct gratification in which case the ego has surrendered to the id forces, or in an intensification of the latency achievements which were carried out under the influence of sexual repression, in which case "the character of the individual during the latency period will declare itself for good and all" (13). These extremes, which coincide with Bernfeld's types (4), leave the adolescent either asocial and incapable of any genuine love relationship or, on the other hand, he becomes rigidly controlled and emotionally impoverished due to the permanent maintenance of countercathexes. "Ego institutions which have resisted the onslaught of puberty without yielding, generally remain throughout life inflexible, unassailable and insusceptible of the rectifications which a changing reality demands" (13).

This changing reality which has been described at great length in the foregoing is in essence represented by sexual maturation and a new social role; both require autoplastic and alloplastic alterations if they are to bring about satisfactory solutions. An ego capable of this ideal attainment will then possess enough flexibility to admit sexual wishes to consciousness and by the same token succeed in repressing incestuous strivings; it could tolerate temporarily partial or substitute gratifications and, if necessary, postpone but not renounce genital aims. Last but not least, it would succeed in channeling psychic energy into socially valuable activities which, in turn, provide a flow of narcissistic gratification thereby keeping self-esteem at a level high enough to dispense with the retaliatory, exploitative and competitive fantasies of childhood.

The strength of the ego is a relative and not an absolute concept. This fact has a bearing on the choice and intensity of ego defenses as well as on their pathognomic character. In recognizing pubertal changes as a determining factor in the unsettling of the psychic equilibrium of the growing individual, it only follows that the rate and mode of physical maturation is of decisive significance (34, 35). Should maturation proceed over a short or long period of time, start early or late in years, result in gross body changes (obesity, height, etc.) or occur in smooth transition, the significance of these factors have to be calculated in terms of Freud's "complementary series."[2] Early and rapid maturation results in sudden and violent intensification of instinctual drives and is quite different from physical maturation which proceeds slowly and steadily with a gradual augmentation of instinctual energy. In these cases the ego is confronted with quite a different task independent of earlier development. In the slow maturing we often notice spontaneous recovery at the time when appropriate sex development takes a spurt. At the period in life when the peer group exerts a normative influence of first magnitude it is only to be expected that arbitrary peer standards can stigma-

[2] Freud has pointed out (*Introductory Lectures,* XXIII) that in the etiology of a symptom two causative factors are usually complementary, such as id strength and ego weakness, constitutional and environmental factors, etc. This is to say, for example, that it is dependent on the degree of ego weakness what increase in instinctual drive will cause anxiety or symptom formation.

tize any difference as an abnormality. Imitative behavior serves to obliterate such conditions. Pseudo adjustments of this type can be understood as attempts at changing oneself as by mimicry; this is done at the expense of the genuineness of emotions and with the result of confusion in ego identity.

Experimentation

Fantasies and thoughts as trial actions requiring the least amount of energy have a limit to their usefulness. The danger of the instinct, the strength of the ego, and the irreducible nature of reality can ultimately only be gauged by action. It is therefore a necessity that fantasies and thoughts which are the conscious representations of impulses find their externalization and are not dammed up for an unduly long time. The condition in which instinctual drives are allowed to progress to the stage of thinking or fantasizing about expression in reality (aim-directed) must not be confused with the defense in which thinking as a process itself is cathected (aim-inhibited) as is the case in intellectualization.

Such bodily changes as size, bulk, strength, proportions, etc., can be evaluated and synthesized into a new body image only by experience and action, never by thinking or learning about it. It also needs mentioning here that the adolescent confusion between role and symbol function of people can best be lifted into realistic appraisal by action and action-interchange. How many an adolescent boy, for example, fails to comprehend the designated role of figures such as a teacher or a policeman, and indiscriminately and automatically reacts to every person in authority and control as to a castrating father. The differentiated response is the result of experience and ceaseless reality testing. The experimentation with instinct, superego, and reality, the triad sources of anxiety, steers the ego toward the attainment of that "rectification which a changing reality demands" (13). The young child had the use of play to master the unintegrated or disorganizing residue of inner and outer experiences, the adolescent cannot resort to play any longer. It is reality which is the sole testing ground of the ego's preparatory solutions achieved in fantasy and thinking. The child can sit in his father's car and play at driving; the adolescent has to drive in actuality.

Prolonged Adolescence

This brings us to the present-day phenomenon of "prolonged adolescence" (Bernfeld) which refers to the fact that social consummation of maturity is being postponed far beyond its biological timing. This has the ominous consequence that adolescent transitory adjustments as described in the foregoing become firmly entrenched and solidify into character structure, thereby becoming an unalterable part of the personality. To prevent this from happening and in order to insure adaptations less rigid than those inherited from the latency period and less transient and radical than those which served their purpose during the emergencies of puberty, it is necessary for the adolescent to modify instinct gratification in harmony with his ego ideal and in cognizance of the social reality of which he feels to be a significant and responsibile part. When this has been accomplished one can say that adolescence has fulfilled its task.

TREATMENT

The theoretical discussion above has outlined the unique condition of adolescence to which treatment technique has to be adapted. In choosing content and form of the following discussion I was guided by the many case conferences, seminars and supervisory sessions which have kept me in close working relationship with social workers. These experiences have demonstrated that certain problems in the treatment of adolescents are basic, focal, and recurrent. From these conferences I have abstracted the fundamental problems of technique which represent most succinctly the contributions of psychoanalysis.

General Remarks

Puberty proves to be a critical moment in the formation and outbreak of emotional disturbances as well as in the resolution of conflicts. "Experiences in puberty may solve conflicts or shift conflicts into a final direction; moreover, they may give older and oscillating constellations a final and definitive form" (12). The psychobiological process of puberty renders the individual extremely labile, introspective and impressionable; by the same token he is also accessible to therapeutic intervention.

The treatment technique has to be maturationally determined. With reference to adolescence this means that the focal task of therapy revolves around the triad of recognition, differentiation, and integration of the self. Recognition refers to the broadened awareness of ego-dystonic and dissociated elements in feeling, thought, and cognition; differentiation refers to the development of that distinct concept of the self which defines its position in space, time, and interpersonal relations and has been described as ego identity (11). Integration alludes to that aspect of treatment in which the expanding mastery of the ego (30) lends a feeling of unity to the self and gives stability, dependability, and economy to psychic events. The maturationally oriented therapist is constantly aware of the meaning of adolescent conflict in terms of a progressive movement toward maturity. Gitelson, therefore, speaks of "character synthesis" as specific for the treatment of adolescents (16). Rather than the reconstruction of the past and its pathogenic experiences, it is their repetition in the present as reflected in the "faulty" maturational adaptations which become the center of the therapeutic effort. Several therapists (6, 16) agree that the present "ego inadequacy" is the object of therapy and "not the infantile conflict." In fact, it is not always a "conflict" which is responsible for the adolescent disturbance but to an equal degree it is the low tension tolerance which exposes him incessantly to anxiety. The treatment of the adolescent, therefore, does not singularly aim at the resolution of conflict but tries foremost to effect structural changes. By exposing the ego repeatedly in treatment to small doses of tension a gradual increase in tension tolerance is achieved. To this we usually refer as strengthening of the ego. "When the specific form of defense can be abandoned, the ego has become capable of bearing a particular kind of tension. 'Strengthening of the ego' and 'working through' are conceptions which describe very similar if not identical clinical experiences" (2).

Due to the climactic conditions which prevail in adolescence the therapeutic goal by necessity becomes limited and often specific. From this it follows that treatment of adolescents often has to have its continuation or conclusion later in early adulthood. This is especially true for those cases in which an infantile neurosis has only temporarily been kept in abeyance due to the adolescent's facility in forming identifications, and as a consequence of the sexual intensification which during puberty crowds infantile fixations for the time being into the background. Anna Freud has described such "spontaneous recovery" during puberty in the case of boys "who all through early childhood and latency fight against repressed wishes of a passive feminine kind" (13). In puberty this fight is partly fought by the ascent of masculine sexuality. It has been my experience that the therapy of the passive-feminine adolescent boy is timed best if taking place during prepuberty or after puberty when either the onrush of physiological maturation is not yet felt in full force or has abated and somewhat spent itself.

In summary, it can be stated that treatment of the adolescent maintains at all times a precarious balance between allying itself with the ego or with the instinct. In fact, technique reflects an adaptation to those shifting foci—namely, on the one hand, to the urgency of instinctual demands in finding representation in consciousness as well as externalization in reality and, on the other hand, to the simultaneous protection of the ego against the indiscriminate break-through of instinctual demands. "The therapist and the therapeutic situation must provide concomitantly and in nice balance, dependable relationship and emotional freedom, dependent security and developmental stimulation, control and ego ideal" (16). Such considerations have led to the almost universal agreement that treatment of the adolescent requires a most flexible technique (1, 16, 36).

Diagnosis

Treatment of the adolescent is a stepchild in psychoanalytic literature. The delinquent has received the lion's share of attention, and lately the schizophrenic adolescent has moved into the center of interest. However, the multitude of transient adjustment problems and neurotic difficulties, the affect disturbances and ego dysfunctions which represent the bulk of individual failures and maladaptations during puberty and the years following, are only meagerly represented in psychoanalytic discussions and case reports. These latter disturbances are diffuse and elude any descriptive order (33). The varied and bewildering symptomatology in adolescence is the result of (a) the constantly fluctuating balance between instinctual forces and ego strength, and (b) due to the incessantly changing vogue of adolescent idiosyncratic behavior (e.g., party style, language pattern) and customs (e.g., zoot-suit movement), each of which assumes a different meaning and significance within a specific social locus (e.g., urban-rural; New England-South; immigrant-native) (11).

The problem of differential diagnostic evaluation of the adolescent becomes acute in those cases in which the ego has either lost all control under the onslaught of the instincts or has erected such rigid defenses that obsessional, stereotyped or bizarre behavior ensues. The clinical picture resembles often that of schizophrenia or psychopathy. It has to be borne in mind that the psychic processes occurring during puberty are similar but not identical to those occurring in psychosis (13). Several cases reported in the literature (15, 19) were first diagnosed as schizophrenic disorders but closer investigation during therapy could not sustain the initial diagnosis. Such disturbances are described as "psychotic-like" reactions to a traumatic experience or to a severely disturbing family situation. Knight has suggested the tentative designation of "acute schizophrenia" as a "semi-serious diagnostic term in contradistinction to such terms as early or incipient schizophrenia, thus recognizing the similarity between the phenomena of severe adolescent turmoil and those of the disorder of schizophrenia."[3] Keiser has attempted a differentiation between schizophrenia and those severe reactive states in girls which clinically look so much alike. It is his opinion that "in the adolescent schizophrenic girl a certain personality growth was achieved and then regression took place. On the other hand, in the cases representing reactive states no true

---

[3] Knight, Robert P., in *Psychotherapy with Schizophrenics,* edited by E. B. Brody and F. C. Redlich. New York: International Universities Press, 1952, p. 13.

personality growth was achieved. These patients reacted merely
as disturbed children might react" (26). According to Keiser, the
"body image concept" (Schilder), namely, the excessive concentration on body parts or the obsessive preoccupation with bodily
changes, as well as the extreme rigidity of affect, as for example,
the unmitigated hate of the mother, add further useful criteria
to differential diagnosis. A careful developmental history is en-
lightening, but attention must also be paid to a possible severe
family pathology. Often only closer scrutiny of the disturbance
during therapy will clarify the diagnostic problem.

Illustration: Ben, age fourteen, a boy of good intelligence and
normal physical development, was referred by his parents because he presented a severe behavior problem at home. He had
started to terrorize his parents and when frustrated threatened
them with violence. The parents did not feel safe in his company
any longer. Ben had become abusive, jealous, and possessive of
his mother. He would kick her, pull her hair, and at other times
throw her on the bed "sitting or lying on her in a sexual way."
He wrestled with his mother, using foul language and trying to
get her down on the floor, dramatizing intercourse. Command-
ing his mother around he would yell at her: "I want you to be
my slave." He would lash her with a belt and soon after ask her:
"Let's kiss like in the movies." He had the habit of smelling his
mother's hair. He never showed signs of regret for his actions;
he stated that he would rather kill his mother to ged rid of the
whole trouble than be bothered by therapy. No complaints from
the community or the school were ever made about him.

The mother reported that she had been father and mother to
Ben because the father had been very ineffectual. Ben was
adopted when three months old. He had the "most beautiful red
hair" which the mother adored. She had spoiled the child according to her own account, fulfilling his every whim; when
older she wrestled with the boy and played baseball with him up
to his adolescence. In the evenings she recited poems to him sitting on his bed. Psychiatric examination showed the mother to
be psychotic.

Diagnostically, this boy was considered schizophrenic or a psy-
chopath. Neither proved to be correct. Upon removal from the
pathological environment to a residential treatment home where
Ben could develop more adequate identifications and controls
while in therapy, the impulsive and infantile behavior subsided
with surprising rapidity.

As soon as he was removed from his home he became anxious, afraid that he had damaged his mother so she might die. Prior to the removal from his family no anxiety nor guilt feelings were apparent in "office therapy." A follow-up after four years showed a remarkable and sustained improvement with a successful detachment from the mother and a more positive relationship with the father. A tendency toward impulsive behavior persisted. The never-abandoned oedipal attachment to the mother broke out with such violence at puberty because the intervening years of latency had never come to fruition and the normal repression of instinct never took place due to the uninterrupted sexual stimulation by a psychotic mother.

Cases of this type cannot be treated in "office therapy" but have to be removed from the pathogenic environment. Cases of the "acting out type" and those in which the ego operates exclusively in the service of the pleasure principle without conscious guilt and without anxiety, require residential treatment and are not included in the discussion on therapy. The treatment of the schizophrenic adolescent is also not considered in the following remarks.

Transference

Few adolescents come for treatment on their own accord but are by some outside agent (parent, school, police, etc.) brought to the therapist. To establish a rapport with the adolescent during the first visits is often the only chance for treatment, especially in those cases where it is not the adolescent but rather the environment which is bothered by the adolescent's symptom. The unique conditions of adolescent object relations gravitate in treatment around four basic considerations: (a) the need of the adolescent for a real, namely personal, relationship with an adult in order to stabilize his self-control at the time when withdrawal from the parent leaves him helpless; (b) the increase of narcissism which reduces any genuine responsiveness to a bare minimum; (c) the ready displacement of relationship patterns from the family to persons in the outside world; (d) the adolescent's desire or fear that the therapist will fulfill or deny his emotional needs.

Transference phenomena are ordinarily interpreted in the

treatment of adults except in strictly supportive therapy. In adolescence, similar to the condition in childhood, transference phenomena constitute an extension of still existing child-parent relationships which—it is true—undergo a profound change but have not yet reached the point of their discontinuance in reality and their relegation to fantasy. It is, therefore, possible and necessary to expose the acute child-parent conflict to direct therapeutic investigation. The inner void which is created by the separation from the parent—or better, from the parent image—can only be filled by the emotional experience which the relationship to the therapist affords. At the time of emotional impoverishment through the withdrawal of cathexis from both the outside world and from the superego it appears that emotional stimulation aroused in the first interview often elicits a strong desire for continued treatment contact. Sessions with adolescents often require a dramatic quality to restore that affective relatedness to the outside world which they are in constant danger of losing. By whichever means a positive transference can be brought about it is always utilized toward progressive mastery of the instinct and the outer world. These changes come about via the transient identifications with the therapist, at least with that part of him which is momentarily experienced by the adolescent as ego-syntonic in terms of his own ego ideal (1). An adolescent of the benign imposter type whose bluff I called very early in treatment replied with great relief: "At last, somebody can look through me!" In other words, he gained confidence that he could with the help of the therapist build his self-esteem on concrete achievements rather than on those faked qualities which were imputed to him by others.

Transference phenomena require interpretation only where they threaten to disrupt the therapeutic relationship. The work with an extremely sensitive, shy and emotionally deprived boy of seventeen was marked by many latenesses and absences until it became clear that the therapist's interest in his unhappiness aroused such strong positive feelings that the boy felt unable to cope with them during the interview. Interpretation was the only means to prevent disruption of therapy. Negative transference due to projections or as a reaction to restrictions or demands has always to be interpreted in order to prevent a break-down of the relationship.

Illustration: A fourteen-year-old boy showed great reluctance to enter a therapeutic relationship; he was negativistic and un-communicative. At the end of the first session it became apparent that he experienced a serious loyalty conflict between his present and his previous therapist. This conflict was modeled closely on his family constellation prior to the divorce of his parents. The woman therapist who had treated the boy years ago in another city had meanwhile moved to the place where he now intended to start therapy with a man. Interpretation of this conflict was however not enough; his wish to call up his previous therapist was granted and a few friendly visits followed. This early resolu-tion of a negative transference paved the way for a most fruitful therapeutic relationship.

Negative phases in treatment are mostly due to premature and consequently disturbing interpretations, to narcissistic in-juries affecting pride and self-esteem, or to wholesale permissive-ness through which the therapist becomes unconsciously identi-fied by the adolescent with his own uncontrollable instinctual de-mands (19).

In order to establish contact with the highly narcissistic adol-escent it is necessary that the therapist resemble as closely as pos-sible the ego ideal of the patient. This technical maneuver of becoming part of the adolescent's highly cathected self-image has been developed by Aichhorn (1) and since then elaborated on by others (9, 20). This approach is based on the formula: I can only love that which resembles my ideal self.

Illustration: Jack, a fourteen-year-old boy, presented the prob-lem of truancy, lying and deception. He had become uncontrol-lable but avoided any open clash by his sneaky and secretive manner. He spent most of his time in the movies. He resented being "taken" to a therapist and he was determined to outsmart him quickly. In order to buy time for further exploits he pre-tended to co-operate. During the first interview the therapist listened with interest to a recounting of movies; the disagreeable reasons for his coming were not mentioned. Finally the time for the next appointment had to be set. Jack asked if he could come at 11:00 A.M., a time which would excuse him from school since the trip to the office required an hour and a half. The therapist answered: "I see your point. But don't you think it's too obvious. If we say 1:30 it still gives you half a day off. In this way I think I can go along with your idea." He answered: "That's it! I see. 1:30 is O.K. with me." This "conspiratorial alliance" represented a relationship in which the therapist became cathected with narcissistic libido; by virtue of this fact an attachment was formed which made the therapist an important part of the adolescent's emotional life. In Jack's case this "involvement" was exploited after several weeks of treatment by telling him that he better attend school regularly; otherwise his parents and the principal would think that the therapist is "just no good and they would stop him from coming to see me." As an act of conspiracy he could return to school and his sessions could be scheduled for after school hours; a new phase of treatment had begun, namely, anxiety became manifest.

In summarizing the establishment of a narcissistic transference I like to quote Hoffer: "Aichhorn's main device seems to be arousing surprise without causing fear, establishing strength without threatening, pretending to attract without promising anything. He utilizes any weakness the adolescent may show, outdoing the impostor's tricks in cleverly conducted fantasies à deux" (20).

Active participation in the transference plays an important part in the work with adolescents. Transference phenomena, such as the belief in the magical power, good and bad, of the therapist, or the fantasy of obtaining the therapist's love by pleasing him—in short, all relationship distortions are dealt with as actualities and not necessarily traced to their infantile origin. The therapist's reaction which deliberately contrasts with the behavior of the parent has the result that the distorted parent image loses its projective universality. The therapist's reasonable, firm, and unaggressive action and attitude gradually modify the superego of the adolescent and patiently educate his ego to tolerate those tensions which growing up entails (2).

Illustration: Michael, a thirteen-year-old boy with a serious learning disability had for some time been evasive and repetitive in his play acting. Nothing of any significance happened in treatment. Michael liked the therapist and never missed an appointment. One day he was told about a conversation the therapist had had with his mother regarding his provocative and aggressive behavior with her at home. He reacted to this by talking in allusions, laughing about imaginary jokes, generally hinting at something but guarding teasingly a most exciting secret. The therapist knew that in this way Michael kept his mother in constant excitement while pretending to assert his independence from her. The mother in her narcissistic attachment to the boy could not bear to be excluded from his private life. Knowing of this constellation and recognizing the transference behavior, the therapist responded to Michael's teasing by saying, "If you think I am curious you are mistaken. I won't play detective nor will I get excited about you having secrets. I want to help you with your learning and the trouble you have at home. If you want to tell me something you will. Otherwise you may as well keep your secrets to yourself." This attitude was diametrically opposed to that of the mother. Through the manipulation of the transference, a relationship of a different character was established and it was possible to approach directly the child-mother conflict which was presently raging in reality.

Interpretation

Strictly speaking, an interpretation aims at making conscious what has been unconscious or preconscious before. In practice, however, the same term is used with reference to explanations, leading questions, inferences, as well as preparatory explorations leading up to giving interpretive insight. Staying within the narrow meaning of the word we usually make the distinction between the interpretation of ego defenses and that of id drives or their derivatives. Any instinct interpretation presupposes an ego which is capable of mastering the new insight and awareness in ego-syntonic terms. Considering the fact that the adolescent ego is relatively weak vis-à-vis the pubertal intensification of instinct and the simultaneous impact of social pressures, it follows that instinct interpretation in the treatment of adolescents with regard to timing and dosage has only a place after the ego has recovered a sufficient degree of self-confidence and adaptive resourcefulness. Therefore, the interpretive endeavor is mainly directed toward the defenses in all their minute and deceptive manifestations. In fact, many interesting leads into the instinctual life of the adolescent are circumvented and only returned to at a time when the maturity of the ego and the reliability of the superego are clearly in evidence. For example, the problem of homosexuality plays in most adolescent cases a more or less significant role because the conflict of bisexuality is part and parcel of adolescence; it is, indeed, the core of the intense identity struggle at this stage of maturation. However, not before the sex-appropriate orientation has appreciably established itself should the homosexual tendency and the related fantasies be subjected to interpretive clarification.

Illustration A (Interpretation of a defense): A thirteen-year-old boy being ten minutes late for his appointment storms into the office and shouts at the therapist: "Today I have a good excuse for being late!" The therapist asks for no explanation. During the interview the boy remarked parenthetically that he had gone to the drugstore before coming to the office. Now the therapist could interpret: "You thought I am terribly angry when you came in. So you yelled at me and shouted me down. I think you were really afraid of me for a moment." This interpretation of a defense (identification with the aggressor[4]) led after many repetitions to a better understanding of his provocative bahavior as an expression of his castration anxiety.

Illustration B (Interpretation of an instinctual drive): A fifteen-year-old girl (depressive, oppositional, learning disability) developed at home the routine of going to the kitchen after midnight to prepare hot cocoa for herself. She did this so noisily that the family had to wake up. A scene between mother and daughter followed which kept both awake for hours. The mother accused her daughter of a particularly inconsiderate behavior because the mother needed her sleep between the feedings of her baby a few weeks old. The obvious interpretation was given, namely, that the mother should feed the patient, that she should respond as kindly and nourishingly to her noisy and jealous daughter as to the screaming and hungry infant. After the all-consuming envy of the baby sister and the destructive fantasies about the mother were worked through, the girl began to identify herself with the "good mother": she took care of the baby, nursing it instead of being nursed herself. It should be added that without a very positive transference these instinct interpretations might have easily been disturbing to the girl.

[4] *Editor's note:* For a discussion of this defense, cf. Chapter 3, p. 37.

Related to the topic of interpretation are those paraphrasing comments or the selective focusing of attention ("spot-lighting") by which the therapist isolates an unusual aspect in the patient's communications, or by which he explicitly relates dissociated conscious and preconscious material (6). This type of therapeutic intervention is of particular relevance during adolescence, because during adolescence it is the rule rather than the exception that diffuse disturbances have not yet crystallized into syndromes. The maturational process forcefully keeps personality development in a state of flux. Symptoms, in fact, are often transient, changing and, generally, have not reached that stage of compromise formation which pays its tribute to the pleasure principle in the coinage of the secondary gain. These transient symptoms have not yet become an integral part of the personality. Indeed, a much larger sector of unconscious and preconscious mental content is often dangerously closer to the adolescent's awareness than is true for the latency child or the adult. By dissociation and magical thinking the adolescent avoids anxiety rather than masters it. He thereby keeps contradictory drives, wishes and ideas in consciousness side by side. This ability of the ego to tolerate discrepancies, incongruities and contradictions represents a primitive adjustment and prevents the progression toward higher integrative processes, such as the formation of defenses and sublimation. In this state of ego primitivity and ego restriction the cognitive and executive functions of the ego are necessarily impaired. The impairment is often quite selective and idiosyncratic. The result is a fragmented or scattered ego rather than a neurotic symptom. The ensuing behavior is closer to acting out than being the outcome of autoplastic alterations. In short, a condition is created which works against the unification of the ego. Treatment attempts to rectify this condition by creating manageable doses of tension or better, by consolidating diffuse anxiety into a conflict—structural or instinctual—which by dissociation or magical thinking was kept in abeyance. The unification of the ego which is stimulated by these interventions liberates psychic energy which so far has been bound up by countercathexis. By confronting the rational part of the ego with contradictions and incongruities, the synthesizing function of the ego is activated and higher levels of integrations are brought about. "The more consolidated and the more healthy the human being, the greater will be the degree of unity in his ego" (30).

The following illustrations are chosen to clarify what has been said but in no way do they represent the only approaches to this problem.

Illustration A ("Paraphrasing"): A diabetic girl of seventeen (promiscuous, neglectful of her diabetic routine, generally without aim or interest) talked during many sessions about her wish to be different, about her desire to go to school and learn something. However, indifference always prevailed in the end and a new escapade followed. I called her attention to this repetitive behavior by saying: "When I listen to you I really believe that you want to do those things you talk about (school, work, study). But you seem so completely helpless as if you had absolutely no influence on anything you do!" The patient was startled, became pensive, and then related a conversation which she had overheard at the age of eleven. It had just "popped into her mind." She overheard her grandmother say to her mother, "She'll never live to grow up." She had then been diabetic for two years. "At that moment," she continued, "I decided to get out of life as much as I could and only live for the moment." Her behavior, then, became comprehensible as a denial of her fear of death.

Illustration B ("Spotlighting"): An eighteen-year-old male adolescent began his first interview with the complaint that he felt uncontrollably angry against his father without any apparent reason. This disturbed him very much and had made him anxious and confused. He described his father as a well-meaning man for whom he expressed a great deal of affection. Toward the end of the interview the patient related that he has a girl friend whom his father does not like; in fact, he has asked his son to break off the relationship. To this the therapist commented that he, after all, had a good reason to be angry with his father. This simple and causal connection confronted the patient with an irreconcilable choice which he had circumvented by dissociation.

This case also illustrates how a conflict is created in treatment by the therapist's intentional reference to dissociated conscious mental content. This is done in order to stimulate the articulation of a conflict; furthermore, it points up the direction toward ego synthesis and, last but not least, it increases critical self-awareness without which therapy is not more than "writing on water."

Acting out

The adolescent's proclivity to action and heightened motility as well as his tendency to excesses and impulsivity are well-known facts. This maturational characteristic often drains therapy of its emotional impact and of a felt need for help. The urgency to experience one's self by action at the time when the ego has become alienated from both the outside world and the superego can be understood as an attempt at restitution. Following this train of thought it seems feasible to provide in the therapeutic situation that stimulating and dramatic quality of experience which makes acting out dispensable or at least less compelling. The problem of acting out is obviously a much larger one.

In this connection I want to mention the necessity which often arises to prohibit the adolescent from taking certain actions. If unrestricted behavior continues to furnish a continuous relief from inner tension, treatment is bound to suffer and to become empty. In fact, since acting out is so often founded on projective mechanisms and contains wild aggressive and sexual fantasies, the permissive and lenient therapist becomes a questionable ally in the struggle for maturity. Hacker and Geleerd say quite categorically: "The fact that adolescents of the acting out type do better in an atmosphere of restrictions rather than of unlimited freedom is an indisputable empirical finding" (19). Acting out is always experienced as ego-syntonic and therefore escapes self-observation (18). In some instances it can be impressed upon the patient that acting out is "a special form of remembering in which the old memory is re-enacted."[5]

Illustration: A seventeen-year-old girl had started an affair with a psychotic man and was constantly quarreling with her family about her right to go out with him. No approach to her "acting out" presented itself in the interview. One day the

[5] Fenichel, O. Neurotic acting out. *Psychoanalytic Review,* 1945.

mother and daughter became engaged in a violent argument
about housekeeping responsibilities in which the girl felt misunderstood and rejected; she left the room in a huff. The therapist said: "I know what you thought when you walked out on
your mother." "What?" "That you will sleep this week end with
Fred." "That's right," she answered. The startle effect brought
her up against a new insight which struck home. Following this
conversation she did not have relations with her boy friend, in
fact, her interest in him died down rapidly. Family conflicts
(oedipal material) began to come to the fore in the subsequent
sessions.

The Parent in Relation to Treatment

In the treatment of children the parent is never excluded
from some participation in the treatment while in adult treatment the reverse is true. With the adolescent a combination of
both is the rule. More often than not it is the parent or some
outside authority which brings the adolescent into treatment. It
is common practice not to keep secret any communication the
therapist entertains with the parent; in fact, such conversations
may be reported to the adolescent in case he so desires, or in case
it seems necessary to counteract the projective elaboration of
parent-therapist contacts. For the therapist to set his standards
or opinions against those of the parent seems less disturbing to
the adolescent than to the younger child. Indeed, it often aids
the adolescent in the critical evaluation of his parents without
the risk of a sudden loss of relationship. The therapist becomes
an ally of the adolescent's critical ego and he, so to speak, holds
out the promise that mastery of the self is possible independent
of parental love or hate. This requires infinite tact at a time of
lowered self-esteem, and a careful avoidance has to be practiced
not to let treatment slip into an infantile dependent relationship
in which the therapist plays the "good parent" who uses his
prestige in order to procure special parental favors and conces-
sions for the patient. The countertransference problem often
reaches a critical impass at this juncture.

A special parent-child constellation deserves our attention. I
refer to those cases in which the adolescent carries out the delinquent, asocial or perverse unconscious fantasies which the

parent entertains about him.[6] The defective parental standards, not necessarily overt, have their counterpart in the superego of the child and these shared defects in the otherwise intact superego constitute a bond of mutual dependency which puts an unsurmountable obstacle in the path of therapy. "The neurotic needs of the parent whether of excessively dominating, dependent or erotic character are vicariously gratified by the behavior of the child, or in relation to the child" (21). In such a constellation treatment of the parent in conjunction with that of the adolescent is always indicated.

In almost every case of an adolescent we encounter features of this problem. The solicitousness, the doubts, the checkups with which parents pursue their adolescent children with reference to their friends, their whereabouts, their habits, their thoughts and intentions, all contain parental fantasies about the child which prove "that there is an alternative to the mother's order and an alternate image of him in the mother's mind" (21). Johnson's paper lucidly describes the dynamics of superego lacunae and the problems encountered in the treatment of such cases (21).

Illustration: A thirteen-year-old boy with strong exhibitionistic tendencies took to the habit of taking off, nonchalantly, his trousers in the therapist's office whenever he could justify such action with having walked in the rain. He obviously enjoyed the partial nakedness and pranced around in his undershorts. The therapist knew that running around more or less naked at home had been a complaint of the parents who had censored this exhibitionistic display. Not until the parents had gained insight into their unconscious voyeuristic pleasure, to which the son responded with exhibitionistic compliance, could the child modify his behavior. Then, and only then, his exhibitionistic tendencies could become amenable to therapy and eventually find expression in sublimated form, such as acting and athletics.

The foregoing considerations lead necessarily to the question whether or not work with the parent of the adolescent alone can influence the family equilibrium in such a way that the child finds himself in an emotional climate more favorable to his maturational needs. Indeed, there are cases on record where the acute conflict between parent and adolescent has been propiti-

6 *Editor's note*: Cf. Chapter 5, pp. 85 ff.

ously changed by rather brief guidance of the parent alone. Such changes are possible whenever the parent can positively and lastingly identify with the therapist in terms of his own "good parent." From my association with Aichhorn I remember many cases of adolescent disturbances which he brought under lasting control solely through his work with the parent. Szurek also reports cases in which the same approach has been used successfully. He adds the cautioning remark: "All this does not exclude in every case the careful evaluation of the accessibility of the child to treatment and even offering such direct treatment for the child as a means toward this evaluation" (36).

The personality of the therapist

The treatment of the adolescent does not only require a special familiarity with this age but also a personality which is peculiarly fit for this work (1, 16, 36). Not every type of adolescent disturbance is equally well treated by the same therapist. Gitelson with candid frankness reports that he "has successfully treated a number of intellectualizing and inhibited adolescents, and has failed with the rebellious and delinquent types" (16). We all have similar proclivities to report.

The empathic and spontaneous relatedness to the adolescent's feeling life transcends mere understanding and insight. In fact, it is this very quality of the therapist's empathic participation in the adolescent's rebellious or apathetic reaction rather than his sympathetic interest—so appropriate in adult therapy—which facilitates the therapeutic contact. Aichhorn once commented on the fact that his own sublimated delinquency was responsible for that keen and intuitive grasp with which he approached his delinquent patients. It is, indeed, the therapist's achievement of mastery which eventually brings about changes in the adolescent's ego ideal. To this end the therapist maintains a twofold attitude: an empathic sharing of emotions and fantasies, and simultaneously a restraint and unyieldingness in order to transform dependent love for the therapist into identification and insight. The easy display of feelings, the ingenuity often needed to make therapy interesting enough to be continued, the shift from dramatization to interpretation, from support to demand, from humor to surprise, these shifting attitudes, always scrutinized by the therapeutic intent, are not qualities which every therapist possesses nor can acquire. Perhaps the kind of adolescence which the therapist has had himself and against which he still struggles successfully, will determine the type of adolescent patient with whom he does his best work in treatment. Gitelson's remark on this question deserves our attention: "For those who work with adolescents, the problem is complicated by the fact that the ego of each is the differentiated product of a particular total life experience. This limits the kind of interpersonal adaptation each is capable of. The type of patient each can work with may therefore be limited by his own life type" (16).

The clinical setting

There is no need to describe the well-known setup of the guidance clinic but a suggestion to its expanding design is perhaps in order. Everyone is familiar with the fact that many cases of delinquency can be discerned several years prior to the manifest condition by antecedent behavior in the school, such as reading retardation (Glueck Study). Adolescent personality disturbances also make their first appearance—certainly not always but in appreciable numbers—in circumscribed ego dysfunctions which are most easily discernible where the adolescent lives under normative group conditions, namely, in high school and college. Cases in this state of limited ego dysfunction will receive therapeutic attention only where such services are available as an intramural setting. Experience shows that only cases of most obvious need are referred to a clinic. Intramural services alone can scrutinize adolescent disturbances as to diagnosis and therapeutic measures at the time they become observable. An advantage of the intramural clinic lies in the ease with which the therapeutic contact can be renewed. A cumulative treatment process, in fact, is complementary to the abrupt maturational spurts which at various times during adolescence push into the foreground the different vectors of the total ego-integrative process (6, 29, 37). This process can be substantially aided by our deepening understanding of adolescent development if practical application keeps pace with the growth of our knowledge.

BIBLIOGRAPHY

1. AICHHORN, A. *Wayward Youth.* New York: Viking Press, 1948.
2. BALINT, M. Ego strength and education of the ego. *Psychoanal. Quart.,* 11, 1942.
3. BERES, D. and OBERS, S. J. The effects of extreme deprivation in infancy on psychic structure in adolescence. In *The Psychoanalytic Study of the Child,* 5. New York: International Universities Press, 1950.
4. BERNFELD, S. Types of adolescents. *Psychoanal. Quart.,* 17, 1938.
5. BLOS, P. *The Adolescent Personality.* New York: Appleton-Century-Croft, 1941.
6. —— Psychological counseling of college students. *Am. J. Orthopsychiat.,* 16, 1946.
7. BUXBAUM, E. A contribution to the psychoanalytic knowledge of the latency period. *Ibid.,* 21, 1951.
8. DEUTSCH, H. *Psychology of Women,* Vol. I. New York: Grune & Stratton, 1944.
9. EISSLER, K. R. Some problems of delinquency. In *Searchlights on Delinquency* (edited by K. R. Eissler). New York: International Universities Press, 1949.
10. —— Ego-psychological implications of the psychoanalytic treatment of delinquents. In *The Psychoanalytic Study of the Child,* 5. New York: International Universities Press, 1950.
11. ERIKSON, E. H. Ego development and historical change. *Ibid.,* 2, 1946.
12. FENICHEL, O. *The Psychoanalytic Theory of Neurosis.* New York: W. W. Norton & Co., 1945.
13. FREUD, A. *The Ego and the Mechanisms of Defense.* New York: International Universities Press, 1946.
14. FREUD, S. Three contributions to the theory of sex. In *The Basic Writings of Sigmund Freud* (translated by A. A. Brill). New York: Modern Library, 1938.
15. GITELSON, M. Direct psychotherapy in adolescence. *Am. J. Orthopsychiat.,* 12, 1942.
16. —— Character synthesis: the psychotherapeutic problem of adolescence. *Ibid.,* 18, 1948.
17. GREENACRE, P. The prepuberty trauma in girls. *Psychoanal. Quart.,* 19, 1950.
18. —— General problems of acting out. *Ibid.*
19. HACKER, F. J. and GELEERD, E. R. Freedom and authority in adolescence. *Am. J. Orthopsychiat.,* 15, 1945.
20. HOFFER, W. Deceiving the deceiver. In *Searchlights on Delinquency* (edited by K. R. Eissler). New York: International Universities Press, 1949.
21. JOHNSON, A. M. Sanctions for superego lacunae of adolescents. In *ibid.*
22. —— and FISHBACK, D. Analysis of a disturbed adolescent girl and collaborative psychiatric treatment of the mother. *Am. J. Orthopsychiat.,* 14, 1944.
23. —— and SZUREK, S. and FALSTEIN, E. Collaborative psychiatric treatment in parent-child problems. *Ibid.,* 12, 1942.

24. JONES, E. Some problems of adolescence. In *Papers on Psychoanalysis*. Baltimore: Williams & Wilkins, 1948.
25. JOSSELYN, I. M. Psychological problems of the adolescent girl. *Soc. Casework*, May-June, 1951.
26. KEISER, S. Severe reactive states and schizophrenia in adolescent girls. *The Nerv. Child*, 1, 1944/1945.
27. LAMPL-DE GROOT, J. On masturbation and its influence on general development. In *The Psychoanalytic Study of the Child*, 5. New York: International Universities Press, 1950.
28. LANDER, J. The pubertal struggle against the instincts. *Am. J. Orthopsychiat.*, 12, 1942.
29. MCBEE, M. A. A mental hygiene clinic in a high school. *Ment. Hyg.*, 1935.
30. NUNBERG, H. The synthetic function of the ego. In *Practice and Theory of Psychoanalysis*. New York: Nervous and Mental Disease Monographs, 1948.
31. REDL, F. Group emotion and leadership. *Psychiatry*, 5, 1942.
32. REICH, A. The discussion of 1912 on masturbation and our present-day views. In *The Psychoanalytic Study of the Child*, 6, 1951. New York: International Universities Press.
33. SPIEGEL, L. A. A review of contributions to a psychoanalytic theory of adolescence. In *ibid*.
34. STOLZ, R. and STOLZ, L. M. *Somatic Development of Adolescent Boys*. New York: Macmillan Company, 1951.
35. STUART, H. C. Normal growth and development during adolescence. *New Engl. J. Med.*, May 1946.
36. SZUREK, S. A. Some impressions from clinical experience with delinquents. In *Searchlights on Delinquency* (edited by K. R. Eissler). New York: International Universities Press, 1949.
37. ZULLIGER, H. Psychoanalytic experiences in public-school practice. *Am. J. Orthopsychiat.*, 10, 1940 and 11, 1941.

Chapter 11

THE CONTRIBUTION OF PSYCHOANALYSIS TO THE RESIDENTIAL TREATMENT OF ADOLESCENTS

RAYMOND SOBEL, M.D.

The treatment of adolescents in a residential setting presents many difficulties which are not present in the usual mental hygiene clinic or social agency program. First, the nature of the symptomatology is quite different. The very factors which have necessitated placement in an institution are usually such that the adolescent has been in difficulties with society. For the most part, such adolescents are either committed by the Court because of the legal nature of their social disfunctioning or else they have been placed by their parents or guardians who have been unable to handle them. Delinquent behavior and acting out of aggressive, antisocial or dissocial impulses are usually seen in by far the large majority of adolescent boys. There are much fewer children admitted to institutions who present withdrawal, detached or bizarre behavior; and if the symptomatology is that of adult clinical psychosis, such as panic, hallucinations, loss of reality testing, etc., such adolescents are usually treated within the framework of a mental hospital rather than an institution for children. As far as the girls are concerned, the most common symptomatology presented at intake is that of asocial rather than antisocial behavior. As is to be expected in view of the mores of our society, sexual difficulties play a larger role with the girls than with the boys. Then, too, aggressive behavior of the girls is usually, but not always, confined to the home.

The acting out of antisocial behavior on the part of both boys and girls is in itself a source of hostility, provocation, and antagonism to the adult world, and it is this fact, namely, that they have been unable to function within the framework of normal society, which has removed them from clinic treatment.

The case of a fourteen-year-old girl is illustrative: The product of a shotgun marriage, she had been rejected from the time of her conception. Both parents focused on her their long-standing dissatisfactions with living and clearly gave her a Cinderella-like role in comparison to her baby sister. Escape into precocious maturity was facilitated by an earlier than usual pubescence. Following the discovery that she was attractive to boys, the girl quickly made use of this knowledge to bolster her inadequate sense of worth and self-esteem. She gravitated toward a fast set of companions from whom she received prestige and status because of her reputation for being wild. Late hours, the intimation of sexual promiscuity, and the inevitable truancy from school precipitated scenes and crises at home which eventually led to psychiatric treatment in the community mental hygiene clinic. Although she attended her therapeutic sessions regularly, the therapist could not compete with the unhealthy satisfactions derived from the acting out of her neurotic conflicts. The vicious circle of this teenager's life spiraled finally into almost complete loss of self-control. Runaways, elopements, and overt sexual promiscuity necessitated an environment with greater limits than could be provided at home. Individual therapy was terminated and the girl was placed in a residential treatment center.

A second feature which differentiates these adolescents from those treated at home is their lack of motivation for change. The children who are institutionalized usually suffer from the more severe personality disorders. I refer more specifically to the groups of mental illnesses variously referred to as primary behavior disorder, sexual perversion, psychosis, character neurosis, psychopathic personality, infantile personality, and the like. With the exception of psychosis (and henceforth I shall refer to childhood psychosis and schizophrenia interchangeably) *society* suffers more from the adolescent's symptomatology than the adolescent himself; although treatment invariably shows that suffering actually is present in the client, but it is unconscious. In more classic psychoanalytic terminology, institutionalized adolescents usually present ego-syntonic symptomatology and the task of treatment is to make it ego-alien. Parenthetically, when this goal is reached, the client is usually ready for discharge, although it is at this point that collaborative psychotherapy first becomes possible. A sixteen-year-old boy who had been committed by the Court because of "mugging" and stealing from the victims, confided to his social worker that he felt he was "getting soft" because he had begun to feel ashamed of his antisocial behavior. At the same time he began to show manifest resistance to attending his psychotherapy interviews and it soon emerged that not only did he *not* wish to change his mode of living, but he looked upon such change with considerable fear and anxiety. This boy had been using interpersonal violence as a defense against any possibility of friendliness, intimacy, and closeness. These more tender integrations were, for him, the most threatening types of experience imaginable. It is therefore not at all surprising that collaborative treatment (in which the client commits himself to a joint goal with the therapist) is difficult with individuals such as he, and the process of working together is late in development.

Although schizophrenia in adolescence is being diagnosed with ever increasing frequency, the attachment of such a diagnostic label to a child often routes the sufferer into a mental hospital rather than to a treatment institution for children. Despite the fact that traditionally such cases are labeled "hopeless" or "very difficult to treat," it has been my experience and that of others in residential work that the schizophrenic adolescent, if he can be contained outside of a closed ward, is usually more amenable to and desirous of collaborative psychotherapy and change than is the allegedly less disturbed adolescent with a character neurosis. It is not at all uncommon to hear such seriously ill boys and girls request extra interviews which they use constructively. This is a relatively rare occurrence in the character and personality pattern disturbances of primary behavior disorder and psychopathic personality.

Another feature which dynamically differentiates "institutional" adolescents from "clinic" adolescents is the authoritative and often custodial nature of their placement. The relationship of the social worker in a Child Guidance Clinic to her client is basically nonauthoritative and to that extent it acts as a neutral ground for eliciting the child's irrational modes of relationship to authority. This is particularly enhanced by the factual absence of authority in the relation of client and therapist. This absence of authority brings out in bold relief the inappropriateness of the adolescent's projected attitude by which he endows the therapist or the clinic with attributes originally derived from the significant adults of his past and present. The perception of this inappropriate response on the part of the client—or, to put it differently, the awareness of his transference—is the feature of the relationship producing a change and allowing a rational and appropriate reaction to authority. Through the medium of his relationship with the therapist, the client learns that indiscriminate hostility to adults is a useless and handicapping mechanism which he is best rid of. However, for the adolescent who has been placed in institutional care, the social worker plays a combination of roles, among which is the important one of rational authority and control. In contrast to her colleague working in the community, the institutional worker is often the delegated authority, the representative of "staff," of rules and regulations. This sometimes occurs to such an extent that it renders the clinic worker therapeutically helpless. For example, the girl who has been placed in a school against her will knows full well that the worker plays a vital role in determining her length of stay in the institution or is decisive in obtaining certain privileges or material things for her. The therapeutic relationship is modified accordingly, with predominantly negative feelings being much more easily transferred to the worker from past significant adults. The residential worker has to resolve not only the client's "tailormade" transference of irrational attitudes toward authority but also her own counterreaction. Due either to their own past misfortunes and bad experiences with authority or to preconceptions derived from other sources, many workers react to their stated institutional role either with denial of their authoritative position or with wielding of their power over the client in an unhealthy fashion. The effects upon the adolescent are clearly predictable: hostile impulses are acted out in either case. In the former it is because of lack of external controls, in the latter it occurs as a reactive gesture of defiance and rebellion.

Very often this authoritative role is even more accentuated than I have indicated. Such is the case among institutions, training schools and reformatories, which are primarily custodial and in which psychiatric treatment (if present at all) functions as if it were "slapped on" to the rest of the program. More often than not, the lack of personnel, the resistance of the staff to change, and the discouraging unwillingness of the client to co-operate, all combine to produce in the mind of the worker a counterreaction of hopelessness and resignation. It is frequently this counterreaction, or poor morale, rather than the case material, which prevents the development of an adequate treatment program under these circumstances.

In addition to the differentiating features mentioned above, the adolescent who has been placed in an authoritative but not necessarily custodial institution rarely has had the opportunity to make the decision of placement himself. The use of power beyond his control usually stimulates an ambivalent reaction of relief from tension and hostility. The relief from tension derives from many sources, the most important of which follow:

First, a sense of security derived from intuitive knowledge that the institution allies itself with the healthy parts of the ego in maintaining control. To a large extent the adolescent has been the victim of forces beyond his conscious influence, forces which are not only destructive to others but also to himself. Such adolescents suffer a double sense of shame and self-contempt as a result: first, because they have truly lost control despite their allegation that "they planned it that way"; and secondly, because their behavior produces guilt—unless they are true psychopathic personalities. It is infinitely reassuring to the boy or girl to know that the "staff" will not allow the acting out of destructive impulses and that they will help to keep such impulses under restraint. It is this tacit insight into the nature of the institution that produces the so-called "miraculous cures" in which a heretofore violent teenager suddenly becomes a quiet, conforming member of the residential school community. Once anxiety over the fear of loss of control is in abeyance, there is no need to strike out!

Secondly, alleviation of guilt occurs. Most children, regardless of preparation, view residential treatment as punishment for badness or bad behavior. In those cases where conscience structure is intact or exaggerated, guilt plays a large role in the genesis of the disturbed behavior. For others, whose feelings of worthlessness are poignantly severe, it is better to be blamed for something they do rather than for what they feel they are. Correspondingly there arises a need to divert attention from one's feelings of self-contempt and worthlessness to bad behavior. Placement often "solves" this conflict by resolving the guilt through the feeling of expiation and by making it unnecessary to behave badly.

Thirdly, there is sanctioned gratification of unconscious dependency needs. Most adolescents in residential treatment centers have a central problem of conflict around dependence—independence which has been distorted into a submission-domination frame of reference. They are vitally afraid of dependence of any kind: real, imagined, healthy, neurotic; and have developed elaborate techniques of overcompensation through irrational self-assertion and rebellion (gangster identification) or have evolved similarly complicated rationalization and plausible justification of their dependency gratification (psychosomatic illness, excessive demands). Placement allows such needs to be satisfied, to a certain extent, through the medium of the impersonal sheltering arm of the institution. Finally, the adolescent has a sense of relief upon placement when he realizes that for the first time there is a disinterested party who has no personal stake in his behavior or problem—namely, the institutional staff. This is felt as a distinct improvement over the previously vicious spiral of guilt—acting-out—guilt.

On the other hand, the adolescent feels justifiably hostile to his institution for he considers that it makes him a prisoner, deprives him of his civil rights and, most horrible of all, removes him from his home, his friends and his school. The difficulties he has recently encountered in all of these relationships tend to dissolve in a roseate haze of wish fulfillment within a short time after placement. An unconsciously determined retrospective falsification sets in rather speedily, depending upon the degree of wishful thinking there was to begin with, and it is at this point that therapeutic difficulties often mount. But before continuing with the specific problems encountered in residential treatment, I would like to mention two additional factors which make it quite different from outpatient therapy. First, the adolescent who lives within an institutional framework comes from a family situation in which the parental conflict is more severe. In most instances the placement is the culmination of repeated unsuccessful efforts by parent and child to effect some sort of peaceful living situation. By the time the case comes to an agency or clinic there have usually been repeated crises and reconciliations, and all methods of resolving the problem have failed, including psychotherapy as well. The residential worker is familiar with the phrase "treatment within the present home situation is impossible." Secondly, the most important feature of residential treatment of children in the adolescent age group lies in the very nature of residential treatment itself as contrasted to the hospital. According to medical tradition, the hospital has always been a place in which treatment was administered to the sick patient; the mental hygiene clinic is part of that tradition, being originally and in many instances still a part of the hospital. Residential treatment differs from this concept in that the institution as a whole is planfully used as a treatment instrumentality for a person rather than being a geographic area in which individual psychotherapy is applied. It must be made explicit at this time that the institution as used here really is not the bricks and the mortar but comprises those individuals who staff it, who are its personnel. Accordingly, residential treatment is a basically multidisciplined approach in which everybody in the institution is viewed as a therapeutic instrument. It must be emphasized that this does not mean that each staff member is a therapist! With such an orientation inculcated and presented to the staff through in-service training and other educational measures, many pressures toward change can be brought to bear upon the adolescent in a planful fashion. In by far the larger proportion of cases, due either to the lack of individual psychotherapy or to unresponsiveness of the adolescent to vis-à-vis treatment, the institution itself, the milieu, must be the primary treatment process. This is in contrast to individual psychotherapy where the process of change is effected mainly through the exploration of the mutual relationship of patient and therapist and environmental manipulation is a secondary consideration. When one considers the environment in residential treatment, one must consider four separate categories of influence; personnel, program, school and work. These four areas in which the child lives are the points at which intervention can be made operative; points at which pressure can be brought to bear so that there will be a change in the customary modes of living. It is said that residential treatment offers a variety of "emotional climate" controls unavailable elsewhere. By utilizing the firmness of one cottage couple, the easygoing qualities of another, and the strict but fair authoritarianism of a third, the therapist can create a frame of reference which selectively can bring forth or at least stimulate the heretofore latent tendencies toward mental health within the child. Thus the personnel of the institution as they function in their roles as cottage parents, plumbers, psychiatrists, and social workers constitute the front line of attack upon the client's maladjustment.

The second point at which milieu or the institution as a whole is used as treatment (rather than as a place for treatment) is encountered in the "program." Every public school has a program demarcated by bells and classroom changes; by schedules and vacation; every home has such a program, too, although not so well defined; and in the homes of children placed for residential treatment, the home "program" has always, without exception, been distorted or disorganized. On the other hand, the institution provides a structured type of living which supplants, by virtue of the separation, the tides of life which have been disorganized or lacking in one form or another at home. The child is swept along in movements which have been established for the entire institution and in which variations have been planned specifically for him. His cottage rises at a certain time; they go to breakfast at a certain time; the cottage goes to class; there are "line-ups," assemblies, and the like. The disorganized adolescent is involved in these structured and organized activities without the use of authoritative methods, in contrast to his previous experience where coercion was the rule. Whereas previously the environment was either too loosely, too rigidly, too inconsistently modulated for mental health, the planned use of program ranging from cottage chores to summer recreation, constitutes a reparative process which counters the effects on the client of previous social disorganization at home and in the community. More technically stated, programming gives a feeling of durability, consistency and continuity to the child's relationships which can be incorporated into his ego structure.

A fifteen-year-old boy with a long history of successive and temporary foster home placements was admitted to the institution because of aggressive behavior. Nuclear in his many difficulties in living was his marked feeling of transience and of the impermanency of all relationships. Originally given a diverse and swiftly moving program involving a multiplicity of clubs, academic work, and extracurricular activity, he showed but little change in his characteristically hostile mode of relationship. However, when it became apparent that his needs were best met by a program involving the least amount of change, he was assigned to the storeroom where the tides of movement were slow, predictable, and of low amplitude. With this more comfortable environment there was considerable alleviation of anxiety with the net result that he was more accessible to other elements in the program which stimulated his drive toward health.

Just as the program is used in a planful fashion to give uniqueness or diversity of life experience to a child, the classroom should be similarly incorporated into the total treatment plan. Most adolescents who must reside in institutions have had school difficulties of one sort or another, depending upon the basic nature of their disturbances in interpersonal relationships. Those whose core of trouble is with authority present disruptive classroom behavior and rebellious truancy. Others who have learned to avert anxiety by projection and paranoid mechanisms are unable to learn save in one-to-one teacher-pupil situations. These children have a long history of blaming others—their peers, their parents, their teachers: everybody except themselves—for their behavior in school and for the most part exhibit an astounding ability to ignore reality. As a consequence of their loss of the capacity for self-criticism and their inability to admit a mistake, trial-and-error learning is almost totally shut off from them and a highly individualized learning program becomes necessary in order to overcome this disability. Additionally, the teacher must be considerably more self-aware than usual in order to tolerate the pupils' hostility.

Still other children whose self-contempt and feelings of worthlessness have taken a masochistic and spiting turn use academic failure to punish themselves and to get even with or frustrate those adults who hold out scholastic aspirations for them. Typical of such a case was the adolescent son of an upper middle-class business man whose life's aspirations to be a doctor had been consistently frustrated by economic circumstances which had prevented his attendance at college. Viewing his son almost directly as an extension of himself, he hammered away at the goals of scholastic success in an unconscious attempt to live his life over again in his progeny. As might have been expected, the boy made a minor career out of failure in school, partly as a passive rebellion against his father's failure to treat him as a person in his own right and partly in a self-punishing maneuver which alleviated some of his guilt over hostile impulses to father.

In addition to the above-mentioned general groupings of educational problems, there is a small but extremely important group of uneducable children who are unable to tolerate any situation in which they are pupils. It is with such problems that the multi-disciplined approach is not only indicated but mandatory. The teacher working within a treatment institution is faced with a group of adolescents whose emotional disturbances have left them with learning blocks as well as severe gaps in their knowledge. Therefore the school work must be correlated with the rest of the treatment plan. The teacher also must have an awareness of the symbolic meaning that his role plays in the unconscious of the student, for without such understanding he will probably be unable to withstand the onslaught of hostility transferred to him from other significant adults of the adolescent's past.

Often it is in the classroom that a salutory experience in group living is begun for the adolescent. Many boys and girls in this age group have successfully acted out their distorted and irrational impulses and drives in other school situations, and it is not at all uncommon to see teen-agers who have never yet had a satisfactory and satisfying classroom learning experience because of their remarkable ability to provoke counterhostility from their classmates or their teachers. The therapeutically and analytically oriented school program attempts to counter the vicious cycle of hostility—retaliation—renewed hostility, by integrating its own program into the treatment program as a whole. This is accomplished in some institutions through workshops, in others by more didactic in-service training, and finally by combined staff meetings on particular problems or in case discussions of specific children.

The last of the well-defined entities in an environmental treatment program is the planned use of work as a therapeutic modality. Every one of the children in residence suffers from poor work habits, which in turn have their roots in the lowered self-esteem universally prevalent in the group. If one does not possess self-respect, it is impossible to respect that which one does and hence one does not attempt to do things consistently or well. This is invariably reflected first in the mastery of the physical world and manifests itself in job and work failure. It is at this point that another of the vicious cycles mentioned above begins. The failure is experienced as further proof of one's worthlessness; self-esteem is further lowered; the possibility of future recovery is diminished. Failure piles on failure and unless the cycle is broken, one sees avoidance of work in order to escape the anxiety and self-contempt engendered by failure. Work assignments are therefore graded according to the degree of personality organization and according to the educational limitations of the child, as determined by the psychologist.

A previously severely disturbed but recovering prepsychotic girl was assigned by her counselor to an off-grounds job requiring considerable initiative in the community. Relatively little supervision was available due to extrinsic factors. What was *not* known at the time was the fact that the girl was countering her anxiety by obsessive and compulsive mechanisms which made independent decisions almost impossible for her and which involved a compulsive, perfectionistic attention to detail on her part. By preoccupying herself throughout her waking hours with thoughts such as, "Shall I cross my right leg over my left, or my left over my right?" or "Does the eraser belong in the left or the right hand drawer of the desk?" the girl had successfully avoided the experience of personal mental dissolution with which she felt threatened. However, she could not carry out any generalized plan of action. Due to the particular form of her difficulty in living and to her already weakened ego structure, the girl was unable to handle the responsibility and was incapable of completing any task. Considerable feelings of anxiety were aroused by the situation, with an ensuing exacerbation of her obsessional defense mechanisms. She felt the failure as reflecting her own worthlessness and also considered it as letting down her counselor on whom she had projected her own perfectionistic aspirations. A minor crisis eventuated with the loss of this job but individual psychotherapy together with assignment to more concrete, highly supervised and routine work was able to restore her previous equilibrium.

Work can also be used planfully to assign social roles which give meaning to the adolescent's concept of self. In every institution there are status- and prestige-laden roles determined by the type of work one does. The work in turn reflects the attitudes of staff and others significant to the adolescent. In most institutions working or studying off-grounds constitutes a sign of approval and tends in and of itself to restore lost self-confidence or self-esteem. Tendencies toward masculine and feminine identification may be strengthened by satisfying work assignments in the manly or womanly occupations, through incorporation into the ego of the social roles that are associated with them. The sublimatory value of work is a subject for several chapters and is beyond the scope of this resume. Therefore I shall proceed with the other main aspects of the therapeutic program, namely, individual and group psychotherapy.

Psychoanalytically oriented psychotherapy is essentially the same process whether practiced in an office, outpatient clinic or residential treatment institution. Generally speaking, it consists of a planned intervention by the therapist into the unhealthy modes of interpersonal relationship of the client or patient; such intervention being derived from a psychoanalytic theory of personality, the skills for its application having been arrived at through adequate training. An understanding of the unconscious motivations for behavior, of the roles played by the significant adults of the client's past in the formation of these difficulties, and of the therapists' own participation in them are basic essentials. The difference between it and group psychotherapy is a matter of considerable theoretical discussion which would be inappropriate here. Suffice it to say that individual and group psychotherapy are conducted in the same fashion as in a clinic setup with the notable exception of the authoritative role of the therapist and the necessity of communication with multiple staff members. As mentioned previously, such a role predisposes toward certain types of transference and countertransference problems. Moreover, the presence of a larger number of participants in the plan makes for somewhat different requirements of the therapists' personality and technique. In the usual mental hygiene clinic the worker is subject mainly to the following interpersonal pressures: the needs of his patient; the needs of the significant adults of the patients' life; his own and his supervisor's needs. On the whole there are relatively few occasions where administrative personnel are brought into the treatment as active participants, particularly in any disciplinary sense. In milieu therapy, such situations are the rule and the worker is likely to have conferences in the course of a day with cottage parents, teacher, recreational director, attendance officer, storeroom keeper, supervisor of cottage parents, director of institution, psychiatrist, supervisor of therapy, group therapist, and a few others; not to mention answering letters to out-of-town social agencies who have placed children in the institution and a few telephone calls to and from parents of children regarding their visits home, spending money, and new shoes. The individual worker in a residential situation is often *in loco parentis* in that he ensures that the physical needs of the child are met. Frequently it is this tangible meeting of needs in the concrete form of shopping for a new suit or obtaining a special home visit, when indicated, that paves the way for the development of a collaborative therapeutic relationship. However, if the worker's own maternal needs are unsatisfied, there is more chance for these needs to produce demands upon the client which cannot be met and which may be returned with malevolence. The role of being *in loco parentis* can thus be a countertransference pitfall, encouraging those unconscious needs of the worker which, used in moderation, promote change but which, used in excess, produce hostile striking out.

Although vis-à-vis psychotherapy is immensely important in the cure of any given child within a residential treatment center, the focus of this paper must remain on those factors in the environment which promote change in the direction of mental health. Some of these factors are specific to institutional life alone, others are enhanced or accented by group living. The first that I shall discuss is one which has immediate increased security as its primary result. This is the fact that the institutional cultural identification is one of "difference" from the "outside." (We are all here because we are "bad boys," "neglected," "emotionally disturbed.") Accordingly, the different person has a greater chance to be different, to exhibit his symptomatology— without anxiety. In this sense the milieu of residential treatment provides the same function as the mental hospital, or, to paraphrase the late William Alanson White, "A mental hospital is a place where a patient can be crazy in comfort." It is this cultural acceptability of difference which diminishes anxiety and which, therefore, renders the individual more susceptible to self-awareness and the development of newer, more constructive patterns of living.

Another factor which allows for healthy change is the fact that within a psychiatrically oriented treatment institution, understanding and awareness of the children's problems always diminishes the general level of irritability of the staff. This, in turn, diminishes the children's need to provoke the adults, and a benign cycle is often begun in this fashion, though seemingly without any visible cause. No staff person can work and live in a therapeutic milieu without assimilating something of "the therapeutic attitude." It is harder to be angered when this attitude has taken root. Along with this diminished level of counterhostility on the part of a multiplicity of adults (in contrast to the single person of the individual therapist), planned recreation provides an increased opportunity for the sublimation of socially inacceptable impulses. At home the disturbed adolescent either obtained direct gratification of impulse through sexual promiscuity or vandalism, or else withdrew from facilities for adolescents which might provide sublimatory or substitute satisfaction. Teen-age canteen or extracurricular high-school activities either were avoided by him or were entered into only to be met with by rejection at the hands of his peers. It is in this aspect of residential living that the therapeutic team serves the same function for the adolescent that a good mother does for her three-year-old at a birthday party: she ensures protection from rebuff and insures some satisfaction through guided participation with the other children. As a result of planned opportunities for sublimation for children in residence, several salutory events occur and they are less prone to the development of loss of control over impulses, due to the decreased pressure of their destructive or socially inacceptable impulses. This has been brought about through their displaced discharge in dancing, sports, etc. In a similar fashion such energies can be drained off through planned work.

Among other features which seem to have a bearing upon the growth toward health in institutional treatment is the setting of limits. One of the most familiar pictures in social work are the parents whose adolescent children have them "over a barrel," so to speak; who have been victimized by their own inability to take a firm stand, to set the limits of behavior. In residential treatment we consider this as one of our main therapeutic considerations and, at Hawthorne Cedar-Knolls School, we have developed what we call "The Accordion Principle of Limits." For those adolescents whose character structure is chiefly inhibited and constricted, e.g., obsessive compulsive, limits are set loosely. For those whose personalities are poorly organized such as schizophrenics and severely anxious children, the limits are set quite tightly. This is relayed to the staff in the form of a therapeutic prescription which carefully delineates throughout the child's daily living the kind of controls which will be imposed upon him from without. And in the same fashion as the accordion expands and contracts with its content of air, so does the prescription for control, depending on the changes within the personality. A recovering schizophrenic is given greater latitude about the routines of living as he develops the inner direction necessary to carry out a 9:00 bedtime by himself. And as he grows more in this direction, he may be allowed to set his own sleeping schedule. This "accordion principle" tends to diminish the anxiety engendered by the fears of loss of self-control and to avoid rebellious acting out because of repressive authority-laden restrictions.

Last and probably the most important of the factors in residential treatment which promote health is the factor of breaking the vicious cycle between the adolescent and the significant adults of his home life.

A fifteen-year-old girl with a severe neurosis, close to psychotic breakdown, was brought to the attention of the Court because of her physical abuse of her mother. Both parent and child were seen diagnostically and it soon became apparent that the child's attacks upon the mother were almost deliberately provoked by the latter. Further study of this family revealed that the mother had a long history of masochistic behavior including final desertion by her alcoholic and brutal husband. That the daughter's behavior served the mother's neurotic needs to be punished became increasingly clear as did the necessity to break up this sado-masochistic integration, if either were to recover from their disturbances. Ordinary foster care was ruled out by the severity of the daughter's disturbance in that her need to tie herself up into such symbiotic partnerships was not only unconscious but also exceedingly powerful. Once placed in a treatment center her indiscriminate need to control and hurt others became manifestly inappropriate to her as well as others inasmuch as the environment refused to complement her sadistic drives. At this point severe anxiety developed for the first time and precipitated her into a search for relief in the psychiatric clinic of the school. It is interesting to note that prior to this time she had been unsuccessfully brought into psychotherapy on several occasions.

It was not until the mutually supporting neuroses were separated, as it were, that therapy could be begun in any constructive fashion.

In a similar way, other mutually interacting unhealthy integrations are dislocated and ended by residential treatment. In contrast to simple separation such as providing board and lodging and possibly case work services, residential treatment offers a contrapuntal device which engenders change. It is contrapuntal in that the planning team has available to it a variety of emotional climates which it can utilize as a counterpoint to the neurotic or irrational integrative tendencies of the adolescent. A child whose main mode of maintaining his security has been to seek domination and then to rebel against it, is no further advanced when he is assigned to a cottage whose structure is along strict authoritarian lines. However, when placed in a cottage where there is no hierarchy of authority and where competitiveness, status and prestige are not very important to the adult, his attempts at power struggles are brought out as distinctly unnecessary; and if insight comes, such attempts are recognized as belonging to the past. As observed in one boy's instance, it became quite embarrassing to him to discover that he was tilting at windmills in his efforts to endow his mild-mannered work supervisor with the attributes of his sadistic stepfather. Similarly, those adolescents who have developed the ability to deny the rough realities of existence in order to avoid facing their own hostility to it have considerable trouble in maintaining such defenses in the face of cottage crises which obviously should have made them angry. This ability to place the client or patient in a milieu which minimally participates in his illness is the unique feature of residential treatment. By using the various personnel, roles, and cultural standards of the institution in a planful way, the therapeutic team can expose the adolescent to new types of living experience which he cannot ward off by seduction, hostility, denial, paranoid projection, and a host of other defensive maneuvers, because the environment, the staff, refuses to be seduced, restrains itself from counterhostility, faces the adolescent with the truth, and through their actions disavows the projected blame. The anxiety engendered by these new experiences is the anxiety of recovery and it paves the way for change.

Before concluding, a word or two is necessary concerning aftercare. Most adolescents who have been placed by the community take a long time to reach the point of independent motivation toward change. Quite often, if they do attain this level, they have reached an age at which the residential center can no longer contain them. This is due most commonly either to their physical maturity and the needs thereof of sexual gratification, self-support and independence, or is due to the danger of developing an "institutional personality" characterized by passive dependency upon authority. Prolonged institutional stay is bad for the adolescent on both counts, yet the therapeutic process is not completed. It is at this point that discharge must occur to the "outside," to the real world, and aftercare begun. Yet in almost every residential program this is the weakest link in the chain of therapy and in some, it is totally lacking. Aftercare is always necessary. At times it marks the beginning of psychotherapy as defined above. At others, it is a period of consolidation of insights learned in the residential treatment process.

Summary

Residential treatment of emotionally disturbed adolescents is a necessarily multidisciplined approach. Psychoanalysis brings to it an understanding of the unconscious sources of the behavior not only of the adolescent and his family but of· the residential treatment process itself. Using such knowledge in a planful fashion by conditioning the interpersonal environment to promote change in the direction of mental health is the essential feature of the residential approach. The manipulation of the environmental field is accomplished primarily through the use of theoretical knowledge of the unconscious transference and countertransference reactions of the adolescent, his peers, and of the institutional staff, including the individual therapist.

BIBLIOGRAPHY

1. AICHHORN, A. *Wayward Youth*. New York: Viking Press, 1935.
2. ALT, H. The role of the psychiatric social worker in the residential treatment of children. *J. Soc. Case Work*, 1952.
3. BETTELHEIM, B. and SYLVESTER, E. Therapeutic influence of the group on the individual. *Am. J. Orthopsychiat.*, 17:684-692, 1947.
4. ――― ―― ―― A therapeutic milieu. *Am. J. Orthopsychiat.*, 18:191-206, 1948.
5. ――― ―― ―― Milieu therapy: indications and illustrations. *Psychoanal. Rev.*, 36:54-68, 1949.

6. —— *Love Is Not Enough.* Chicago: The Free Press, 1950.
7. JEWISH BOARD OF GUARDIANS. Conditioned Environment in Case Work Treatment. New York: 1944.
8. KRUG, O. The application of principles of child psychotherapy in residential treatment. *Am. J. Psychiat.,* 108:695, 1952.
9. REDL, F. and WINEMAN, D. *Children who Hate.* Chicago: Free Press, 1951.
10. —— —— —— *Controls from Within.* Chicago: Free Press, 1952.
11. ROBINSON, J. F. Use of residence in psychiatric treatment with children. *Am. J. Orthopsychiat.,* 16, 1947.
12. —— MAXWELL, A., and DOMINIQUES, K. E. Resident psychiatric treatment with children. *Am. J. Orthopsychiat.,* 17:458-467, 1947.
13. —— The role of the resident professional worker. *Am. J. Orthopsychiat.,* 19, 1949.

Chapter 12

MEDICAL SOCIAL WORKER IN A HOSPITAL SETTING

S. MOUCHLY SMALL, M.D.

During the past fifty years medical diagnosis and therapy has become extraordinarily complex. The need for expensive special diagnostic apparatus and numerous laboratory examinations requiring highly skilled technicians has led to a sharp increase in the number of hospitalized patients. Concomitant with this development, physicians have turned away from the general practice of medicine in favor of specialization. These trends have led to more accurate diagnoses and fostered research which is so essential to progress in medicine. However, it also inevitably resulted in the physician losing sight of numerous personal, familial, social and economic aspects which play significant roles in precipitating or prolonging illness.

With the increasing recognition of the relationship between life situations, emotions and disease, physicians began to feel handicapped in their treatment by the lack of such knowledge. Factors such as these led to the development of medical social service. It is not mere coincidence that this first developed in large busy hospitals such as the Massachusetts General Hospital and Bellevue Hospital, for it was particularly in such institutions that the overwhelming pressures on the doctor led him to lose intimate contact with his patients. Patients had to be given detailed explanations concerning their illness and how to cooperate in a treatment plan. Unrealistic suggestions had to be adapted to social and economic possibilities. Community resources, many of which were unknown to the physician, were not being properly utilized. The doctor was often handicapped in his understanding of the ill patient as a person because of his lack of information concerning social and psychologic determinants. It was only through the elaboration of medical social services that these defects have been gradually overcome. Today, no modern progressive hospital can function efficiently without an active social work staff.

The study of human behavior, both in health and disease, requires an understanding of its biologic basis. A general frame of reference is provided by the recognition of the existence of certain essential similarities in structure and function upon which environmental forces exert significant modifying influences. Fruitless arguments concerning heredity versus environment lose sight of the need for a successful fusing of these concepts to appreciate man as a living organism in a given society. While general laws may be elaborated, their ultimate value rests in their application to the individual. The infinite complexity of man as a living organism, further complicated by innumerable life situations and limitless variations in ways of experiencing them, necessitates detailed studies of individuals to discover meaningful relationships that may explain behavior. Modern dynamic psychology (psychodynamics) attempts to show how structural (somatic) and environmental influences are related to each other. The study of motivation at different levels of mental functioning, be they conscious or unconscious, helps to bridge this gap. Through the knowledge of psychodynamics, biologic drives such as instinctual forces, the highly significant early environmental influences, and the adaptive needs required by current life situations may be integrated.

The general practitioner who serves as the family physician is privileged to observe individuals in their natural environment. As a member of the community, the doctor is often intimately acquainted with many of the social problems and emotional conflicts which may be contributory to a patient's illness. In addition, he may be in possession of pertinent facts relating to heredity and early development that may have a bearing on the present difficulty. When the patient is hospitalized and the responsibility for his care is transferred to a group of specialists such opportunities for first-hand observation is lost. Too much emphasis is placed on studying the disease process rather than the ill person who, all too often, is caught in a maze of complicated laboratory procedures. One must not depreciate the value of such studies but we cannot accept them as a substitute for a detailed personal history sufficient to give us insight into the needs of the sick person.

During the past decade, recognition of the importance of social and psychologic factors in illness has been reawakened under the banner of psychosomatic medicine. Physicians are becoming aware of the intimate relationship between emotions and all types of illness and how personality problems may upset a well-planned therapeutic regime. The psychosomatic approach is dedicated to a sympathetic understanding of all facets of the patient's personality and how it is related to physical disturbances. More effective use is made of the medical social worker's contribution in properly evaluating distressing financial, familial and situational factors and an attempt is made to control them. The following case history illustrates the importance of obtaining adequate psychological and environmental data in order to aid in the proper diagnosis and treatment of a patient with a long-standing complaint.

Jane B., a thirty-six-year-old housewife was admitted to the medical service of a New York City hospital with the complaint of intermittent diarrhea for the previous eighteen months. Bowel movements were watery and accompanied by cramplike pains. In the preceding two months they increased in frequency up to seven a day but the stools contained no pus or gross blood. On physical examination her abdomen was slightly tender on deep pressure over the area of the descending colon but no masses were felt. Repeated stool cultures were negative for amebae and dysentery bacilli. A barium enema X-ray of the colon and sigmoidoscopic visualization of the lower bowel did not reveal ulceration although the mucosal lining was reddened. Since the patient appeared tense and anxious and had difficulty in sleeping, a psychiatric consultation was requested.

At this time, she told how her diarrhea first began when her son contracted scarlet fever following a tonsillectomy. At that time it lasted only about four days and she had infrequent attacks up until two months before her admission to the hospital when the diarrhea became more persistent. She slept poorly, was often awake for hours during the night and was troubled by nocturia. She expressed concern over the fact that she was more irritable with her son and on one occasion slapped his face for no good reason. She was troubled by disturbing dreams which often involved her son being burned or injured in some manner.

About five months prior to her admission to the hospital, she missed a menstrual period. She realized she was pregnant and tried to abort herself with various types of medication but was unsuccessful. For the next few months she was nauseated, ate little and smoked a great deal. She spontaneously aborted two months before her admission but had no return of menstruation since that time. She expressed deep concern over the fact that there must be something wrong with her genitalia.

The patient was born in the South, the second of six children. She was a normal full-term baby and her early development was not unusual. She attended school up to the ninth grade and then went to work as a switchboard telephone operator and following that worked as a dress saleswoman. She was first married at twenty-four years of age to a man who was unreliable and could not keep a job. She divorced him five years later because of nonsupport. She had one child in this marriage, namely, her son, who is now ten years of age. The following year she remarried. Her sexual relations were unsatisfactory with both husbands. She never used contraceptives but would only have intercourse the week before and the week following her periods. However, this scheme failed when she last became pregnant.

Her husband is a beer salesman and is often away from home. At times she drank a great deal of beer to the point where she would become tipsy. When feeling this way, she talked quite freely about anything that was on her mind—occasionally expressing resentment against her husband because of his "know it all" attitude. This infuriated him, so she stopped drinking and rarely argued with him. When she expressed her feelings of anger she would often start to cry and so she stopped doing that. Whenever others interfered with her way of doing things, she reacted with a silent type of resistance but was aware of mounting hostility within herself.

When she aborted, her husband asked his mother to come up from the South to help his wife with the housework. The mother-in-law is a meddling, garrulous individual who was constantly telling the patient how to manage her life. The patient stated that for the few weeks before she came into the hospital, this became so bad that she often felt like screaming or slapping her mother-in-law in the face. Since the patient expressed consider-able concern about how her son was getting along, the medical social worker paid a home visit and interviewed the mother-in-law. The social worker found the latter to be "impossible," criticizing the way the household was run and constantly com-plaining about the son's manners. She had no hesitancy in tell-ing the social worker that the patient must have injured herself by taking these medications in order to abort herself and she positively stated that the diarrhea must be due to these drugs. She further added that she had told the patient her opinion in regard to the diarrhea on many occasions. Subsequent to this home visit, the social worker interviewed the husband and sug-gested that his mother return home and in her place a part-time housekeeper be hired. She also explained the relationship be-tween the patient's diarrhea and her inability to express her feel-ings whenever a subject came up for discussion. He was quite co-operative and followed out these recommendations.

A gynecological examination was arranged for her and no evidence of pelvic disease was found. This was explained to the patient and seemed to give her a great deal of relief. After about three weeks in the hospital, during which time her diarrhea practically disappeared without the use of any medication, the patient's menstrual period returned. A follow-up visit one year later revealed the patient to be free of diarrhea although it was apparent that she readily became tense and anxious whenever faced with any difficult situation. However, this was not suffi-cient, either in intensity or duration, for her to feel that she wanted any further help.

The relationship between the patient's pent-up resentments and hostilities and the exacerbation of her diarrhea was quite apparent. No attempt was made to analyze deeper feelings of guilt and anxiety in relation to her abortion and what sig-nificance it might have in terms of disturbed bowel functioning. The relatively superficial environmental modification plus the reassurance of not having any pelvic disease was evidently suffi-cient to give her relief from her symptoms to the point where she could return to her ordinary household duties. While it is still difficult for her to express her hostile feelings, she is able to do so in part by virtue of her husband's greater comprehension of her need to do so.

FUNCTIONS OF THE MEDICAL SOCIAL WORKER

The medical social worker functions most productively as a member of a group of specially trained individuals who are concerned with the prevention, diagnosis and treatment of illness. While the physician is nominally the person responsible for the proper integration of the various services, major contributions toward effecting the patient's adaptation frequently depend on other members of the therapeutic team. To qualify as a competent medical social worker one should be able to face serious illness, physical handicaps and disfigurements in others with a sufficient degree of objectivity and equanimity to avoid becoming personally overwhelmed. The social worker can be most helpful if she is kind, sympathetic and tolerant of the liabilities of human beings under stress. The ability to feel into the problems of patients, to empathize, without overidentifying with them to the point where she becomes personally involved is essential. Ideally, the worker should be a mature individual, happy, healthy and relatively free of neurotic problems. Since medical social work is usually carried out in a hospital or clinical setting, she must learn to work in co-operation with other professional personnel and understand the ethics and practices of the related fields such as medicine, nursing, dietetics and occupational therapy.

An essential aspect of the medical social worker's activities is case work in which the individual and his problems are approached through his social environment. Since these clients are usually ill or handicapped, the behavior and reactions of people to sickness, disability and therapy should be clearly understood. While there is considerable variation in individual reactions to illness, certain general patterns of response may be observed. Irritability and resentment are frequently misunderstood as a personal attack by those who work with patients. It is much more commonly a generalized nonspecific response protesting against the injustice of fate which incapacitated him. Often times the more anxious the patient is, the greater are his demonstrations of hostility. Getting involved in arguments destroys the worker's usefulness. Other patients may adopt a giving-up attitude with a passive dependency that is out of proportion to the realities of the situation. They refuse to take any active part in helping themselves. Closely related to this type of reaction are those who welcome illness as an escape from duties and responsibilities. They appear content in the hospital until plans for discharge are considered; at this point, they react with anxiety or a return of symptoms which is often the precursor of a tendency toward chronic invalidism. More serious emotional reactions such as severe depression or confused excitement may also complicate somatic illness.

The Individual Patient

With the individual patient, the worker's approach is of a combined medical-social nature. The sick person is unable to make the most effective use of the medical care offered because of personality problems or environmental difficulties. Visualizing the ill person against the background of his family, occupation, social environment and community resources enables the worker to obtain a comprehensive picture of interrelated facts which can be used constructively for the patient's benefit. Those who are physically handicapped or suffer with chronic ailments such as tuberculosis, diabetes and heart disease or those in whom emotional and social causes contribute heavily toward their somatic illness (psychosomatic disorders) are especially in need of social service. At times, case work with both the patient and relatives may help to ease the remaining days of those unfortunates in whom inoperable cancer or leukemia lead inexorably toward death. With surgical patients who refuse operations necessary for their recovery or alleviation of symptoms her social information may enable the physician to analyze the reasons for refusal and help the patient to overcome his conflicts.

Once the patient is cured or sufficiently recovered to return home, the social worker's focus is now directed toward rehabilitation and the maintenance of the healthy state. Many a cardiac child has become a physical or psychological cripple out of proportion to the actual disability by the fear unwittingly engendered in the hospital. Adults with amputated extremities may keep their artificial limbs in the closet no matter how perfectly they fit unless they are urged to use them and encouraged through help with vocational placement. It may be necessary to explain to a potential employer the fact that an epileptic, whose convulsions are well-controlled with medication, may be a valuable employee in certain nondangerous occupations. The types of problems are legion but each individual returned to a self-respecting, independent, happy and healthy life is a source of considerable gratification to those who have assisted in the process.

Relatives

Conferences with relatives to explain the nature and extent of an illness may materially aid in eliciting their co-operation. Not infrequently parents are only vaguely aware of attitudes which lead to exacerbations of symptoms. Overly strict or coercive approaches to the patient may result in unconscious rebellion against medical advice given by the physician. If relatives do not make allowances for an occasional minor dietary indiscretion by a diabetic, the patient may try to sneak improper foods. If apprehended the resulting emotional reaction may do more to upset the metabolic balance than any ordinary breach of diet would ever cause. Blind and inflexible insistence on rest hours may harm rather than benefit the convalescent tuberculous individual. Particularly with psychosomatic disorders such as peptic ulcer, bronchial asthma and ulcerative colitis, a salutary emotional climate at home is of the essence. Relatives have to be coached to engage in discussions rather than arguments. Formulating the importance of safety valves for emotional steam in the form of verbal expression, rather than through body language with resultant physical disorders, may enable those close to the patient to accept such occurrences more gracefully. To be sure, this may place an undue stress on the relatives but the knowledge that they are actively participating in helping the patient to get well may ease the strain.

The Physician

Physicians are utilizing social workers to an increasing degree to ascertain facts about the patient's social situation and adjustment that may be pertinent for diagnosis and therapy. At times, the practitioner's primary concern with symptomatology and treatment may cause him to overlook social factors. The physician may be familiar with society at large and its general political, economic and cultural trends, but it remains for the social worker to interpret for him the specific manner in which a given individual in a particular social environment deals with it as differentiated from the variable responses of others. She should clarify, for the doctor, those social factors which led to the patient becoming ill, the problems his illness creates for him as well as for his family, and those hurdles which stand in the way of his being able to accept and use medical advice. Disregard of such information may lead to ridiculous advice by the doctor such as advising an indigent patient to take long vacations in another state with a desirable climate when the latter is more concerned with paying the next month's rent. Lack of knowledge concerning religious practices may create more problems for the patient through giving blunt advice at variance with the latter's beliefs. Only by integrating all the information available to him from various sources can a comprehensive, utilizable therapeutic regime be formulated.

Community Agencies

The function of the medical social worker in relation to the use of other community agencies and resources may appear deceptively simple. It is not sufficient to be acquainted with the various organizations and their particular fields of interest or work. If this were so, any well-trained clerk could use a directory of social agencies and refer clients to the proper ones in rote fashion. This type of routine referral often proves to be wasted effort for everyone concerned. Many patients find it difficult to accept help when it is offered directly and bluntly. Others tend to become excessively dependent on agencies to the point where they contribute little effort of their own. Only after the social worker has achieved a satisfactory working relationship with the patient and appreciates his needs, can a skillful utilization of resources be made. Proper preparation of the patient through explanation of the reasons for referral and what one hopes to achieve will lead to a more productive use of the agency. Likewise, preparing the agency for the client's visit by outlining his problems and briefing them about his sensitivities or idiosyncrasies will make for a smoother and more successful contact.

The social worker has to learn to strike a happy balance between the wholesale and indiscriminate use of community agencies and the meaningful exploration of psychologic factors that play significant roles in the patient's illness. It is uncommon for the client's difficulties to be based entirely on external factors. The interplay of the individual's inner emotional difficulties with environmental pressures is much more likely to be the determining force that leads to difficulties.

Education

In addition to the social work functions directed toward patient care, the medical social worker has an educational and training responsibility. The primary focus is ordinarily concentrated on social work students but present trends in medical education have made increasing demands on social service departments. Among nonsocial worker personnel, medical students, internes and residents, as well as nurses, physiotherapists, occupational therapists and dietitians are increasingly concerned with medical social problems. The medical social worker is charged with the duty of clarifying the social implications of illness and disability. She interprets the significance of family relationships and its influence toward health or disease. In some medical schools, the freshman students are assigned to families whom they follow for the duration of their medical education. The medical social worker assists with home visits and participates in conferences interpreting various aspects of family life and evaluating the social and environmental pressures on the individual patient.

INTERVIEWING

The foundation of successful social work rests upon the worker's competence in interviewing. Professional skill in this area requires not only theoretical knowledge about the psychology of human behavior but also considerable case work experience in which the worker's technique is repeatedly analyzed. Observation of proficient interviewers at work is by far the most desirable method of learning interviewing methods. Certain general principles may be taught but specific rules that cover the infinite number of situations that may arise between the two people concerned are impossible to formulate.

Goals of Interviewing

Interviewing is a special situation involving communication between people. Much talk is for the mere pleasure or satisfaction that is derived from such contacts. The interview, however, is a serious communication directed toward definite purposes. Essentially, it strives to help the individual deal with his problems in a constructive fashion. The interview is used for securing information about the person as well as his illness including his relationships with other persons in his social and familial environment. Through the interview situation, the case worker attempts to instruct and guide both the patient and others who play significant roles in his life and attempts to manipulate the environment for the benefit of the patient. Finally, through the use of various techniques in the interview situation, one tries to influence or motivate the client for the purpose of achieving a better adjustment.

These goals have important implications, both as an aid in diagnosis as well as being integral parts of therapy. The particular approach in the interview will naturally vary with the purpose in mind and may change from time to time as contact with the patient progresses.

The medical social worker in a hospital setting will most frequently focus her efforts in the direction of understanding the patient's symptoms and complaints and to utilize this knowledge toward returning the patient to an active and happy life. Therapeutic fervor may lead to premature attempts in making decisions or giving advice without first having a basic understanding of the various emotional problems involved. Inexperienced interviewers are often prone to do this without recognizing that a great deal of information will only be forthcoming after a good relationship has been established with the client.

General Considerations

How the interviewer's own prejudices and attitudes may distort information that one obtains from a client was clearly illustrated in a study by Stuart Rice, involving two thousand destitute men in a municipal lodging house. Twelve different skilled social workers were asked to interview these men. One of the interviewers was an ardent prohibitionist and found that the downfall of 62 per cent of the subjects was chiefly due to liquor. Another interviewer favoring social issues, found only 22 per cent affected primarily by liquor and 39 per cent whose plight was due to industrial causes.

Despite the fact that each interviewer was a trained and conscientious investigator, his personal bias affected not only his reports but the statements made to him by the clients he interviewed. It appears that the bias was imparted to each subject unconsciously, perhaps through subtle forms of suggestion carried by changes in tone of voice, facial expressions, gestures or bodily posture. The interviewers were not aware of expressing any prejudices or biases, at least at a conscious level. This type of contagious bias may so distort information obtained from the patient that an objective evaluation of his difficulties may become impossible.

Another factor which one must be aware of is the fact that there are constant errors which creep into an interview situation. This is particularly true when one tries to elicit judgments or attitudes on the part of the client. For example, it is a well-known fact that if you carried out an experiment in which various members of an audience are asked to estimate the interval of time that elapses between two signals, the great majority of answers will tend to be longer than the ten or fifteen second interval which elapsed. In other words, the experimental situation by focusing the attention of those members of the audience on the lapse of time tends to make the time that passes seem longer than it actually is. We have all experienced the much longer time it seems to take for water to boil when we are watching the pot as compared with a situation in which we are not in any particular hurry. In like manner, the specific situation of the interview will tend to show a constant error in a given direction when you ask patients for opinions about themselves. Most individuals tend to overestimate desirable traits and to minimize undesirable characteristics when they are asked to rate themselves.

It is always far more desirable to elicit facts rather than conclusions. For example, when a patient is asked whether or not he gets angry very easily when kept waiting, he may answer either "yes" or "no." However, this is not a meaningful answer unless the patient is asked for an example in which he is able to give the facts which the interviewer may then interpret herself. It not infrequently appears that the patient's conclusion is at variance with the interviewer's interpretation based on the given example. Asking for factual details of situations in which the particular personality trait is exhibited will tend to reduce constant errors of this nature which would otherwise lead to a distorted picture of the individual's personality.

The physical setting in which the interview takes place may determine success or failure in achieving one's goals. A sense of privacy and the confidential nature of the interview must be imparted to the client. Frequent interruptions are very disturbing to the patient, destroy his trend of thought and may at times give him the feeling that the social worker is not particularly interested in his problems. It is desirable to set aside a specific amount of time and to let the client know approximately how much time you have for him. This gives both the client, as well as the interviewer, the feeling that the time allotted is important and makes for a more efficient use of the interview period. Lengthy interviews lasting more than an hour are usually not as productive for the time spent as those which last between one half to one hour. It is usually desirable to talk to the client across the corner of the desk or table rather than separating interviewer and interviewee on either side of the desk. It is difficult to impart a sense of close contact and interest when one is physically separated in this manner.

The question often arises about taking notes or writing during an interview. This varies with the patient. Generally speaking, there is little reason for taking voluminous notes in the patient's presence. If the client is really given full attention and only an occasional word or phrase is jotted down to serve as a sign post, it is fairly easy to dictate a detailed report immediately following the client's departure. To be sure, certain factual information, such as name, address, dates and ages are important and there is usually little interference with the interview when this is noted. However, should the interviewer start writing in detail, the patient notes certain topics which seem to interest the interviewer. It may influence the client to talk more about a given subject than may be worth while or it may work in the reverse manner. If the patient notes that you are writing down everything that he talks about, he may hesitate to discuss certain sensitive subjects which he prefers not to have on his record. There is no question but that it is impossible really and adequately to observe the patient and listen to his content of thought if one is going to pay excessive attention to note taking.

Interviewer's Attitudes

Of basic importance in the interview situation is the continuous emotional interplay of forces which takes place between the social worker and the client. The patient often comes to the interview with preconceived attitudes and ideas based upon previous life experiences which exert their force without his being aware of them. Factors such as the sex, age, manner of dress, physical appearance and activity of the case worker may unconsciously reanimate behavior patterns which were utilized in the past with individuals who had similar characteristics.

In addition, there is a tendency for sick patients to show regressive behavior under the impact of their illness so that they may behave in childlike fashion. Under these circumstances, it is particularly important that the medical social worker impress the patient with her sincere interest and encourage him to talk about his problems. There must be a true willingness to accept the patient's behavior based upon an understanding of the emotional and reality problems involved. Unless the interviewer is able to feel into the situation, namely to empathize with the patient, she may appear cold and detached or even worse if she becomes maudlin or overly sentimental the client will recognize that her sincerity is spurious and hesitate to give necessary information. The social worker must carefully avoid the role of censor, moralist, judge or minister but focus primarily on what is healthy versus unhealthy without tending to pass judgment.

In instances where asocial or unusual behavior presents a major problem it may be helpful to discuss the pros and cons of such behavior with emphasis upon the reality situation. The social worker must always keep in mind that we are interested in causes and what makes the patient behave as he does, rather than allow herself to become indignant or indulge in a lecture on morality. A knowledge of one's own prejudices and sensitivities will go far toward controlling the interviewer's intolerance and make for a better control of her feelings. The patient must be made to feel that you are "all for him" and that your quest for information is primarily motivated by a desire to obtain a well-rounded picture of his personality and how it plays a role in his illness.

Communication with the patient is not confined to the verbal area but many nonverbal aspects of the interview often play determining roles. Factors such as attitude, gestures, facial expression and tone of voice can do much toward giving the patient a sense of warmth and interest. Leaning forward, an appropriate nod of the head or the repetition of a key word, which the patient has used, accompanied by a rising inflection of the voice may stimulate the patient to further verbalization. Through the use of such techniques, it is often possible to focus the patient on relevant topics concerning which more information is desirable. The case worker must be sufficiently sensitive to the patient's reactions and emotional responses so that she may evaluate its significance in the context of what is being discussed. This ability will further aid in directing the development of an effective relationship with the patient to the point where he will be willing to return for further interviews and assistance.

Some patients have the facility for turning the tables by asking the interviewer many personal questions. This is often an attempt to find out more about the interviewer before the patient feels free to disclose things about himself. One can often handle this by smiling in a friendly fashion and asking why the patient is interested in these personal aspects of the interviewer's life. If this does not successfully lead to further movement in the interview, it may be necessary to give the patient a frank and brief answer followed by a re-emphasis on the importance of the interview in terms of trying to help the patient. Such personal questions often have a significance of their own and may be the patient's way of introducing a problem.

At other times, the patient may try to inject some humor into the interview situation. The tense and inexperienced interviewer may take this as a signal to relax and be inveigled into a similar trend of thought. Ordinarily, patients who are ill do not enjoy the interviewer being too humorous or funny or ridiculing his symptoms. Essentially, the interview is serious business for the patient and this must be repeatedly corroborated by the social worker's every action, demeanor and attitude.

Technical Aspects

It is essential that both the client and the social worker be as relaxed and as comfortable as the situation permits. The interviewer who appears calm and at ease will often impart a similar attitude to the patient. In a medical setting, it is usually easier to allow the patient to begin talking about his illness and his experiences in the hospital. If the patient does not begin to talk spontaneously, some general question concerning his illness may help him to get started. It is desirable to allow the patient to talk freely since if he is given "free wheeling" he will often lead the social worker to important sources of his difficulties. This, however, does not mean that the interviewer sits back and allows her thoughts to wander. On the contrary, it is important to listen very actively, both to the substance of what the patient says and to see how it relates to his complaints and the over-all picture. Not infrequently the opening remarks of the patient will give important clues to significant emotional relationships that play an important part in his illness. For example, an alcoholic who was hospitalized because of gastric complaints spontaneously remarked that his mother would rather see him dead than drunk. This information was given early in the first interview and it would have been premature to investigate his relationships to his mother at this point. However, the social worker should make a mental note of such a statement and keep this in mind as an important area to be investigated subsequently. Blanket reassurance given early in the interview before the case worker has ascertained many of the important facts may have the effect of shutting the patient off. In addition, he may feel that such reassurance is based upon ignorance, rather than facts and it may interfere with the establishment of a good relationship.

Encouraging the patient to talk freely also gives the interviewer the opportunity to determine how the client speaks, his choice of language, and give her an indication at what level she can make effective contact. In talking to young people or patients who have not had much education, the use of a word like "masturbation" instead of "playing with one's self" or more common slang terms which can readily be understood by the patient, may become a definite drawback in terms of getting the patient to express himself. At times, the patient may not understand what is meant but because of embarrassment may hesitate to ask for clarification. Differences in background and education may lead to the misuse of certain words. In talking to a physician who had recently arrived in this country, a woman was trying to tell him how much she liked to do housework, how much she enjoyed cooking and baking. The doctor, trying to be sympathetic and pleasant replied, "You are a very homely woman." His intention was good, his choice of language was poor and the patient became quite disturbed at this remark. While an example such as this may be exaggerated, it illustrates the point which often arises in far more subtle ways in the interview situation.

Some interviewers seem unable to tolerate a minute of silence. They become uneasy and experience a strong urge to fill in the gap with a question which may have little significance or direction. If the interviewer is able to be silent for a minute or two and observe the patient in a friendly pleasant manner, the patient may take this opportunity to bring up a subject which has been on his mind but which he has hesitated to speak about. It is not an uncommon experience to find, even after a number of interviews, that a patient will give some very important information and when asked why he had not told about it previously may remark that he had never been asked or never been given the opportunity to tell about it. A patient who is full of strong feelings about some acute situation may also take this kind of opportunity to express his emotions and obtain some relief by virtue of being able to do so. This is not only therapeutically beneficial to the patient but also gives the social worker the opportunity to observe the type of emotional responses the patient characteristically exhibits.

A common but subtle form of suggestion is often conveyed by the wording of a question. In its extreme form it is described as "a leading question." There are many ways in which an interviewer can influence responses without anyone else being aware of it. Unfortunately, sometimes not even the interviewer is aware of how this distorts responses. Elmo Roper, who conducts public opinion polls made a pretest of the wording of a question relating to governmental efforts to maintain peace. In response to the question, "Should the United States do all in its power to promote world peace?" 97 per cent of those polled gave affirmative answers. With a similar group, the form of the question was slightly changed to, "Should the United States become involved in plans to promote world peace?" only 60 per cent answered in the affirmative. Evidently, the use of the word "involved" disturbed many of the people who were interviewed and confused the issue. During the initial interviews, it is far better to keep questions general rather than making them more specific. However, once the patient has opened up a particular area for discussion, the interviewer may then go ahead and ask pointed and pertinent questions on the subject to obtain a more comprehensive picture.

Proper timing is of the essence. A premature probing into sensitive areas in the form of direct questions may lead the patient to give incorrect information. Since there is a certain need to maintain a consistency in his answers, this may persist even when the relationship between interviewer and client has improved to the point where the patient would ordinarily talk more openly. It is, therefore, advisable to take one's cue from the patient and if a general question concerning certain subjects seems to increase the patient's tension or causes him to become more restless, it should be taken as a signal to defer further probing. With patients suffering from certain types of psychosomatic disorders, such as ulcerative colitis, it is necessary for the social worker to recognize that persistent questioning of a probing nature might precipitate exacerbations of the disease caused by emotional distress. By the same token, the medical social worker should avoid a confessional type of interview, particularly during the early contacts because once having divulged a great deal of intimate information all at once, the patient may be embarrassed and refuse to return for further interviews. In addition, flooding the interviewer with a plethora of information prevents her from properly absorbing and evaluating the significance of the patient's productions. Such a tendency on the part of the patient may be stopped by taking advantage of a slight pause in the patient's recitation and returning him to the subject just previously under discussion.

The interviewer must be constantly on the lookout for meaningful relationships as indicated by slips of the tongue, spontaneous remarks or the observation of specific physical reactions, such as blushing or restlessness, accompanying the discussion of certain topics. One must listen, both to the manifest content of what the patient is talking about as well as the unconscious significance revealed by the context in which certain information is given. Ever present, in the interviewer's mind, should be the question of how is the present difficulty related to what the patient is revealing both directly and indirectly. Meaningful relationships may be revealed by a repeated chronological association, such as migraine headaches which occur only on Sundays when the patient is at home or the appearance of physical or emotional symptoms in a given type of situation, such as being exposed to a domineering authoritative type of person. Essentially, we are looking for common denominators which underlie distressing emotional reactions or physical symptoms. Recurrent themes or patterns of behavior are often intimately related to the nature of the complaint. A patient may complain about being discriminated against by the nurses and subsequently reveal that he felt the same way in school or that he repeatedly leaves a job after only working for a short period of time because of similar feelings. He may have perfectly good excuses for each time that he left a certain job and each instance taken by itself may appear to be quite reasonable. However, when one views the total picture, particularly if the pattern has been repeated a number of times, it is much more likely to be related to factors which are not immediately apparent rather than the glib rationalizations given by the patient.

Striking omissions in giving information are apt to be of particular significance. For example, a patient may discuss various members of his family and consistently omit the fact that he has a younger sister. Such an apparent omission is often quite pertinent. For example, in one such instance, with a patient whose presenting complaint was impotence, it was subsequently revealed that he had had intimate sexual play with this sister over a period of years. In the case of another patient, who had symptoms of a duodenal ulcer of six months' duration, it was only after the social worker had seen him five times that he finally revealed that he had moved in with his in-laws just prior to the onset of his symptoms. Previous questions concerning living arrangements had given the impression, without his actually stating so, that he was living in his own house.

Chronological inconsistencies are often unconsciously determined by the need to hide or conceal revealing facts. At one time a patient may state he was married on a given date and subsequently mention that he has been married for a certain number of years which is at variance with the original date given. This may be a cover for the circumstances under which the marriage took place. The same significance applies often to gratuitous information repeatedly given as though the patient wishes to emphasize a certain point. This may be part of the mechanism of denial. For example, a patient may insist that his symptoms are on a neurotic basis, when in truth it is quite apparent he is suffering from a serious organic illness.

Certain clients seem to verbalize freely and easily without much show of emotion even when talking about distressing incidents such as the death of a parent, a child or a marital partner. This reaction may appear all the more incongruous when he further describes his close relationship or deep attachment to the deceased individual. In such instances of dissociated feeling, if the interviewer is able to supply the missing affect by remarking how distressing or upsetting this incident must have been, the patient may be encouraged to reveal his true feelings and experience considerable relief in doing so.

Throughout her contact with the patient, the social worker should try to integrate all the information obtained from the patient in an effort to establish tentative formulations concerning the relationship between the patient's illness and behavior on the one hand and his attitudes, emotional reactions and social situation on the other. Subsequent interviews then provide the opportunity to confirm, disprove or modify these hypotheses. Even though a significant relationship may appear quite obvious to the social worker, interpretations to the patient should be kept at a minimum until such time as the patient is on the verge of establishing the connection himself. A premature interpretation will only heighten resistances against seeing a meaningful relationship. When one is in doubt a tentative hypothesis may be presented in the form of a question so that if the patient is not ready to accept it, the interviewer may go on to other relevant issues.

PSYCHOANALYTIC ORIENTATION

Social work is one of many disciplines which attempts to gain scientific insight into human behavior as a means of influencing both the individual and his environment for constructive purposes. Implied in these various approaches, is the concept of causality which insists upon a relationship between cause and effect. Neither symptoms nor behavior in any form arise "out of the blue" but are to be viewed as reactions to inner drives modified by various factors such as life experiences and social reality. The psychoanalytic frame of reference requires that all behavior, whether rational or irrational, be finally revealed as understandable human reactions.

Human beings do not exist in a vacuum. The social world in which we live is a complex structure which exerts various pressures on the individual. An individual's particular state of emotional distress is the resultant of both internal and external factors. To evaluate which influences play the major roles, we depend on the study of many individuals exposed to similar situations and note the variations in response. Most persons exposed to a large dose of virulent tubercle bacilli will contract the disease. In like fashion, overwhelming long-term emotional stresses, such as are encountered in modern warfare will probably lead to psychiatric disorders. Given sufficient stress everyone has their breaking point. In these examples the deciding factors are primarily external. However, psychologic forces may be the determining element in unconsciously leading the individual into difficult reality situations. Some individuals manage to get themselves repeatedly involved in the same type of trouble. A woman who had been beaten up on many occasions by her alcoholic husband was finally helped to obtain a divorce. Within the year she was remarried to an aggressive, sadistic man who also drank to excess and was again seeking assistance for her marital problems.

As an integral part of the medical social worker's training, she should be familiar with the facts of personality development, the common emotional constellations and defense mechanisms which are often the source of difficulties. Such basic knowledge is helpful in arriving at tentative hypotheses and assists the social worker in directing the course of the interview. Unfortunately, such information may not be an unmixed blessing. Certain insecure case workers may tend to force individuals into diagnostic pigeon-holes, overlooking information which seems to be at variance with her formulations. A single slip of the tongue in which the patient substitutes the word "mother" for "wife" should not be taken as conclusive evidence of a deep-seated incestuous conflict. An out-of-wedlock pregnancy is not always undesired. Deeper motivations may be operative which would make it dangerous to consider abrupt termination of the pregnancy. In situations such as these, the social worker may too readily identify herself with the client and project her own feelings onto the patient.

A therapeutic plan must take cognizance of all the facts and be based upon well-founded dynamic formulations before an attempt is made to manipulate the environment or influence the patient's attitudes. Initially, one must try to grasp the meaning of the presenting problems, what led to the acute situation and how the patient became involved in it. As the social worker then gathers background history she must evaluate various life experiences in the light of their effect on the present situation. The inexorable repetition of specific patterns of behavior may indicate the hopelessless of a naïve giving of advice. The life history assists in highlighting the particular danger points where the patient characteristically fails. By the same token, it is just as important to analyze what factors have made for success in past endeavors. A personality inventory should include both assets and liabilities. With this in mind, the social worker is prepared to outline her goals and how she may achieve them. No matter how well the problem is formulated in a report, the essential point is to enable the patient to accept advice and to follow through with it.

DYNAMIC FORMULATION OF THE PATIENT'S PROBLEMS

To illustrate the importance of a psychodynamic understanding of the patient's problems and how they are handled by the medical social worker two cases will be described.

Mrs. T. had always been a proud, quick-tempered, tense person. For months she had a dry hacking cough which she attributed to excessive smoking. Although she was aware of tiring more easily and lost some weight, it was not until she coughed up a small amount of bloody sputum that she consulted a physician. The latter sent her into the hospital where a diagnosis of pulmonary tuberculosis was confirmed.

On the ward she was irritable, restless and complained about the food. She was not friendly with the other patients and kept to herself for the most part. When it was finally decided that she should receive sanatorium care she interposed one objection after another. At this point, she was seen by the medical social worker who was to explain the importance of sanatorium care and assist her in working out arrangements for the care of her eight-year-old daughter.

When first seen, Mrs. T. sat back with a somewhat haughty attitude as though flaunting a challenge. Ostensibly, she was willing to listen but attempted to convince the worker that she could get as much rest at home as she could by going away for a rest cure. She tried to minimize the fact of her stubborn refusal to co-operate, characterizing the whole idea of sanatorium care as "silly" and "not really necessary." Any explanation or appeal on the grounds of what was best for herself fell on deaf ears. The first indication of how deeply upset she was became apparent only when the danger of infecting her daughter was approached. Although this was mentioned as a matter of course during the discussion, she reacted to it as though she had been accused of not being concerned about her daughter's health. Mrs. T. became quite resentful and insisted that the worker had implied she was selfish. A denial by the social worker of any such intimation was followed by an extended account of all the patient had done for her daughter. Having unburdened herself in this manner with sympathetic acquiescence by the worker, she felt relieved. No further attempt was made to discuss sanatorium care. Mrs. T. was amenable to the worker's suggestion that perhaps it might be desirable to get the husband's point of view.

Mr. T. was most co-operative and was willing to accept any recommendation given by the physicians. He thought that his married sister would be willing to care for their daughter. His attitude was warm and friendly with a sincere appreciation of the worker's interest. He thought it was wonderful that the hospital was so solicitous of the family's welfare. Following his interview, he visited with his wife and evidently told her about his interview and his suggestion for the care of their daughter.

The following day when the social worker returned to discuss the matter with the patient, she was again quite hostile. She was adamant about her refusal to send the daughter to her sister-in-law. When pressed for reasons she divulged that the sister-in-law had been opposed to her marriage. She also made some sarcastic remarks about "how sweet" the social worker had been to her husband. Mrs. T. was apparently quite jealous of the social worker who was younger and more attractive.

The worker seemed upset by the turn of events and a consultation with the hospital psychiatrist was arranged during which it was felt that Mrs. T. had a deep-seated anxiety about leaving town because of her insecurity with her husband. It was decided that the social worker should approach the patient directly and understandingly by denoting her recognition of the patient's anxiety about leaving her home. When this was done, the patient tearfully acknowledged that she had always been jealous of her husband. She originally met him on a blind date when he was much sought after. The marriage was a forced affair because of a premarital pregnancy. At times she suspected her sister-in-law knew about this although her husband denied telling his sister. While the patient obtained emotional relief through telling this, the social worker surmised that it would be inadvisable to probe further. Since her attitude about going away was bound up with so much anxiety, it was deemed best to re-evaluate its importance.

It was felt that since her apprehension would probably negate much of the value of sanatorium care this should be discussed with the doctors. When this was called to the attention of the tuberculosis specialist, he agreed that she could be treated with pneumothorax and chemotherapy at another general hospital in town which had facilities for such care. When news of this decision was transmitted to the patient at a subsequent interview, she felt greatly relieved. The patient spoke about her own parents, how her father showed her very little affection and her mother favored her younger brother. It seemed clear that she had felt rejected by her own mother and that there was a deep need to overcompensate in her care of her own daughter. Since the patient refused to place her daughter in the care of relatives, arrangements were made for a housekeeper who would visit the patient at the hospital and report to her how the daughter was getting along. This arrangement was satisfactory and the patient was then transferred to the local general hospital. There she reacted well to therapy and after a period of approximately two months, she was able to return home and again take up some of her duties.

A much more complicated situation is illustrated by the following case. Mrs. S., a forty-eight-year-old colored housewife, was first referred to the medical social service department in December 1950 from the outpatient gastrointestinal clinic because she had not accepted a recommendation for hospitalization. The patient had been under treatment for a peptic ulcer and had recently completed a course of penicillin therapy for latent lues. The family was known to the department of social welfare and information from them indicated that the husband was a chronic asthmatic but that his illness did not seem adequate cause for the patient's refusal of hospitalization.

The onset of her present difficulty was in 1947 at which time she suffered from nausea, vomiting and gastric pains which were severe enough to awaken her from sleep. When first seen in the hospital clinic, she stated that she had been unable to eat solid foods for a few years and that she had previously consulted a spiritualist who first told her she had stomach trouble. He instituted some kind of healing ritual but the patient did not improve. In the outpatient department they diagnosed her as having both a duodenal and gastric ulcer. In December of 1950 the patient admitted that she went off her prescribed diet and ate some highly spiced foods. A few hours after this she became violently nauseated, vomited and began to have back pain. This led to the decision to admit her to the hospital.

Mrs. S. was born in Georgia and was told that her father was burned to death when she was about two years of age. It seems that at that time he was recovering from smallpox and being disturbed by the noise of the children moved into another room which had a fireplace. He fixed a bed for himself near the fire and some time during the night the bedding went up in flames.

The patient was the youngest of six children and shortly thereafter her mother remarried. The stepfather provided well for them but he was strict, drank to excess and often fought with her mother. Evidently, the ties at home were not very strong since the patient left Georgia at the age of nine to live with a maternal aunt in the North. In her late teens she had various jobs as a domestic as well as an aide in a hospital. At sixteen years of age she first met her future husband in a night club. After a one-year courtship, during which he was very attentive, she married him. Since the patient was quite short and thin he would often pick her up and toss her around like a baby to her great enjoyment. Once they were married he changed and she has regretted her decision ever since then. Although she has now been married thirty-one years, she told her physician how her husband refused to have intimate relations with her on the wedding night and remarked that he was sorry he had ever married her. Subsequently, sexual relations have never been satisfactory.

The husband is fourteen years older than the patient. He worked as a waiter on the railroad and has been away from home a good deal of the time. After several years of marriage, he became more cranky and began drinking heavily. In this setting the patient obtained a job and began to go out with her own friends, indulging excessively in alcoholic beverages and not eating regularly. Since 1949, her husband has been unemployed because of his respiratory difficulty. The patient states she worries constantly about her husband and particularly about the fact that he often falls asleep while smoking in a bed or a chair and he may be burned to death as her father was. There was some indication in the interview that perhaps the patient assumes some sense of responsibility for her father's death since as one of the children who disturbed him she was the cause of his moving the bed near the fireplace.

Following a number of broken appointments, the patient finally came into the hospital for her first interview with the social worker three weeks after the initial referral. She appeared as a thin and anxious-looking woman with a whiny voice. She said she was ready to enter the hospital because of a severe aggravation of her pains caused by dietary indiscretion. She was seen by the physician but because of a bed shortage she could not be admitted to the hospital. The following week the patient kept telephoning repeatedly to inquire about her diet. She stated she did not know how to figure out menus from the bland diet list. It seemed that she wanted to maintain some contact with the hospital through the worker. In addition, she obviously knew what foods to avoid but could not resist the highly seasoned and fried foods. The worker's attitude was sympathetic over her inability to tolerate the foods which she enjoyed and encouraged her to believe in the hospital's interest in helping her to get well. Her intolerance of her husband was hinted at but not clearly defined since it was felt that this was premature. A general formulation was given to the effect that both she and her husband had medical problems which were increased by worry and friction between the two of them.

Since the bed shortage continued at the hospital and the patient was unable to be admitted, the social worker sent the patient letters at intervals so that she would know she had not been forgotten. A favorable point in the patient's make-up was that she seemed to have ambitions above and beyond continuing on social welfare care. It was felt that both the patient and her husband were in competition to be the invalid member of the family and that it would be most difficult to modify their basic personality problems. It was hoped, however, that the situational factors could be alleviated.

The patient was finally hospitalized in February, 1951 for a period of two weeks and instead of being worried about leaving her husband, she seemed to enjoy the experience. While in the hospital she heard that her husband had become worse as a result of her being away. However, she was consistent and frank in her attitude that he was at the bottom of her difficulties. She sneered at him as being old enough to be her father and wondered why she ever married him. She talked about his shaking, his productive cough and the resulting nauseating sputum. His forgetfulness was so extreme she couldn't trust him to do a single errand. There was very little expressed tolerance for his difficulties. Quite spontaneously she indicated that he has little to live for and his death would be a solution to her problems.

When the husband was interviewed by the social worker, he expressed the belief that his wife deliberately worries him. On occasion she would appear anxious and say that she was going to die and then would drop off to sleep leaving him wide awake and worried. He thinks she frequently makes out that she is sicker than she really feels in order to torment him. He told about his own background with considerable pride in his past performances. However, the social worker focused toward developing tolerance for each other and again tried to clarify the extent to which their physical difficulties were increased by emotional factors.

Following her discharge from the hospital in March, 1951 the patient complained of a backache which she ascribed to the spinal tap which had been done while she was an inpatient. She wanted to have a corset prescribed for her. She was seen by the orthopedic consultant who advised admission to the hospital to determine the extent of motion in her back under anesthesia. The end of May, 1951 she was again admitted and during her stay it was determined that she had a full range of motion and that her back difficulty was probably on a hysterical basis. However, the doctors prescribed a back brace.

During her hospitalization, the patient was placed next to another colored patient who was being seen by the same social worker. Mrs. S. was quite jealous of the social worker's relationship with the other patient and made obvious bids for the worker's attention. When she saw her husband she told him she was threatening to sign her own release ostensibly to take care of some minor matter concerning a welfare check. It seemed likely, however, that her feelings of being rejected motivated this desire to leave against advice. As an indication of the patient's dependence on the social worker and her inability to share her with other patients the following incident is helpful.

A former client of the medical social worker had been admitted to the hospital as a possible suicidal risk and it was imperative for the worker to spend considerable time with her. Even though it was quite late in the day, the patient kept signaling the social worker imperatively. At the conclusion of the interview with the suicidal patient the social worker went over to Mrs. S. to see what was wrong. Mrs. S. stated that she had received her supper tray and wanted to complain that she was tired of the bland diet and wasn't going to eat "that junk" anymore. At this point, the worker told the patient that she had no intention of becoming involved in the question of her diet at that late hour. While the patient felt rejected at the same time it seemed indicated as part of giving her a better appreciation of the reality of her own situation. The social worker may not have thought the matter through in this fashion and her reaction may have been the result of an unusually long and difficult day's work. Fortunately, it did not interfere with her subsequent relationship with the patient. When the patient was again seen she was very friendly with the worker and pulled up her clothing to show how complicated the lumbosacral support was. She was delighted at the fact that the doctors thought her condition warranted so much support. She remarked that she had only wanted a little band and here she was encased from just below the breasts to the lumbar area in a large corset-like arrangement. The symbolic meaning of this incident as part of her dependency was clear to the worker but not expressed to Mrs. S.

The patient continued to visit the gastrointestinal clinic and because of the persistence of her symptoms gastric surgery was recommended. All the attention she was receiving pleased her but she was also terrified as to the operative recommendation. On the day that she was to be given the verdict, the patient was tense throughout the morning and when finally called into the consultation room, two doctors and a few students talked to one another using such terms as "intractable ulcer," "psychosomatic features." With an apparent increase in fear her eyes grew bigger and bigger. When one of the doctors asked questions about her most recent attack, she stated she had become angry with her husband and had drunk a whole bottle of brandy to get even with him. Subsequently, the doctors left without telling her what the decision was. Perhaps as part of her anxious anticipation, the patient spoke to the worker about her desire to return to the South. Another colored patient who was suffering from ulcerative colitis had made a dramatic departure from the hospital to live with her family in South Carolina. Despite the worker's attempt to point out the unrealistic aspect of her belief that she could pick up threads dropped some forty years ago, the patient persisted in her desires and an attempt was made to contact a social agency in Georgia to see what help could be given in locating her relatives. However, this was fruitless. When this form of escape was closed, the patient vacillated about surgery but there was no real question about her finally accepting it. As part of her defense against anxiety she ruminated in childlike fashion about the joys of being able to eat corn on the cob, fried fish and various other spicy foods to the point where she became really enthusiastic about the surgical procedure. During the same period, she received an eviction notice along with other tenants because the board of health had condemned the house in which she was living. She began to think of the hospital as a refuge and was not too kindly disposed toward a suggestion made by the worker to help her get an apartment in a housing project. With the exaggeration of her symptoms she was admitted to the hospital and in December, 1951 a subtotal gastrectomy was performed.

Postoperatively, she was extremely uncomfortable with nausea, diarrhea and hot flushes. To her this was a sign that the operation was a failure. Her apprehension was increased when she had to be reoperated on for incision and drainage of a subdiaphragmatic abscess. Every slight comment was seized upon and added to her concern. For example, when one of the surgical residents started to change a dressing he remarked, "Oh, you're infected, I had better leave you to the last." She evidently associated this with her previous history of lues and wanted to know what he meant by this.

During the time she was in the hospital, her husband required much assurance and he was bolstering his courage at the corner saloon. In view of the shortage of beds an abrupt decision was made to discharge her even though she was still having difficulty in gaining weight. Again she reacted to this by rationalizing that she could eat better at home than in the hospital. The social worker obtained information as to the type of high caloric, high protein diet she should have with various types of interval feeding and explained this to the patient. For the two days prior to her discharge, she made a number of trips down to the social worker's office which indicated her dependence on the latter. However, it also indicated the fact that she felt strong enough to walk up and down the stairs that many times. She found all sorts of reasons why she could not go home at the time; talked about the cold weather, the wind and the difficulty in arranging for transportation to her home. The social worker explained that many patients who had been in the hospital for some time were often a bit scared about leaving it. The patient agreed this was true and after a number of further minor complaints, about such things as galoshes and getting her belongings together, arrangements were finally completed and she was discharged.

Her convalescence continued to be stormy during the early part of 1952. She taxed her husband's strength and patience by her insistent demands and grudgingly recognized his solicitude. She subsequently developed an incisional abscess which ruptured spontaneously and drained. When there was a recurrence of another incisional abscess in February of 1952, she was readmitted. She was quite pleased when she heard the X-ray man describe the surgery as being "a beautiful job." She continued to see the social worker but insisted on individual allowances, both for herself and her husband, rather than having a joint income from the department of social welfare. Special arrangements were made whereby she would have supplementary milk, cream and eggs and she gradually showed some improvement both as to gaining weight as well as the absence of symptoms. As part of weaning her away from the social worker, the intervals between visits have become longer but as yet she is not ready to take on a job as a domestic.

In her relationships with the social worker, there were certain aspects of the case which were never verbalized but which seemed to play an important role in the establishment of a close positive maternal type of transference. The social worker spoke with a definite Southern accent which must have been quite apparent to the patient. The latter often asked the worker for her old clothes and in many ways behaved like a dependent child without being willing to recognize the extent and intensity of her demands. It is of note that the patient rarely talked about her own mother even when asked direct questions concerning her. Her marriage to a much older man seemed to be part of her seeking for the kind of a father that she had hoped to have; someone she could depend upon and who would look after her. Unfortunately, he himself had a similar type of difficulty which led to each partner looking for a loving parent in the other. The obsessive fear about her husband burning himself to death was part of this identification with her father. The courtship was the happiest time of her relationship with her husband for it was at that time that she was treated most like the child, being tossed around in the air as one would do with an infant.

The strength of her oral demands, despite the knowledge that she would suffer for it, is indicated by her repeatedly going back to highly spiced foods, complaining about her bland diet and utilizing the same type of mechanism to express her resentment against her husband as in the instance where she drank a whole bottle of brandy to get back at him. A knowledge of her emotional needs indicates that it would be desirable for the patient to obtain a job as a domestic with the kind of an employer who would be maternally inclined and be willing to overlook some of her childish attitudes in return for the excellent domestic service which she is capable of giving.

PARTICIPATING IN THERAPY

The medical social worker participates in therapy in varying degrees depending upon the nature of the physician's request for service. The doctor is nominally in charge of the patient and is therefore primarily responsible for his welfare. Depending upon his knowledge of social work functions he may be able to specify the particular areas in which he desires assistance. Many physicians still look upon social workers as philanthropically minded individuals whose main purpose is to provide some type of economic assistance for the underprivileged. The worker's skill in dealing with people and understanding human behavior may be buried under an avalanche of clerical duties because of similar misconceptions concerning her role. The reverse situation in which the medical social worker is expected to handle complex emotional problems beyond the limitations of her training may lead to dangerous consequences. Her usefulness to the hospital and patients depends upon her ability to define her functions for the doctors with whom she works.

When a patient is referred to social service it is incumbent upon the physician to outline the nature of the medical problem, the kind of information or assistance he desires and the ultimate therapeutic goal he hopes to achieve. This is best accomplished through a personal interview between the doctor and case worker. Should the referral be made in a routine note, the social worker should seek out the physician to clarify these points. This provides a basis for exchange of information and future co-operation.

The need for self-knowledge and the importance of transference manifestations have already been stressed. The patient may derive considerable benefit from the opportunity to discuss her feelings. Following such an experience combined with environmental modification to make for an improved real life situation, the social worker may be able gradually to withdraw from her supportive role with the maintenance of improvement. It is usually more beneficial to get the patient to participate in doing something for himself. In this way he maintains his self-respect, avoids becoming too dependent and sets the stage for self-reliance in the future. The patient seems to derive benefit by learning through doing with the ever-present opportunity for correction of his attitudes by the worker.

Suggestion, persuasion and education are all part of the medical social worker's therapeutic armamentarium to be utilized as the occasion demands. Explanation and clarification of problems is an essential part of treatment. In this way, the patient's feelings and attitudes are more clearly defined so that he may handle his problems more effectively. Interpretation in the sense of offering the patient deep insight into unconscious material should be utilized only by those social workers who have had adequate psychoanalytic training.

BIBLIOGRAPHY

1. BERNSTEIN, S. S., SMALL, S. M., and REICH, M. J. A psychosomatic unit in a general hospital. *Am. J. Nursing*, 49:516, 1949.
2. BINGHAM, W. V. and MOORE, B. V. *How to Interview*. New York: Harper & Brothers, 1941.
3. FINESINGER, J. Psychiatric interviewing. *Am. J. Psychiat.*, 105:187, 1948.
4. FRENCH, T. M. and ORMSBY, R. *Psychoanalytic Orientation in Casework*. New York: Family Service Association of America, 1944.
5. GARRETT, A. Historical survey of the evolution of casework. *J. Soc. Casework*, 30:219, 1949.
6. HODGES, M. B., ed. *Social Work Yearbook*. New York: American Association of Social Workers, 1951.
7. MILES, H. W., COBB, S., and SHANDS, H. C., eds. *Case Histories in Psychosomatic Medicine*. New York: W. W. Norton & Co., 1952.
8. *Outlook for Women in Social Case Work in a Medical Setting*, U. S. Department of Labor, Women's Bureau No. 235-1. Washington, D. C.: U. S. Government Printing Office, 1950.
9. ROBINSON, G. C. *The Patient as a Person*. New York: Commonwealth Fund, 1939.
10. WAELDER, R. Scientific approach to casework. In *Personality in Nature, Society and Culture* (edited by C. Kluckhohn and H. A. Murray). New York: Alfred A. Knopf, 1950.

Chapter 13

THE APPLICATION OF PSYCHOANALYSIS TO PSYCHOSOMATIC ASPECTS

FELIX DEUTSCH, M.D.

The use of the psychosomatic concept in medicine opened the medical wards and clinics for the psychiatric social worker. Without exaggeration, it can be stated that the social worker grasped the importance of emotional factors in disease earlier than the average physician, largely when psychoanalysts brought these factors to her attention. Owing to her psychiatric training, she, in turn, aroused the interest of the residents and interns in the medical departments in this concept and became the mediator between them and the psychiatrist. At present, this team work is indispensable in hospitals for the diagnosis and therapy of psychosomatic disorders which, since the last war, are by far better understood than before.

Psychiatric social work rests today on the understanding of the dynamics of human behavior, on the right evaluation of the social and cultural environment, and on the correct use of the client-worker relationship. These are the presuppositions for the effective management of the client and for a sound approach to the problem. Nevertheless, the understanding of the psychodynamics has its limitation. From psychodynamic instruction which she cannot assimilate, the social worker is likely to emerge more confused than enlightened. The value of analysis to the social worker will only be practical when psychoanalytic principles become more clearly adapted to her technique and to the client-social worker relationship.

Therefore the criteria for selection of psychosomatic content for case work students should be of a basic and general nature with the emphasis on those aspects which have to do with the client's current problems, reality adjustments and interpersonal relationships, including the one with the case worker himself. Avoidance of resistance and anxiety on the part of the student can be aided and genuine assimilation be encouraged by keeping the presentation of case material as much as possible related to the student's actual field work experience, and by limiting dynamic formulations to those which the student can actually, through school or experience, digest. She must be taught basic theories but at the same time she must see these theories confirmed in daily practice. Otherwise the theory is something she resists or denies. Since students are having such diverse experiences in practice, the task of selection of dynamic formulations to meet the student's level is very difficult. Case work teaching will probably tend toward a greater recognition of the "levels" at which students are working, and leave some of the content it now seems valuable to teach to be taught later to those students who want to specialize in this field. Material concerning the functioning of the ego and its defensive system in everyday living is in general more basic for case work than genetic formulations.

By and large the whole teaching should be considered from the point of view of:

1. The adaptability and usefulness of this material to the total group of case workers.
2. Its suitability in relation to the background and readiness of the students.
3. Its emphasis on the social implications of psychosomatic illness.
4. Its practical applicability to situations in which students as workers will encounter psychosomatic problems.
5. Its weight and emphasis in relation to the total psychiatric, medical and case work sequence.[1]

It is an experience annoying as can be to find after a long time spent in toil and effort that the problem which has been preying on one's mind is totally incapable of any solu-

[1] These formulations correspond in essence to the conceptions of Mrs. Alice B. Hyde, Professor of Social Work, who has been in charge of the seminars on psychosomatic concepts given at Boston University School of Social Work.

tion at all—either because there exists no indisputable method to unravel it or because considered in the cold light of reason, it turns out to be absolutely void of all meaning—in other words, it is a "phantom problem."

This is the statement of the famous physicist Planck in reference to the mind-body problem and to the physical or mental processes. Since they are the selfsame processes, but viewed from two diametrically opposite directions, there can be no such problem, when one speaks of conscious states only. But, since many processes, perhaps even the most decisive ones, take place in the unconscious, the question arises whether they can be reached by scientific analysis.

Psychoanalysis as the science of unconscious mental processes has been the method of formulating psychodynamic terms for biological events which, if expressed in physiological terms, would not explain the emotional feelings of a human being. Hence, without the acceptance of the unconscious the psychosomatic concept is untenable. As we know, the unconscious comprises all mental and bodily experiences of the past, which, once conscious, had been repressed and forgotten but still exert their power on the consciousness, simultaneously motivating and determining psychosomatic behavior. If one adheres exclusively to the principle of the conscious, one must arrive at a concept of reality in which everything is taken at face value.

From the psychoanalytic point of view the psychosomatic concept comprehends the problem of bodily ego behavior under the impact of id and superego demands on one hand and of environmental factors on the other hand. Furthermore it is the concept of how the ego makes use of bodily structure and bodily functions for its defenses, which may be called the ego's body politic, in contrast to the ego's sociopolitic for social adjustment problems and to the ego's mind politic as far as intrapsychic problems are concerned.

In a more general way the psychosomatic concept comprises the systematized knowledge of how to study and understand biological processes, which are fused and amalgamated with emotional processes.

A schematic sketch of the antagonizing relationship between

the instinctual forces—the id and the objecting ones—the super-ego—on one hand and the continual influence of this unconscious psychologic process on the body on the other hand can illustrate how the ego may use the body for its defense against the demands of these forces and of those of the outside environment to achieve the adjustment necessary for the equilibrium. The outside world exists only in so far as and in what way the ego makes use of the sense perceptions for the contact with the reality. It depends on the politic of the body ego, whether it withdraws from or whether it seeks closer contact with the reality. Accordingly certain bodily functions can become functionally more or less active depending on the ego's adaptive pattern of keeping peace.

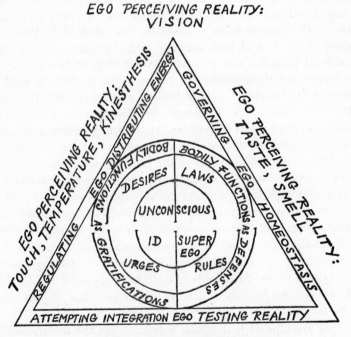

TABLE I

This sketch illustrates how psychosomatic symptoms can develop. The more sense perceptions are used by the ego for its defenses, the more solidly will the symptom complex be formed and the more resistant will it be against the treatment.

To an individual the body represents "reality," which he cannot deny because he would have to deny his existence. A newborn child knows only one reality, i.e., his body, which he can feel, touch and reach, and the whole world for him does not go beyond this sphere. Later he begins to use the other senses—kinesthesis, hearing, taste, and vision for the awareness of his own body. The child soon learns that what he thought was a part of himself is sometimes gone and he has to give it up. This loss is the first and deepest source of that which we call fantasy, because what is no longer seen or no longer in the realm of ourselves has disappeared and can only be imagined from memory or in fantasy. It therefore belongs to irreality. The small child therefore reacts to the loss of both animate and inanimate objects (that which he imagines is a part of himself) with protest or sorrow and expresses these feelings in crying. This reaction is used to retrieve the imaginary part of himself and he is reconciled only when it is reunited with himself. In this sense the whole outer world was once a part of ourselves, in our imagination, and therefore the objects of the outer world remain, and are used as, the deposits of our emotion and of the fantasies which we once had about them because we thought they were part of ourselves.[2]

The old experience that the world—which was once a part of ourselves—has been gradually taken away from us, is never completely forgotten. The unconscious wish to incorporate it again leads to different emotional attitudes toward our own body. For these reasons we can produce and exercise all our feelings toward our bodies as we do to objects outside of us—and we do that. Moreover, the feelings which we direct to other objects must have originally been experiences in ourselves.

This assumption is the basic condition for the understanding of the fact that our emotions are continually at work in and on our bodies, whenever and because they cannot always find objects

2 *Editor's note:* Cf. Chapter 3, pp. 29 f.

in the outer world and have to return to our bodies in which they can create sensations whose origin is so often completely obscure to us, viz., unconscious.

The interrelationship between the individual and the environment is therefore always reflected in and answered by bodily sensations which can be changed and influenced, depending on the fantasies which play a role in this relationship. The confrontation of the social worker with the person to be interviewed can produce visible and invisible bodily reactions on account of the transference.

It is easily understood that the continual contact between members of the family creates to some extent a mutual correlation in the functions of their bodies. We see the continual attempt of sons to resemble fathers, of daughters to resemble mothers, and we know that this process, which we call identification, means not only resemblance in character qualities, but also in the bodily actions and functions. Identification is often accompanied by an imitation in bodily behavior, not only of the healthy parts of the partner-object of the identification, but also of the sick parts.

In every normal human being, certain emotional processes are always at work; there is an attempt to control them and to find a balance among these different emotional processes. To give an example: the bodily musculature has a certain task in these emotional processes which is easily understood. If someone is confronted with a dangerous situation which comes from the outside, he has three possibilities, either to attack or to defend himself or try to escape. In all these situations, he may use his musculature and if he is not able to do either of these things, he may develop anxiety. Sometimes we see explosions of anxiety in people who are deprived of the free use of their muscle movements, for instance, in persons who because of fractures are in a plaster cast for a rather long time. In addition, we may observe outbreaks of anxiety in jails where prisoners sometimes revolt, although there is no possibility of gaining anything thereby. The revolt is merely an outlet for the accumulation of anxiety. On the other hand, we sometimes see the opposite, for instance, people who seek restrictions on the free use of their movements.

Some types of criminals who are in reality kind and gentle persons repeat crimes so that they will be imprisoned. The restrictions on their freedom imposed by the jail are, for them, a protection against the abuse of their freedom which may lead to actions connected with anxiety.

All this means that the musculature serves a definite purpose, namely, to release anxiety by action, not only in situations in which an individual moves with a definite purpose, but also in situations in which movements have no obvious purpose. The latter betray the extent of an individual's inner anxiety and the need for preventing an accumulation of the anxiety. In some neurotics who develop what is known as a shell shock-neurosis, the only symptom is a permanent shaking either of parts of the body or of the whole body. It seems as if these movements were an attempt to make up for the flight which they could not make in the face of the danger when they were surprised by the sudden shock.

The use of the breathing musculature in anxiety states is very often expressed by rapid respiration, which does not serve the need for more oxygen, but is the expression of attempts to get rid of anxiety. In our civilization we are compelled to inhibit free movements of our body, in contrast to primitive people and infants, who make much greater use of muscular movements to express emotions. These conventional restrictions are in some part responsible for the readiness to develop anxiety.

Grownups with greater self-control show their inner tension only in the facial muscular movements.

The inhibition of the use of our musculature by inner laws leads to the same or to an even greater reaction on the emotional side, in so far as this inhibition is then expressed in attacks in which the meaningless movements are a mixture of the rebellion against this forced inhibition of movements and the aim to get rid of the anxiety. People climb mountains, athletes fight in competitive play to get rid of anxiety.

To summarize, the muscular movements which we can observe in a person betray to some extent the emotional state of the personality, an exposure which we may use in the judgment of the individual.

There exist no bodily functions which cannot be used for the expressions of emotional needs. Certain primitive biological needs are common to all individuals. In infancy they center in the feeding, secretory and excretory functions. Some of these needs are satisfied within the organism independently of the environment. Others, such as feeding, are dependent for their fulfillment on the environment, as mother and nurse, and soon become intimately related to and conditioned by the environment. They thus become secondarily emotionalized. Without discussing the full theoretical implications of these statements, one may state that patterns of emotional behavior are thus laid down, which contain both psychological and somatic components. The infant reacts to the gratification or frustration of these needs with emotional responses. The gradual adaptation to reality begins at this period, and specific, emotional significance is attached to an individual in the environment according to the role he plays in the fulfillment or frustration of these needs. The manner in which a person reacts to conflicts is greatly influenced by his reactions at this time. These conflicts may be solved either normally or neurotically.

A simple example of a normal conflict and its solution in a child's life is the following one: a child may have a marked preference or wish for a certain type of food. The mother denies the child's wish. The child may react to this denial with hostility. Since there is a need to retain the mother's love, this hostility may not be expressed because of a fear of punishment or loss of affection. The conflict then ensues between the wish for the food and the fear of losing the mother's love. The child's solution may be the acceptance of a substitute for the desired food or the acceptance of the denial. The role of the forbidding parent may even be assumed by the child itself through the mechanism of "incorporation," and one sees in this mechanism a prototype of the pattern of conscience formation. Should this happen, subsequently in a similar situation there may arise a purely internal conflict involving the child's conscience. During the further development of the child, various other biological needs appear. The gratification or frustration of these needs gives rise to new conflicts to which the individual reacts in terms of his past experiences. The type of conflict may be similar in different persons and thus modes of behavior may universally have characteristics in common.

Among these universal experiences are anxiety, shame, embarrassment, disgust, rage, pleasure, the need to be loved, and various forms of psychosexual satisfactions. Each of these complex emotional states has physiological correlations: shame may be accompanied by blushing; disgust by nausea; anxiety by pallor, increased blood pressure and accelerated heart rate. These physiological responses are not invariable, but tend in each individual to repeat the psychophysiological characteristics laid down in early life. The degree to which psychological factors distort or inhibit the somatic component may determine whether the bodily functions of an individual will respond normally or pathologically.

The case worker should recognize that the age period in which somatic illness occurs is of great importance, because of the difference in the ego strength of the given periods. An illness occurring at three or five may have a significance to the individual that is different from the same illness occurring during the latency period or during puberty. Coming at the height of an unresolved hostility to a parent, it may be interpreted in fantasy as retaliation or punishment. In another situation in which the need for sympathy and affection from the parents is threatened by the arrival of a new sibling, the illness may provide a solution for the rivalry. Environmental stresses, cultural factors, social needs present at any given period in the life of the individual play an important role.

An illness gives rise to a certain immediate gain in terms of gratification of various needs, and this exploitation of illness or "secondary gain" plays an important role and may often determine its course and outcome. The gain here involved, however, arises after the onset of the illness, and should not be mistaken by the student for the etiological factor. There is a tendency to overvalue immediate reality factors as etiological rather than as precipitating causes of psychosomatic processes. The bodily symptoms which appear are the defenses of the ego and represent the unsuitable attempt of a conflict solution.

A neurotic conflict solution in the example cited above would be as follows: the child, not receiving the food it wishes, is forced to accept the substitute food because it fears either direct punishment or loss of the mother's affection. It eats the food and may then vomit. In this way, the child both accepts the command to eat and at the same time rejects the unwanted food. The pattern of vomiting laid down at this stage will subsequently be revived in any situation which is reminiscent of and associated with a similar type of conflict. If the current conflicts are of such a nature that the ego organization cannot arrive at a satisfactory solution, a regression to older patterns of behavior, i.e., to conflict solution mechanisms at a more primitive level, will result. This formulation is in accord with the concept of regression. In these attempts at solution, the individual responds with the same somatic patterns utilized in the earlier development of his personality.

The significance of early experiences vary from person to person. Conflicts which arise during the suckling period lead to psychosomatic responses which give a different direction to the development of personality than conflicts and experiences arising at a later date.

A very important pattern is the patient's relationship to his own body, which he had before he fell sick. Every illness disturbs the balance of the personality, which must be recovered when the illness is over. What upsets the balance is the psychic reaction of the patient to the body which is endangered by the sickness, a reaction which consists of certain emotional factors. This upset in the emotional life is what responds to the handling, management, and therapy of the patient. We must realize that every person reacts differently to an illness, and that this reaction is not accidental, that it is defined by the personality structure of the person. Therefore, the reactions will be different in different persons. As we know, some people react to physical illness with anxiety, others with impatience, and still others are not affected very much. Some lose hope from the very beginning; others do not lose self-confidence in spite of a chronic or recurrent illness. Moreover, some people are very eager to be nursed and petted, and show a very passive attitude in this condition. Others rebel against this, and resist giving up, so to speak, their independence. They distrust those people who want to make them admit they are ill, and it sometimes takes a long time before they surrender. It is a common experience to find those people who lose their self-confidence too readily remain ill longer than those who resist this loss more. What we are confronted with then, in the illness, are expressions of the personality such as anxiety, fear, hypochondriacal ideas, despair, loss of confidence, and resentment. What we see then is not really a change in the personality under the influence of the illness, but only an accentuation of certain character features which have not been on the surface as long as the patient was in a healthy condition. It seems to be true that every somatic illness creates at the same time a so-called neurotic reaction of the personality which has to be taken into consideration during the treatment. What we have to realize is that it is the whole personality which reacts to the threat of any kind to the body. Every human being settles in any illness a certain amount of emotional conflicts and uses the opportunity of being sick for settling some of his emotional problems. Either it is asthma, or it may be typhoid fever. The danger of an illness for the personality rests in the tendency of the patient to derive, for instance, too much gratification from the illness that is called the secondary gain of the illness, and further, the tendency to divert interest from the outer world completely to the body itself. Drawing attention thus from the outer world to the endangered organism is then used as a kind of protection of the body and creates a situation which is often not easy to dissociate.

There are those patients who show from the very beginning a tendency to return to a very passive behavior and who want to be mothered. Others, on the other hand, reject this approach to their personality, and do not want to be treated like children. In these cases an approach must be used which is different from the former one. Persons with illnesses, which are accompanied by pain, are usually more resistant to any kind of approach. On the whole, we have to realize then that any patient looks, to some extent, for a secondary gain from the illness. Some escape very readily into the illness from unpleasant realities; others see in their illness a kind of punishment which should solve some of their guilty feelings, and generally, all patients regress more or less deeply into an earlier period of their lives.

In psychosomatic disorders, we find that the illness itself represents a conflict solution which the patient prefers to exhibit as an emotional expression. This kind of conflict solution can be expressed either in disturbance of the whole body or in special organs, but we must realize that since this is a solution, the patient, therefore, is not able and not willing to give up this solution until a better one is offered. This implies that those patients will show a resistance against the cure and will prefer to remain sick. This is, of course, not a conscious process, because the patient himself is not aware that the sickness itself represents such a solution. However, there are those patients who are so afraid to speak of their own anxiety, which they would exhibit if they gave up their bodily expression of their conflict, that they find many ways to confirm their illness as independent of their emotional conflict, so that they prefer, for instance, to remain invalids for the rest of their lives. There are others who have the need to look for a conflict solution by turning to the surgeon. There are patients who have so many operations that it impresses us as a need to be punished for guilty deeds, for which they use the surgeon as the executioner.

The different kinds of reaction to sickness depend on the patient's relationship to his own body in the past. The experiences sustained in his childhood determine very often his relationship to his body. It might have been a very transient and harmless but frequent involvement of the body in a process of organic disease in the earliest childhood which laid down the pattern for the later behavior, in which the patient uses the body, and always the same part of the body, for the expression of a struggle or conflict. What is important to know is that the coincidence of emotional processes with a harmless bodily disorder in early childhood might lead to such a fusion of those processes with the whole personality, so that they will always show the same pattern of psychosomatic behavior in later life.

We also have to realize that many of those patients use their illness not only to punish themselves, to get rid of guilty feelings, but also in order to place the blame for their sickness on a person

in the environment, whom they want to feel sorry and responsible for their being sick; that means that they want to punish
the person in the environment for that which happens to themselves, and want to take advantage of the guilty feelings of the
persons in question. Very often, on the other hand, they are the
victims of the aggressions of other persons in so far as a family
member might use a patient as the object of his very covered-up
and hidden hostility; that is, some family members may need
those patients to be sick, and to keep them sick, in order to act
out on them their hostility by overcompensated loving behavior.
They keep the patient sick, so to speak, in order to show, through
their overprotective behavior, that nobody can accuse them of a
hostile feeling against the sick person. On the other hand, a patient who is the victim of this approach, often very readily accepts this kind of approach and wants to remain sick because he
can then enjoy the love of which he is in such need.

What we have to take for granted is that every patient regresses to an earlier period of life in illness. Regression of bodily
functional behavior can take place at any age. We can have it
even in infants who, as we know, when the nurse is changed or
when they are left by the mother, regress very soon to a behavior
which might be expressed in the giving up of progressive attitudes and of the body training which they have gained. Those
infants might suddenly refuse to eat, or they might start to soil
again; they might lose weight or again wet their pants. They
might use this bodily behavior either to express their sorrow or
their frustration of love. They might use the functions of intake
or elimination to express their resentment against the environment.

Any elements of those babyish and childish behaviors we find
in the so-called psychosomatic disorders. Seen from this point of
view the case worker has to realize that the client whom she
handles in the case worker-client relationship is always a child
to some extent.

The practical application of the psychosomatic concept to case
work and the problems of the extent to which the case worker
must confine herself, on the one hand, and to which she must
manipulate with knowledge and professional skill, on the other

hand, shall be illustrated with a case chosen at random from many others which had been used for teaching purposes:

It deals with a psychosomatic disorder, which is as a rule most resistant against treatment and management by all people involved.

The psychosomatic story of this client, a woman, who was thirty-five years old when she was referred to the social service, contains the essential factors for which one is looking in a case of atopic dermatitis, viz.:

1. Skin disease in the earliest childhood, probably originating on a genetic basis.
2. Deviation and fixation of instinctual drives during the earliest psychic development and fusion of these with the different sense perceptions related to the skin, being used by the ego for the pathologic conflict solutions.
3. Complementary neurotic traits of the environment which decreased the strength of the ego.

In selecting those pertinent data from the psychiatric history of the client, it was elicited that in her third year an accumulation of harmful experiences occurred: she was hit by a truck, badly frightened, anuric for several days and developed her first skin eruptions. Shortly afterwards her mother died and her skin condition became worse. She became very disturbed, since the attachment to her father met many frustrations. He was a compulsive neurotic, overconscientious, strict, punitive person, who wavered between affection and withdrawal of love to the girl, who was the only child. She clung to him, but was often sent away to relatives. After two years of hope and despair, the hardest blow occurred when the father remarried a likewise compulsive person, a puritanic domineering, nagging and cold woman. The skin condition took a turn to the worse. The unexpressed hatred against the stepmother found its outlet in attacks of furious scratching and in temper tantrums. Since those outbursts met with punishment, the anger turned against the skin. The need for hiding the "bad" skin led to a secretive behavior on the one hand, and to exhibitionistic and voyeuristic tendencies on the other hand, expressed in intense sexual curiosity. She liked to be fondled by older men, to be looked at and to look at them. In her adolescence she emerged as a very religious girl with sharp repression of any sexual and aggressive feelings. Since the ego needed stronger defenses to maintain the repression, the girl developed apart from her maltreatment of the skin, the punishing attitude of slapping her face, particularly her eyes, with one hand and covering her mouth with the other hand. This kind of punishment gave her the permission to give in to the forbidden erotic wishes toward the father, by keeping company with older married men. For that she had again to atone by being very conscientious. She married finally, thirty-one years old, a father figure, the dream of her earliest childhood. Shortly afterwards her stepmother died. During all the conflictuous periods of her development her skin's appearance changed accordingly. However, the last blow that again "a mother" has to die just when she married a father image and when she moved to her father's home, made the skin worse than ever because of her furious scratching against the itching. But scratching was not enough, she had to slap her face, i.e., nose and eyes. She developed cataracts on both eyes and became partially blind. This self-destructive behavior appeased her conscience, allowed her to become pregnant and to fulfill her infantile wish to have a child from father. That raised again her guilt feeling like in a vicious cycle. To expiate for this sin she scratched and slapped the eye on which she was operated, bringing about a complete blindness on that eye. That was sufficient expiation. She could have the child, a girl, could give up her scratching and her skin healed up. She remained symptom free for almost one year. However, when the father engaged in relationships with another woman, whom he finally married, the skin symptoms became worse again, the scratching and the slapping penance started again. An operation on the other eye was contemplated. She counterbalanced this threat by achieving her purpose of becoming pregnant again. Since this operation led to complications with further diminished eyesight, she did not need to act destructively against herself as she had done before in an identical situation. A boy was born.

The contact with the case worker began before this second pregnancy occurred. What situation did the social worker meet and what task as an adjustment adviser was expected from her? It was certainly a very complicated one.

She had been informed by the psychiatrist about the past history and the psychosomatic implications. She understood what had been the trigger situations for a relapse of the psychosomatic skin conditions. These situations had appeared in the past several times, though not with all precipitating factors involved at each time in reality, but always with the same unconscious wishes in the background. These unconscious wishes began when she was three years old—when her mother died—and then were stirred up when she was five years old—when her father remarried—and much later when she had relationships with older married men and then when she married a father image and her stepmother died, and finally during pregnancy. The case worker had to be aware of the severe guilt feelings of the client for her hostile attitude against all mother figures and her need to punish herself for these attitudes and for her unconscious wishes toward father figures. It was apparent that the patient had chosen her skin and her eyes as the part of the body for the pathologic conflict solution. The following questions arise:

1. What are the social implications of the client's condition?
2. What kind of transference relationship shall the case worker expect to happen and how shall she behave in this relationship?
3. What is the effect of the client's emotional and bodily behavior on the husband and the child?
4. What kind of service, financial aid, attention, support can the social worker give to the client?
5. How can the worker relieve burdens in the patient's daily living, which will lessen her helplessness because of her poor eyesight and what activities should she propose to her, which will relieve her guilt feelings and her need of punishing herself?

With all these questions in mind the case worker had first of all to manage the home situation. She helped her to obtain a housekeeping service which relieved the client's feeling of helplessness and gave her the permission to be dependent. It prepared her also for being able to meet the separation from her father, with whom she lived and whose house she had to leave very soon because of his plan to remarry.

Already a few months earlier the client had been handled by a social worker, who had played the role of a good mother by driving her around in her car, eating together with the client and giving her other opportunities of having common enjoyments together. Furthermore, by suggesting to her to become an active worker in the League for the Blind, the case worker deflected the aggression from the client to others, on whom she could overcompensate her destructive tendencies by love and support.

Since the client mourned for the loss of this case worker, the new one had to restore the loss. She had to follow the footsteps of her predecessor for the development of a favorable transference relationship. She had to commend and praise the client whenever possible.

What could she do to alleviate the unconscious resentment of

the client for having been left by her father who preferred another woman, and what to offset her unmerciful scratching?

The social worker gave her the opportunity of denying the loss
by encouraging her to go away on a vacation and to leave the
home and the family for a time. That represented an act of
revenge as if she would have said to father: "Not you are leaving
me, I am leaving you." The influence of such an emotional experience on the skin condition was apparent. It made it also possible for the client to find in the social worker an ally, to whom
she could express her feelings against the father. If enough of
this hostility could be poured out, the way would be open for a
reconciliation with her new stepmother.

Manipulating this difficult relationship, the case worker assigned to the client a role, in which she could see the father as a
sick man, whom the new wife would lose soon any way. That
made it possible for the social worker to bring the client and the
future stepmother together on equal footing—so to speak. The
client could minimize the loss, since on one hand her rival could
have the father only for a short time and on the other hand she
herself would survive the father, gloating over the retaliation.

On account of it the relationship to her husband improved
considerably because he remained alive as the living father image,
who stayed with her and who gave her the girl-child. This child
was in some respect she herself and in loving her and in magni-
fying her virtues she restituted herself. The social worker acted
accordingly and strengthened the client's opinion of the girl.

When the client returned from the vacation her skin was clear
and her mood more stable. She was prepared to move to new
quarters, although she looked forward with mixed feelings to
the separation from her father. When the father's marriage occurred she reacted with a cold, wheezing, and hostile feelings.
These she was able to express. The case worker deflected them to
the activity in the League of the Blind. There she could release
her guilt feelings by being a good mother to the blind and could
heal indirectly her self-inflicted wounds.

In the regular weekly contact with the client the case worker
used every opportunity for an expression of aggression as prevention against turning it against the skin. The ambivalent relationship to the little daughter gave such occasion. Since she was a
representation of the client herself everything that she said about
the child was only a projection of her feeling about herself. The
girl according to her age was very active and destructive, which
was of great concern to the client. Being daily confronted with
this behavior it became a source of guilt feeling, which had to be
prevented from repression. It had to be verbalized and the social

worker as the moderator had to listen with cautiousness and permissiveness.

Just when this favorable situation had developed the eye specialist advised the patient to have the eye operated on in the near future. At that time the social worker-client relationship had already continued for nine months. The client agreed to have the operation, but saw in it also the danger of losing the eye. To compensate for it she succeeded in getting pregnant. She looked forward to having a baby. In the interviews with the social worker this wish was in the center of their conversation. However, when the operation was unexpectedly postponed by the eye specialist for a few months, it threw her out of balance, because the operation and the pregnancy were closely linked up. Whenever the case worker wanted thereafter to talk about plans for the baby, the patient became anxious and wanted to talk about the eye operation. She could not accept the pregnancy without the imagined sacrifice of the eye. The guilty feelings mounted, the need for punishment increased. The aggression against herself had to be discharged. The scratching bouts recurred, likewise the nose slapping and the eye rubbing. The psychiatrist intervened and tried to confront her with her unconscious guilt and with her self-destructive needs. The social worker induced her to talk about her little daughter and the curiosity of the child from where babies were coming. She spent much time with mother and child. She encouraged the client to take the girl with her to the obstetrician and to tell her about the forthcoming baby. The client told the social worker with great satisfaction that the girl expressed the wish of having a brother or sister and already was playing sister and brother with the dolls. The client joined the little girl in this game. The social worker guided the client into those consoling thoughts—by using the little daughter as the mouthpiece—saying that it is not wrong to have a baby. Thus she fulfilled on the one hand the very task of the social worker of acting with the client together in the reality situation, and on the other hand influencing indirectly favorably the psychosomatic symptom. That also brought about a better relationship with the new stepmother and permitted her to release old resentments against the former stepmother and to settle the repressed grief for the loss of her own mother. In the fifth month of her pregnancy the eye operation was performed and although the need of scratching made her skin condition worse, she no longer slapped her eye due to the continual motherly permissive behavior of the social worker. The guilt feeling became sufficiently relieved. However, the success of the operation, which restored the eyesight almost completely, was too much pleasure gratification for her. Although she did not scratch her eye, she denied the eyesight to herself, keeping her eyes closed or walking around as if she were blind. She felt angry against the psychiatrist, who confronted her with her denial, and against the social worker, whom she avoided. Her skin symptoms returned and she disclaimed any confidence in psychiatry and the social worker, showing discouragement in her behavior. She even began to speak in a childlike way, acting like a naughty child. This mood changed gradually after her return to her home, where the social worker again deflected her angry feelings onto the little daughter whose naughty, demanding behavior the mother began to criticize. The skin condition improved particularly when another eye operation became necessary. She indulged in the hospital care, having special nurses provided by the social worker during the first days. She felt loved and accepted by the doctor who had performed the operation without charging her. She behaved like a spoiled child and wanted to go on a vacation again, acting as if she were not pregnant. She made no plans for the baby and remained in this regressed condition until the social worker made the little daughter again a partner in the relationship with the patient. It was the child talking about the baby she was looking forward to see, and who played with her dolls by dressing them up with nice baby clothes. In the interviews with the social worker the client was always induced to talk about the child's ideas in relation to the little brother she expected to see soon. The girl herself assumed a motherly role toward her mother, behaved bossy and even told her not to rub her eye. The social worker encouraged the client in resuming her activities in the League for the Blind, to which she readily agreed. Throughout that time the client remained free of skin symptoms. Helped by the social worker, her social relationships improved and she began to participate in social events. Finally the client gave birth to a baby boy whom she nursed for three months. The social worker happened to be on vacation when the baby was born, but a substitute was provided in case the client should need help. The regular contact with the social worker was reduced to occasional visits. On these occasions the client proudly presented her baby boy, giving the impression of a happy mother. She remained free of skin symptoms so far.

It can be assumed that this improved condition was brought about chiefly by the efficient handling of the client by the case worker. Furthermore, it may be rightfully stated that the skillful management of the transference relation in which the case worker played the role of the understanding, good mother contributed largely to the success. That could be achieved only by indirectly relieving guilt feelings during the interviews, and by guiding the client into activities with blind people on whom she could undo the self-destructive and self-punishing attitudes against herself. Last but not least, the guidance of the client during the acting-out periods of her infantile pregnancy fantasies and the concomitant needs of atonement made further bodily expressions of the still not fully resolved infantile conflicts superfluous, since the changed reality—father's remarriage and the birth of her baby boy—gave sufficient opportunities for adjustment.

Not always can the management of a client with a psychosomatic disorder turn out as successfully as this case did. However, it was not only the skillful handling of the client which achieved the adjustment. There is more to it, which could not be demonstrated in this brief excerpt of the case history: that is the kind of interviewing and of guiding the client's thoughts.

One of the great difficulties in obtaining the right information about the meaning of the symptoms lies in the fact that the interviewed person does not know that he is using his symptoms as a solution of conflicts, or what he wants to express with his symptoms. As the motivations for them are unconscious they are repressed and cannot be revealed consciously. They can be brought to light only indirectly in the interview.

Obtaining the material and writing the case history of psychosomatic disorders cannot simply follow the well-established pattern of the ordinary medical case history. In medical diseases we are interested not so much in obtaining as many facts as possible, as in getting information that has not been prepared for the occasion. If one elicits properly this kind of history taking, one learns how the symptoms developed and what the symptoms meant to the client from early childhood. The client is stimulated to give the information needed when asked to describe his organic complaints without being aware of a psychological background in his illness. He will give the material necessary for proof of the psychosomatic unit in his illness only if he is unaware of what he reveals to us about his emotional life. If the examiner allows him to talk without asking leading questions, the client will usually give a detailed account of his complaints and ideas about his illness. Having exhausted his ideas and recollections regarding his organic disturbances, he will stop and wait to be questioned. The examiner waits until it seems clear that the client will not continue spontaneously, and then he repeats one of the points in the client's last sentences in an interrogative manner. The examiner usually repeats one of the last-mentioned organic complaints, being careful to use the same words as the client. The client then usually gives new information about his symptoms and is stimulated to further associations. He drifts into a communication in which he inattentively mixes emotional and somatic material. References to persons in his environment, present or past, begin to appear.

This is the critical phase of the examination. Here usually appear the first important hints leading to three essential points in establishing the case history: the old conflict, the recent conflict, and the time factors. The person who appears first in the case history is very often a relevant person. Somatic and emotional symptoms with reference to this person should be used as a word stimuli for new thoughts. From here, the client himself usually correlates the organic illness with his emotional life.

In this type of interview we learn a great deal about the conflict of the client, how it motivates his life and how he reacts to people with whom he is and was living. We get hints about the family relationships of his early life; clues as to why and when the symptoms developed; how the psychic make-up was influenced thereby; how the organic disturbances were utilized in conflict situations; and finally, the role of the afflicted organ's function in the psychosomatic pattern.

It will become apparent that the already premorbid personality used in its development certain parts of the body and bodily functions for the expression and solution of emotional conflicts which later become symptoms of the organic condition, and that the subjective body sensations are simultaneously symptoms of the neurosis and of the organic disease. This implies that the subjective symptoms of the disease are following the pattern laid down in the bodily and personality make-up. On the whole, the interview will show the fundamental, dynamic, uninterrupted interrelations of the client with his inner and outer environment. From this point of view, the term "psychogenic" which was at first so fruitful for, but later on seriously blocked, the application of the psychosomatic concept becomes outmoded. There does not exist an alternative to "psychogenic or not psychogenic." The fundamental question is: What is the interrelationship of certain psychological factors with certain biological ones?

It has to be borne in mind that the words used by the client during the interview always have manifold meanings: i.e., an intentional one and an unintentional one—a conscious one, and an unconscious one. Therefore, it is important during an interview to familiarize oneself with the client's vocabulary. This is done best by listening without interrupting. The interviewer then picks out a few of the words or expressions most often repeated, incorporates them into his own sentences and observes the client's reaction. The client may react unmistakably positive. He may become willing to talk, bringing new material. He associates to some extent to his own words which had been used by the interviewer.

The associations bring him nearer to the emotionally colored material he has suppressed or repressed. Sometimes it may seem as if this were leading away from the introductory material—but on the contrary, it only shows the ramifications of the material. The client himself then feels that he has wandered off from his original intention. This is the moment to take up anew the words and expressions used earlier by the client and thus, through this repetition, one establishes the continuity of this material. These words and phrases may or may not have a visible connection with the previous content. The purpose of this technique is to prepare for the identification of the client with the interviewer and to facilitate the transference relationship. The essential thing, however, is the intensification and continual guidance of the associations and the maintenance of their continuity. Pointing out this continuity to the patient prepares him for an insight into certain connections which he may have to face later. Often it leads to a kind of self-revelation, springing from interrelations which have become conscious to him. The use by the interviewer of words and expressions of the client has still other consequences. During the interview these word representations become inevitably intermingled with the words of the interviewer and thus bring into play new associations which did not exist before. As the interview progresses, one soon notices the person using the new word connections himself. They are thus carried over and anchored to other chains of associations. This facilitates the emotional discharge for the client, as the associative material has been thinned out, so to speak. It loosens and breaks through thought connections which had an important part in the formation and the rooting of the neurotic disturbance.

The timing of the repetition of the cue words is of decisive importance, but if one prematurely forces on the client the meaning of the words he just used, repeating them questioningly, he will often tend to retract or replace them by others, or change their meaning or deny having used them at all. He acts as if he were caught in a trap and becomes completely silent or very cautious in his choice of words, so as not to betray himself. Above all, some clients do not want to be pinned down, for, to be confronted with their own words is to them, so to speak, equivalent to a definite decision. They react with hostility to this confrontation. On the other hand, others regard it as a sign of acceptance which makes them ready to furnish more details to the stimulus word. For them, the words become magical signs which they welcome as being related to their fantasies. Others feel flattered by the repetition, feel appreciated and on equal footing with the interviewer and express this by emphatically taking over words of the interviewer.

This kind of interview with a client suffering from asthma may take the following course: the client relates the story of his illness, describing the various sense perceptions corresponding to his complaint—smell, taste, hearing, or pressure feelings on the chest. Stimulated by the sensation of smell, he associates different odors and reveals his attitude to the odors of his body, going back from the present to the past. He reveals some of his habits in this direction as well as some features of his character. Repeated use of the patient's organic complaints as a stimulation for further association leads to problems of secretion—the quality, quantity and consistency of the fluids, first of his nose, then of other excretory organs. He expresses fantasies concerning the origin of these and other fluids, including birth fantasies and his attitude toward water. Brought back to the subject of sensations in his nose, he may talk about adenoids, their removal and re-growth, and go on, for example, talking about swelling and growth in general, hinting at other problems of growth and shrinkage. At this point he may jump from one period of his life to another. After discussing taste sensations there usually follows a description of the color and consistency of phlegm. There are fantasies about infections in the respiratory tract and reports about the difficulty of getting rid of the "sticky stuff" associated with coughing spells, choking sensations, and leading to temper tantrums and stubborness.

This in general is the content of one interview in which there is included a great deal of life history, with organic and emo-tional data, showing the respiratory response to certain emotional crises. This sketch of a history obtained in this way describes to a certain extent the characteristics of a psychosomatic unit in an asthmatic, and suffices to clarify the co-ordination of the respira-tory symptoms with certain psychic complexes.

An interview with a client suffering from any other psycho-somatic disorder takes a similar course depending on the symp-toms around which the patient's complaints are centered. The method of interviewing is intimately connected with the treat-ment of a psychosomatic disorder. It is in some way a treatment by itself.

The methodological treatment of psychosomatic disorders has a goal. It aims to disassociate, to free, the afflicted organs from their unconscious meaning, from their symbolizations, from their abuse for defenses against anxiety, from the inhibitions as well as from their use for substitutional gratifications. When that has been achieved, we must realize that in addition nothing more can be done by psychotherapy to restitute the functions. By and large, the treatment always aims at strengthening the ego and to enable it to give up the use of a function and to change its "body politic." In that way, even the perception of unpleasant and painful sensations, based on organic tissue changes, can be re-lieved.

What has to be borne in mind is that a person will not give up his symptoms and, therefore, a psychosomatic disorder cannot cease as long as the emotional setting is not reshuffled and the psychic economy rearranged and psychic energies redistributed. The disappearance of the symptoms proves that such a process has happened. It has further to be realized that in the course of the therapeutic process the gradual disappearance of the organic expression of the psychological unbalance will be accompanied by the appearance of emotional symptoms. This is due to the fact that the person is still ill at ease in giving up the protective use of the body against danger from within. These dangers are:

1. Desires and forceful wishes which are rejected and suppressed because of their contradiction to reality.
2. Fears and anxieties regarding the gratification of these desires and wishes.
3. Guilt feelings and self-accusations because of these desires and wishes.
4. Accusations against the object of these desires and wishes.
5. Punishment for these desires and wishes.

It is an axiom that a person will resist any change of his choice of conflict solution as long as he feels uncertain of a better solution or as long as the conflict is not solved. Therefore, the assurance given to the person with a psychosomatic disorder, i.e., that nothing is wrong with him organically—can rarely help him. What he needs is a better and more acceptable conflict solution than the one through his bodily symptoms. The acceptance depends on whether he can get back what he lost, or whether he gets a satisfactory substitute for what he lost, or whether he can become reconciled with the loss, or whether what he wants is no more forbidden to him. Then the symptoms will have no further purpose and meaning and can be abandoned.

The outline of what the social worker should know about the psychosomatic concept, may be summed up in a nutshell as follows:

1. Bodily symptoms are expressions of emotions and these symptoms should be understood.

2. Why these symptoms are conflict solutions of emotions, how they should be handled, and how the bodily expression of the emotions can be changed to a verbal expression.

3. The psychological and social implications of a psychosomatic disorder; what they are, why and how they develop, and how they lead to personality patterns and personality deformations.

4. To what extent the ego is in need of its defenses.

5. That the approach to these disorders depends on the kind of neurotic factors involved.

6. What leads to the choice of a specific psychosomatic disorder.

7. The technique of interviewing clients with psychosomatic disorders, how to uncover the earliest roots and unconscious motivations of psychosomatic interaction.

8. What information she is expected to elicit for further evaluation of the disorder.

9. The management and adjustment of clients with psychosomatic disorders within the family frame.

BIBLIOGRAPHY

1. ALEXANDER, F. *Psychosomatic Medicine.* New York: W. W. Norton & Co., 1950.
2. BIBRING, G. Psychiatry and social work. *J. Soc. Casework,* June, 1947.
3. CANNON, W. B. *Bodily Changes in Pain, Hunger, Fear and Rage.* New York: Appleton-Century Co., 1936.
4. DEUTSCH, F. Present methods of teaching. *Psychosomat. Med.,* 2, 1940.
5. —— Social service and psychosomatic medicine. *News-Letter, Am. Assn. Psychiat. Soc. Work.,* 11, 1942.
6. —— Psychological methods of obtaining medical information. *Acta Medica Orientalia,* 5, 1946.
7. —— The psychosomatic concept. *Ibid.,* 7, 1948.
8. —— *Applied Psychoanalysis: Selected Objectives of Psychotherapy.* New York: Grune & Stratton, 1949.
9. DUNBAR, F. H. *Emotions and Bodily Changes.* New York: Columbia University Press, 1938.
10. FRENCH, T. M. and ORMSBY, R. Psychoanalytic orientation in casework. *The Family Welfare Association of America,* 1944.
11. GARRETT, A. Transference in casework. *The Family,* April-May, 1941.
12. —— and ROBINSON, V. P. Contributions of Freud and Rank to casework. *Ibid.,* January, 1940.
13. JOHNSON, A. and ROSS, H. The growing science of casework. *J. Soc. Casework,* November, 1946.

14. MAEDER, LEROY M. A. The concept of normal and abnormal. *The Family,* October, 1941.

15. —— Generic aspects of the intake interview. *Ibid.,* May, 1942.

16. PLANCK, M. *Scientific Autobiography.* New York: Philosophical Library, 1949.

17. RADO, S. Psychodynamics as a basic science. *Am. J. Orthopsychiat.,* 16, 1946.

18. REYNOLDS, B. *Learning and Teaching in the Practice of Social Work.* New York: Farrar & Rinehart, 1942.

19. SEGUIN, C. A. *Introduction to Psychosomatic Medicine.* New York: International Universities Press, 1949.

20. WAELDER, R. The scientific approach to casework. *J. Soc. Casework,* October, 1941.

21. WEISS, E. and ENGLISH, O. S. *Psychosomatic Medicine.* Philadelphia: W. B. Saunders, 1943.

Chapter 14

CONTRIBUTION OF PSYCHOANALYSIS TO THE PROBLEMS OF THE AGED

JOOST A. M. MEERLOO, M.D.

INTRODUCTION

In the handling of old-age problems many things today seem a matter of course as a result of a more advanced psychotherapeutic attitude. However, when I first was introduced to the psychiatric problems of the old-aged (1924), things looked very gloomy indeed. At that time available articles on mental afflictions of older age conveyed a sense of futility: intervention was hopeless and cure nearly impossible. We were shown the degenerative processes in the brain and other organs and that was all. Most senile patients had to be hospitalized in the end. Psychotherapy was not used; psychoanalysis was considered of little help—patients were estimated to be far beyond the age in which results could be expected. Sedatives and nursing were the only means that could be used.

Three important developments, however, changed our insight into what happened in old age and what could be done.

Increased Interest in Gerontology

Gerontology or geriatrics is the science of what happens in the old-aged and how difficulties can be treated and cured. There were special reasons why medical attention became sharply focused on this section of the population. Thanks to advancing medical knowledge and improved methods of hygiene and treatment, the division of the different age groups among the population has changed. Age dispersal shifted as opportunity for longevity increased the proportion of old-aged people. This situation presented new problems for general medicine, for psychology, and for sociology.

Statistical life expectancy has risen with startling swiftness. In Greek times it was 29 years; by 1900 it had moved upward to 44 years, and in our lifetime to 62 years. For women this expectancy is even longer, and this implies special problems for them. In 1945, statistics tell us, because of greater mortality among older men, 32 per cent of all married women were widowed by the age of 60, and 55 per cent by the age of 64. Beyond the age of 64, more than two-thirds of all women in the United States are either widowed or unmarried. This short and incomplete statistical survey alone points to a forced deprivation of love relations. The old-aged are compelled to live alone during a period in which they become more dependent and in need of help.

As a result of this shift in age groups, a new set of physical diseases and mental afflictions required the attention of the physician, diseases determined by biological decline. It was known that various impairments in bodily processes take place in the organism: decline of sharpness of the senses, increasing arteriosclerosis, increased blood pressure, declining sexual libido, more heart impairments, heightened irritability and lessened adjustment of cells, and a decline in regenerative potency of tissues. During declining years, more malignant tumors appear. However, there is no direct parallelism between such physical deterioration and the neurotic and psychotic disturbances we observe. Mental responses to gerontological changes in the body vary greatly.

The growing study of old-age afflictions, both physical and mental, has brought profit for both aspects.

It is difficult to affix a numerical definition to the terms *old* or *senile* because people vary so. Senility, or the process of involution, begins at different ages in different people. The time of the beginning of senility depends upon the person's biological and mental life experiences. As has been said already, the proportion of elderly people in our population is increasing rapidly. Our mental hospital population shows corresponding increases. In response to an inquiry (10), the Director of the Bureau of Statistics of the New York State Department of Mental Hygiene reported that as of October 1, 1949, there were "31,519 patients aged 60 or over on the books of the New York State Hospitals out of a total of 92,231." This is roughly one third of the mental hospital population. He further informed us that "patients aged 60 or over have an average duration of hospital residence of about one and one-half years. The per capita cost of maintenance per year during the year ended March 31, 1950, was $956.78." McGraw (15) points out that in the ten-year period 1936-1946, the percentage of patients aged 70 and over increased from 15 per cent to 26 per cent of the total patient population of New York State hospitals. The cost of this hospitalization is all the more expensive when one realizes that it is avoidable in many instances. As McGraw states, "Formerly if a person over 70 developed mental disturbances manifested by abnormal behavior, disturbance of mood, abnormality of mental trends as shown by delusions or alterations in the perceptive attributes (such as questionable hallucinations), and in addition exhibited memory disturbances, the prognosis was considered rather hopeless. . . . However, recent experience has shown that many mental disturbances of the elderly are transitory in character, are the results of emotional upsets, environmental stress, or toxic conditions, and that in a great many instances they may be favorably influenced or treated. . . ."

The Application of Psychoanalytic Knowledge to Old-Age Problems

If one is educated medically and familiar with the terms of "biological decline" and passive anticipation of the final "processes of death," one develops unwittingly a resignation to the manifold psychosomatic problems coming to the fore in the old-aged. Because of this prejudice, the scientific eye overlooks the remarkable fact that there are old people who have full command of their physical and mental capacities. The question arises: why do some have such good command and others such a poor one?

Among early students of psychoanalysis, Abraham (1) and

Ferenczi (6) in particular, began to throw new light on the psychological processes of the aged. Previously, Freud in "Mourning and Melancholia" (7) had laid the foundations for their research.

Psychoanalysis teaches us that the same psychological dynamisms come to the fore in the old-aged as in younger people. It is, therefore, possible by means of therapeutic measures used in normal psychoanalytic treatment, to lessen and change the impact of these dynamisms. Special circumstances in the old-aged often force us to change the technique, but treatment is possible and improvement is likely. What form the mental approach takes, I will explain in the second part of this chapter.

Intensified Occupational Therapy in Mental Institutions and Increased Use of Social Workers in the Field

In a recent article, Grotjahn (8) mentioned the prevalent hostile attitude toward the old-aged, concealed by a thin veneer of esteem and love. This attitude is related to anxiety-provoking identifications. "The aging people of this country feel more apologetic than proud of their age and try to keep up with the younger ones. . . . The young don't have the image of a wise old man. . . . The old have to compete, and cannot sit back. . . ." This presents an unrealistic (and hence neurotic) solution of the problem to an old person. Mental hospitalization is often resorted to for senile patients who show some depressive or paranoid trends, when actually intensive psychiatric and social guidance could stave off institutionalization.

It is a matter of course that such hospitalization influenced the old fatalistic psychiatric attitude. However, therapeutic measures underwent a change when the general attitude toward the mentally sick began to change.

Within mental institutions, a more active therapy started; thanks also to analysis, the psychiatrist got rid of his anxiety-provoking identification with the mentally ill. The inertia of the bed treatment was replaced by many variations of occupational therapy. Psychotherapy entered the asylum and patients were encouraged to be more social. I remember so well the amazement of doctors and nurses at the change in attitude of the senile dementia patient when he was able to do some work that suited him. An old continuously shouting woman, who had been confined to her bed for months, livened up the moment she was allowed to scrub floors, to sew and to work, as she had done all her life. Another patient livened up when she was allowed to work and to accept some responsibilities in the children's department. Even when patients were not able to take part in all the activities, the development of new social life and prestige did something to them and staved off the process of mental decline.

Improvement became even more evident when the social worker was called upon to overcome environmental deficiencies. Among special difficulties to be contended with were the loss of social ties, the increased struggle for social adjustment, loneliness, loss of love, the more difficult contact with reality, and lack of security. All these troubles provoked or worsened mental deterioration in the aged. Here especially the social worker can rebuild confidence and even cure where there was failure before.

In the course of experiences in the Vanderbilt Clinic, we have been able to bring several old people back to normal adjusted life by giving them the social care and advice they missed before. In this way, for instance, a formerly psychotic woman of 72 was even able to return to her job.

All these changing factors in general medicine and psychiatry have proven that mental disturbances can be prevented and treated with rising success. Increased psychological understanding with well-organized social psychiatric service now makes better approaches toward mental treatment of the old-aged possible.

PSYCHOLOGICAL PROBLEMS OF THE AGED

Now that we are more aware of the changed factors in our approach to the problems of the old-aged, it is easier to follow a survey of related problems. For an extensive clinical description of this field, I refer the reader to textbooks on psychiatry.

The onset of involution and decline differs widely among people. We may say this is dependent on the underlying neurosis and the degree of current frustration in finding a happy life.

JOOST A. M. MEERLOO

Usually one speaks of involution as starting in the period of decline, after the menopause in the woman, after the man, too, is warned by his body that he has reached the limit of his physical possibilities. However, it must be said that in many people the process of psychosclerosis may start in their late teens, and that others are still able to develop new capacities in very old age. This is the core of the problem of old age: why are there such tremendous personal differences in declining functions? Physiology and psychology both will, in the future, give their answers to this question. At the moment we can merely be descriptive. Many conflicts of the old-aged center around the failure to have found a more stable outlook on life, mentally and physically. In addition to our psychological investigations, philosophy, religion and sociology will be called on to contribute to the final solution of our question.

Originally it was believed that the decline and deterioration of life functions were mainly organic. However, more and more frequently, it has been found through experience that there is a much closer relationship between psychological functions and environmental influences. There is no direct simple parallelism between mental changes and physical decline. Some old people with chronic illness, even with brain disease, may still find their highest mental functions available; in others we find early mental involution without knowing yet the corresponding bodily changes. Psychologically we may expect that the failure of rigid defensive systems provokes the involutional mental disturbance. In several early involutional breakdowns, I found evidence of a lifelong compulsive defensive ritual.

Among the psychological changes of the old-aged, I want to call attention to the following categories:

A. *Changed attitudes toward the environment*
B. *Changed attitudes toward the body*
C. *Sexual problems*
D. *Other psychodynamics*

A. *Changed Attitudes Toward the Environment*
We often find that many involutional disturbances begin as a

reaction to some outside occurrence. The person is no longer able to deal with the troubles he had been able to overcome in his previous life. This increased sensibility to environmental influences is a result of a general weakening of ego and ego defenses. The front cannot be upheld any more. There is impaired adjustment, a dislike of change, a dislike of new things and ideas. The whole field of social relationships narrows. Although we may attribute the weakened ego in part to the organic process in brain and body, there is also a mutual relationship between changing elements and attitudes in the environment and the changed response of the old-aged. Cultural values determine to a great extent the place held by the old-aged in any society, and these influences vary greatly. Where mutual competition and immaturity are in high esteem, old age has become taboo; people dread losing the attention to which they have been accustomed. They become lonelier but also poorer in self-esteem. For most people, the struggle for life grows more difficult; through death of beloved ones, the world becomes a lonelier place, one begins to feel more and more superfluous and no longer needed. On the other hand, we have to be aware of the fact that there are cultures which cherish a growing esteem for the ripeness of old age (e.g., in China before the revolution). Under these circumstances, psychological problems involved will be very different.

The conflict brought on by retirement from business has a strong trigger effect on involutional disturbances. Besides the decline in financial income, the loss of a job has a tremendous symbolic meaning to the person. It involves loss of self-respect, accompanied so often by more hours of leisure without means to make them productive in a new way. The work one does in the world also has a sexual meaning: it represents one's value in the eyes of the sexual partner. It represents prestige and power; it is helpful in resolving aggressiveness and in repressing neurotic feelings. Outliving one's usefulness means loss of anticipation, of the tremendous drive to look forward and to expect what reasonably might not be expected. The result is a breaking through of feelings of defeat and failure, and repressed hostility cannot be repressed any longer. Because there is a repressed outlook on progression, people regress. Through lack of regular

work, they lose the opportunity to sublimate, another reason why
hostility breaks through. Many a man or woman who reaches the
age for a pension has anticipated a golden period of leisure; but
instead he gets lost in emptiness through lack of inner depth.
To find a new hobby, a new study, a new interest for these people
is the first aim of social therapy.

Another change which has a great trigger effect on older
people is moving. Because of loss of income or through death in
the family, or because of other reasons, a change of housing becomes necessary. But now suddenly hell breaks loose. The person could adjust to previous losses, but the change of familiar
surroundings becomes for him a symbol of nearing death; it increases awareness of being bereft and of loneliness. I saw several
cases of involutional depression in which the person stood his
difficult circumstances courageously till he had to move. During
wartime we became even more aware of this aspect when evacuation forced older people out of their familiar surroundings. They
had been able to adjust themselves to all other deprivations of
war, but the removal from the home caused depression and even
suicide. Younger people were more flexible—they did not find it
so hard to build a new nest.

For old persons the neighbor assumes a peculiar role: he becomes the symbol of the lost paternal relations toward whom ambivalent feelings are revived. The negative part of the ambivalence is projected onto the neighbor. I would like to call this
process "the totemization of neighbors." As a result, feelings of
persecution by neighbors develop, as is obviously found in the
so-called senile paranoia, but is apparent in lesser degree in
many mental disturbances of the old aged.

But the most important provocation of involutional disturbances is the death of one of the beloved. This too has more a
symbolic meaning than has the actual grief. Especially the unconscious relationship to the lost one determines the degree of
the shock effect. If there was much ambivalence, much latent
hostility, the weakened ego is no longer able to synthesize these
feelings—a sudden split in the tense feelings takes place. The
dead person is overidealized and the hostile counterpart is identified with; a typical introjection mechanism is provoked, so

beautifully described in Freud's "Mourning and Melancholia." The resulting self-hate and suicidal tendency are common symptoms in old age.

My impression is that especially when death of the beloved one is caused by a sudden unexpected accident, the trigger effect is most outspoken; a sudden totemization of the dead and the living takes place, in which the living person represents the hostile part of the old ambivalence.

Knowledge of this increased sensitivity to environmental changes is so important for our social therapy because we often see what can be accomplished by offsetting or overcoming the effects of the changes. Many of the involutional disturbances disappear when we introduce group work and give the patient new aims, or when we provide substitutes for his lost love, or bring him back to familiar surroundings.

B. *Changed Attitudes Toward the Body*

In all involutional disturbances conscious and unconscious concepts of death play a role. The different somatic warnings of the body remind us of the end of life and as a result various defense reactions against death are mobilized. The body asks for more attention, old hypochondriacal attitudes become fortified. The person grows more narcissistic. On the other hand, the coming of old age may be denied and the aged plays the role of being young. Impairment of vision and hearing is denied; hearing aids are refused. The old man tests his memory repeatedly in order to deny his failing perception and memory. There is a greater seeking after prestige combined with less productivity. Every real disease may be felt as a personal insult, an affront to the defensive system. One of my patients started his involutional depression at 72 after an appendix operation. The same defensive denial is found in those who begin zealously to test their libido. They become more licentious, return to homosexuality, want to prove their potency with young mates. Infantile perversions return. I saw several involutional depressions start after the onset of impotency in men with a typical narcissistic character structure.

Another example of withdrawal of interest from reality toward the body is shown in the heightened concern with body functions, covering the individual's more unconscious hostile attitude toward his own body. Eating becomes a new ceremonial to evade death. In a world that provides less satisfaction, his old oral dependency returns. Bowel evacuation is meticulously observed lest impaired body control should hinder the control against death. Loss of feces and loss of money signify, for some individuals, loss of life. The delusion of being poor is common. Depending on the patient's early psychosexual development and early infantile fantasies, these defenses against the fear of death may acquire different symbolic meaning for him. Consequently, in all patients we find the return of compulsive control of functions. One of my patients, who had had a hoarding compulsion at the age of five, started doing the same thing after he had to move to another home when he was sixty-nine. In many, the fear of insomnia actually symbolizes the fear of unconscious experiences during sleep, the fear of the loneliness of the dead.

Under the influence of organic disturbances of the brain, the body image may undergo other changes which may be expressed in fantastic dreams. A patient who recovered from a stroke became plagued by dreams of mutilated puppets.

C. *Sexual Problems*

If ever there is a time when sexual advice and information are needed, it is when people reach old age. Nevertheless, this period is a dark chapter in psychiatry because our countertransference attitude wants to deny sexual pleasure to the old-aged. We do not have detailed information regarding this period although we know there is a continual involvement in sexual yearnings and fantasies. Organic changes in sex organs (shrinkage, atrophy, arteriosclerosis, hormone changes, kraurosis, prurigo) cause changed feelings, which are again reacted upon with the changed and more infantilized sexual needs of the old-aged. In senile paranoia we encounter illusions of rape and incubus. Symbolic fertilization fantasies are expressed. Infantile scoptophilia is reversed so that the paranoiac woman believes that people are peeping at her. Eventually, the hallucinations assume a special form: the patient feels he is being beaten, pinched or flirted with. These changed and perverted sexual feelings and hallucinations must, in former ages, often have led to accusations and self-accusations of being bewitched. A gradual change takes place between normal and pathological sex feelings. The growing feelings of impotence, combined with increased needs for gratification, may cause a daily struggle. Patients who again find themselves fighting with their guilt feelings about masturbation must be instructed and reassurred again. I once treated a case of involutional depression who had been treated years before with electroshock, but had never been able to talk about her changed sexual needs. The knowledge, new to her, that masturbation was no sin and a very usual habit at that age, changed the whole aspect of her continual worrying.

Another woman, who lived alone and was full of paranoid ideas expressed in sexual suspicion, changed her attitude when she was allowed to kiss motherly the young male social worker on his weekly visit. In her fantasy he played the role of lost son and father, but this new tie did the trick: it got her out of her delusions, her libido found outlet through normal channels.

The advice sometimes given older lonely people that they get married can be useful if they are prepared for the special difficulties of mutual adjustment. I once had to give advice to a newly married couple of over seventy when the man suffered from his impotence and the woman explained his abstention as unfaithfulness. In discussing their mutual inhibitions and shyness, they gradually reached a phase of mutual masturbation with great gratification for both parties. This stimulated the man to normal potency from time to time. The common transference on the accepting, benevolent therapist played the greatest role in the mutual adjustment.

The study of sexual problems in the old-aged is just in its beginning. Superficially it looks as though there were less demand for help with their sexual problems. On deeper analysis, however, we find that here is a sleeping volcano full of underground turmoil.

D. *Other Psychodynamics*

Unconscious anxiety or the conscious fear of death may be

expressed in manifold symptoms. In most patients it is concentrated around the fear of sleep or the denial of sleep. Old long-buried fears are reactivated: the fear of becoming dependent, of intrusion of other people into their lives. The oedipal fears return. Patients displace such fears to the different noises they hear. Irritating noises may symbolize the voice of the superego. They dream of thieves and murderers, or they symbolize this persecution in the fear of being poisoned.

The ego reacts to the feelings of decline with growing suspicion and even paranoid feelings. Some patients begin to mull over all the rejections they received in their lives. Primal scenes become vivid and the castration fear is projected on all unpleasant interference by the environment. One patient suddenly awoke hearing fire engines in the street. This started an anxiety attack which in analysis could be traced back to early homosexual fears of the brother. The return of infantile fantasies is also related to old oral aggressive tendencies. Food becomes a symbol of the deceased. Some patients cannot eat because food is taboo; in others it becomes part of their hoarding compulsion.

Special fears are aroused by memory gaps which are often compensated by secondary fantasies (confabulations), but behind this artificial filling of mnemonic emptiness there is always fear. There is weakened emotional control, tears come easily, concern or attention for others is lessened, the same conversation is often repeated, hiding the unconscious identification with the dead.

Increased aggressiveness is often evident as people approach old age and may be shown in a rather paradoxical way: greater aggression toward their own body, a neglect of decorum, increased accident proneness. But the hidden aggression comes more to the fore in the fight to master the returning ambivalence toward the lost love objects. Sometimes the repressed death wishes toward the deceased are openly expressed, sometimes the deceased are highly idealized and the hostility displaced toward the living. The image of the dead is split in two, the loved one is buried, the hostile one projected onto a living person. In order to have better relations with the dead, such patients must have enemies among the living.

As a result of these difficulties the patient isolates himself more. In one of my involutional patients depression and self-isolation broke out after a neighbor started a fight with her and she suddenly began to fight back in a furious way. This occurrence provoked various delusional ideas.

The hidden aggressive attitude comes to the fore in a change of voice, in a more growling querulous conversation, broken through by spells of crying self-pity.

When there is fear and aggression, there is a feeling of guilt. This arises from self-reproach because of having lived longer than the lost ones. It is a normal expression of all mourning to feel guilty because of all the good things we failed to do for the deceased. Those who cannot mourn honestly become depressed. But the deeper guilt is related to the revival of repressed infantile material. This type of guilt and the accompanying remorse we often find in narcissistic types who have been able all their lives to keep the mask of health and pseudo happiness; but now, in their loneliness and bereavement, they become aware of their egocentric attitude. In their remorse, they feel they deserve what they provoked. The remorse is the greater because of the lack of love they themselves must endure. But at the same time, they fight against these consequences in human relationship. They ask for more love than usual and greater consideration, and feel, of course, more guilty. One such patient, a lifelong Don Juan and bachelor, perpetually retreated from all friends and subjected himself to all kinds of symbolic penitence. In his analysis the fear of ultimate punishment was the dominant theme.

Another patient, who suddenly expressed all his pent-up aggression toward his son, reacted to this a couple of days later with a deep melancholic self-reproach, refusal of food and other signs of self-punishment.

In such cases, a peculiar battle with the superego arises. Through the return of infantile ambivalence, the superego is identified with the hated parental figure. There is increased disinhibition but also increased guilt and self-punishment. Remorse and suicide may be the outcome, through which, at the same time, union with the hated parent and killing of him are attained.

In every treatment of involutional disturbance there is the risk of sudden suicide.

The return of the infantile ambivalence and the need for totemization lead to peculiar symptoms belonging to the varied symptomatology of senile psychosis. The clearest examples are to be seen among old people living in slovenliness and squalor, with loss of all decorum. At the same time they are hoarding all their possessions, their money; in the end they starve in the midst of plenty. Symbolically this is the ultimate protest against oral deprivation and against the last deprivation, the deprivation of death.

THERAPY

It is often amazing to find what good results one can obtain in the psychological treatment of old-age problems. Psychoanalytic concepts are applied, but the treatment differs from the treatment of common neuroses. However, one has to keep in mind that part of the impaired biological function cannot be reconstructed. From the outset, our aim in therapy must be the solution of the psychological impact of changed circumstances. One of the goals must be a form of re-education which assures the person that he can be useful again. In such a case environmental therapy can be just as important as working through of the inner difficulties. In a psychiatric outpatient clinic, many cases were seen (10) in which the social worker and her guidance in the home and the community contributed tremendously to the healthy readjustment of the patient. What always amazes the therapist is how much of the lost mental functioning can be repaired.

Analytic therapy of involutional disturbance is, in some ways, easier, in other ways, more difficult than therapy for younger age groups; much depends on the amount of contact that can be established. The technique is the same. Often, a positive transference relationship develops easily because of a greater transference need (16). The therapist and the social worker, both, replace the lost love and the lost contact. In the transference, the analyst often becomes an imaginary child of the old patient. One old patient justified his coming to me by saying he wanted to teach me the facts of life. He remained proud of the fact that others might learn from his life experiences. Through my acceptance of the role of being his student, tremendous improvement in his symptoms was attained.

Among older patients there is also less resistance because approaching death presses them unconsciously to a reviewing of life and a comparison between early goals and actual achievements. My impression is that because of the weakening defenses, there is a better and more direct contact with the unconscious.

Older patients react more easily to interpretations and feel more easily relieved by relating the actual conflicts with those of the past. Yet the very weakness of defenses which, on the one hand, makes it possible to reach the patient's unconscious, on the other hand makes it more difficult to diminish the ties with the therapist. However, in this greater dependency need, the social worker can take over and be a part of the transference process. The patient in his deep identification with the dead, may cause some difficult countertransference reactions in therapist and social worker. Therapists are reluctant to give so much attention or to be so patient when their own fear of death is involved.

I would like to stress this point of countertransference because the degree of our accepting attitude toward the aged will have much to do in determining our success. The relative weakness of the patient and loss of usefulness provoke in others the bossing paternal attitude they resent so much. The social worker who is asked to help in a home for the old-aged has to be very careful not to fall into this common mistake. If she is able to reconstitute the family sphere, transferring responsibilities to the members, organizing groups and using occupational therapy; finding the right middle road between need for privacy and the desire for company, for the longing for freedom and the need for dependency—if she can accomplish these things, the social worker will indeed be a blessing to the old.

As to the prevalence of psychosis in old age—it is as common among men as among women, but we have found (10) that men are more apt to require hospitalization. Some reasons for this discrepancy are the following: women come to treatment earlier than men do when they feel ill; men hesitate longer to ask for guidance. In women, the inner battle for prestige centering around penis-envy has been fought long ago; in man it is still in full swing because of the retirement conflict. Women are usually more accustomed to staying at home and to being alone than are men. As a result, when elderly men manifest psychiatric traits which interfere with their employment or their environment, they tend to need earlier hospitalization. However, a well-equipped psychiatric social service, with workers trained to go regularly to homes, can prevent many such discomforts. The presence of the helping social worker is a sustaining reality which drives the image of persecuting parents into the background. Her visits become expressions of affection given by the community; she becomes a protective presence between the old patient and his fears. As a result, such patients stop withdrawing and once more take up the adventure of social intercourse.

In concluding, we find that the beginning of involutional mental disturbances is often emotional and traumatic. Because of the weakening of the ego and ego defenses, integration and synthetizing of concepts begin to fail. As in every neurosis, we find a breakdown of defenses. However, the breakdown is not directly parallel to underlying organic processes. The premorbid neurotic potential determines the symptoms we will observe, the degree of deterioration, and the strategy of our therapy. In the readjustment of the patient, environmental therapy will be an important factor.

Old age can bring readjustment. There are people who become more active and less rigid and even more creative in old age. The further study of these personalities will direct us to the core of the psychological problems of the old-aged.

BIBLIOGRAPHY

1. ABRAHAM, K. *Selected Papers on Psycho-Analysis.* London: Hogarth Press, 1927.
2. COMMITTEE ON HOSPITALS OF THE GROUP FOR THE ADVANCEMENT OF PSYCHIATRY. *The Problem of the Aged Patient in the Public Psychiatric Hospital.* Report No. 14, August, 1950.

3. BROWN, D. J. et al. *The Aged and Society.* Madison Industrial Relations Research Association, 1951.
4. DOWNING, T. C. and BURNS, G. C. Involutional illnesses. *Am. J. Psychiat.,* 108, 1951.
5. FENICHEL, O. *The Psychoanalytic Theory of Neurosis.* New York: W. W. Norton & Co., 1945.
6. FERENCZI, S. Beitrag zum Verständnis der Psychoneurosen des Rückbildungs-Alters. *Bausteine,* III. Bern: Huber, 1939.
7. FREUD, S. Mourning and melancholia. *Collected Papers,* IV. London: Hogarth Press, 1925.
8. GROTJAHN, M. Psychiatric observations in a case of involutional melancholia treated with metrazol. *Bull. Menninger Clin.,* 6, 1939.
9. —— Some analytic observations about the process of growing old. In *Psychoanalysis and the Social Sciences,* III. New York: International Universities Press, 1951.
10. HERKIMER, J. K. and MEERLOO, J. A. M. Treatment of mental disturbances in elderly women. *Soc. Casework,* 32, 1951.
11. KAUFMAN, M. R. Psychoanalysis in late life depressions. *Psychoanal. Quart.,* 6, 1937.
12. LAWTON, G. *New Goals for Old Age.* New York: Columbia University Press, 1943.
13. MALAMUD, W. et al. The involutional psychoses: a sociopsychiatric followup study. *Am. J. Psychiat.,* 105, 1949.
14. MALZBERG, B. (Personal Communication) Director of the Bureau of Statistics of the New York State Department of Mental Hygiene.
15. MCGRAW, R. B. Recoverable or temporary mental disturbances in the elderly. *J. Gerontol.,* 4, 1949.
16. MEERLOO, J. A. M. and COLEMAN, M. The transference function. *Psychoanal. Rev.,* 38, 1951.
17. MONROE, R. T. *Diseases in Old Age.* Cambridge, Mass.: Harvard University Press, 1951.
18. RUEMCKE, H. C. *Life Periods of Man.* Amsterdam: Arbeiderspers., 1938.
19. —— The borderline of virilitas and presenium. *Netherlands Med. J.,* 1938.
20. SANDS, T. J. The neuropsychiatric disorders of the aged. *N. Y. Med.,* October 15, 1951.
21. SCHILDER, P. Psychiatric aspects of old age and the aging. *Am. J. Orthopsychiat.,* 10, 1940.
22. STERN, K., WILLIAMS, G. M., and PRADOS, M. Grief reactions in later life. *Am. J. Psychiat.,* 107, 1951.
23. WAYNE, G. Modified psychoanalytic therapy in senescence. Accepted for publication in *The Psychoanalytic Review.*
24. —— Psychotherapy in senescence. Accepted for publication in the *Annals of Western Medicine and Surgery.*

INDEX

Displacement, 17-18, 40, 42-45, 144, 218, 256, 332
Distortion, 17
Dominiques, K. E., 260
Downing, T. C., 337
Dream, 17, 19, 141
Dream work, 18
Drug addicts, 27, 156
Dunbar, F. H., 319

Eating difficulties, 38, 137, 174
Economics, 54
Ecstasy, 29, 46
Education, 73, 110, 120, 129, 151-153, 248-253, 270
Ego
  and anxiety, 42-43
  and body, 296-298, 302, 307, 319
  and depression, 17, 19-20, 23, 40-42
  and flight, 49-50
  and group formation, 67-68
  and interpretation, 231-235
  and superego, 32, 54, 212, 218-219
  and therapy, 100-104, 121, 139, 223
  at puberty, 218-227
  autonomous functions of, 56
  boundary, 29
  deformation of, 24, 50-51, 233
  development of, 22, 25-29, 56-57, 61-62, 74, 177-178
  deviation, 58-59
  functions of, 22-52, 67-68, 219-221, 295
  history of concept of, 22-25
  ideal, 214, 222, 224, 229, 238
  identity, 66, 183-184, 206, 221, 223
  impoverishment of, 47
  inhibitions of functions of, 40-42, 44
  mechanisms of defense, 17-20, 25, 42-51
  oral phase of, 35-36, 334
  restriction, 50, 133, 235
  strength of, 23, 141, 220, 224
  synthetic function of, 50, 139, 219, 233-235
  unconscious part of, 19-21
  weakness of, 23, 211, 220, 327-328, 336
Egocentrism, 65
Ego psychology, 22-52, 110, 119
Eissler, K. R., 107, 229, 240, 241

Empathy, 38
English, O. S., 320
Enuresis, 137, 162, 165, 187
Envy, 34-35, 43, 45
Epilepsy, 106, 134
Erikson, E. H., 66, 75, 123, 183-184, 206, 208, 223, 225, 240
Erogenous zones, 55, 61
Escalona, S., 175-177, 208, 209
Exhibitionism, 45, 61, 212, 237

Fabian, A. A., 80, 111, 116, 124-152
Fairweather, M. E., 178-180, 208
Falstein, E. I., 105, 107, 240
Family
  and child, 59-64, 112-117
  diagnosis of, 112-117
Family agency, 83, 109-123
Family romance, 206-207, 217
Fantasy, 45-49, 71-72, 129, 141, 206-207, 212, 221-222, 298, 302, 330
Fatigue, 40, 120
Feces, 43
Fenichel, O., 39, 222-223, 235, 240, 337
Ferenczi, S., 324, 337
Fetishism, 44
Finesinger, J., 293
Fishback, D., 105, 107, 240
Fixation, 27-28, 32-33, 61, 70, 86-87, 94, 105, 307
Foreplay, 71
Forgetting, 39-40, 42
Foster homes (-parents), 117, 120, 153-168, 174-175, 250
Free association, 24, 48, 129, 315-319
Freed, S. C., 195-196, 209
Freedom, psychological, 6, 8-9
French, T. M., 51, 123, 133, 152, 293, 319
Freud, A., 37-38, 45, 49-50, 51, 64-65, 75, 123, 138-139, 152, 168, 174, 208, 211, 215, 218, 219, 221, 224, 225, 230, 240
Freud, S., 5, 16-18, 21-25, 27, 34, 39, 43, 48-49, 51, 56, 67-69, 75, 123, 124, 129, 152, 168, 211, 217, 220, 240, 324, 329, 337
Friedgott, A. H., 123
Fries, M. E., 123, 168, 174-175, 209

Garrett, A., 293, 319

Josselyn, I. M., 133, 152, 241

Kaplan, L. K., 153-168
Kaufman, M. R., ix, 337
Keiser, S., 225-226, 240
Klein, E., 22-52, 54, 162, 177, 230, 298
Kluckhohn, C., 293
Knight, R. P., 197, 209, 225
Kraepelin, E., 126
Kris, E., 48, 51, 52, 62, 68, 75
Kris, M., 123
Kroger, W. S., 195-196, 209
Krug, O., 260
Kubie, L. S., 3-14, 60

Lahor, J., 74
Lampl-de Groot, J., 215, 241
Lander, J., 241
Language, 9-11
Latency period, 117, 144, 210-212, 219, 233, 302
Lawton, G., 337
Learning
  difficulties, 150, 251-253
  in infancy, 25-29
  program in institutions, 248-252
  through repetition, 5
Leibniz, G. W., 15
Leitch, M., 175, 209
Leites, N., 68, 75
Levy, D. M., 108, 176, 200-201
Libido, 55-56, 331
  see also Instinctual drives
Liebault, A., 15
"Little Hans," 43
Loewenstein, R. M., 51, 52, 62, 75
Love
  infantile, 59-64, 70
  mature, 69-71
  see also Object relationships
Low, B., 26

Maeder, L. M. A., 320
Malamud, W., 337
Malcove, L., 209
Malzberg, B., 337
Masculinity, 34-35, 41
Masochism, 88-89, 133
  moral, 70
Masturbation, 102-103, 162, 215-216, 277

Maturation, 54, 154, 162-163, 177, 211, 220
Maxwell, A., 260
McBee, M. A., 239, 241
McCleery, S., 182, 204, 209
McGraw, R. B., 323, 337
Medical patient, dynamic formulation of problem, 281-291, 303-319
Medical social worker, 261-293
Meerloo, J. A. M., 321-337
Melancholia, 324, 329
Memory, 23, 39-42, 56, 139
Mental defectives, 136, 138
Mental health, psychoanalytic concept of, 3-14, 51
Meyer, A., 124-125
Michaels, R., 193, 197, 209
Miles, H. W., 293
Moore, B. V., 293
Monroe, R. T., 337
Mores, conformity to and mental health, 3
Mother-child relationship, 54, 56-58, 85-94, 112-117, 133-134, 177-179
Murray, H. A., 293

Narcissism, 21, 29-31, 54-56, 69-70, 74, 200, 215-217, 229, 329
Narcosis, 46
Nazism, 64, 66
Negativism, therapeutic, 147-148
Neubauer, P. B., 8, 109-123, 124, 132, 138, 139
Neurology, 106
Neurosis, 3-14, 22, 105, 115, 257, 322
  distinguished from normality, 7, 51
  experimental in animals, 9
Neurotic potential, 9-10, 13
Neurotic process, 6, 10-12
Neurotic state, 12-13
Nirvana principle, 26
Normality, concept of, 3-14, 71
Nunberg, H., 223, 234, 241
"Nursery morality," 20

Obers, S. J., 240
Obesity, 220
Object choice
  anaclitic, 60
  narcissistic, 60, 70-71
Object love, 69-71, 74, 177, 211
Object relationships, 53-75

343